Queer Justice at School

Queer Justice at School

A Guide for Youth Activists, Allies, and Their Teachers

Elizabeth J. Meyer

TEACHERS COLLEGE PRESS

TEACHERS COLLEGE | COLUMBIA UNIVERSITY
NEW YORK AND LONDON

Published by Teachers College Press,® 1234 Amsterdam Avenue, New York, NY 10027

Copyright © 2025 by Teachers College, Columbia University

Front cover by adam bohannon design. Photo by Vladimir Vladimirov / iStock by Getty Images.

All rights reserved. No part of this publication may be reproduced or transmitted in any form or by any means, electronic or mechanical, including photocopy, or any information storage and retrieval system, without permission from the publisher. For reprint permission and other subsidiary rights requests, please contact Teachers College Press, Rights Dept.: tcpressrights@tc.columbia.edu

Library of Congress Cataloging-in-Publication Data is available at loc.gov

ISBN 978-0-8077-8688-8 (paper)
ISBN 978-0-8077-8689-5 (hardcover)
ISBN 978-0-8077-8297-2 (ebook)

Printed on acid-free paper
Manufactured in the United States of America

This book is dedicated to all youth and educators who are working to transform their schools and communities to end all forms of oppression and to create learning environments that affirm and celebrate LGBTQIA+ people and communities.

Contents

Preface	xi
Acknowledgments	xv
1. Queering Your School: Youth-Led Change	**1**
Introduction	1
Early Activists: 1980s and 1990s	2
Millennial Change-Makers	4
Partnerships: Adults and Youth Together for Change	6
Solidarity Work: Building Coalitions for Justice	8
Conclusion	12
Discussion Questions	12
Key Terms	12
2. Making Your Case: Evidence to Support LGBTQIA+ Equity Work	**14**
Impacts of a Negative School Climate	15
Features of a Positive School Climate	23
Collecting Evidence From Your Community	28
Conclusion	30
Discussion Questions	31
Key Terms	31
3. Queering Learning and Classrooms	**32**
Queer Pedagogy	32
Queering the Curriculum	35

Social-Emotional Learning and Character Education	43
Flags, Stickers, and Other Displays: Visibility Matters	44
Conclusion	47
Discussion Questions	47
Key Terms	48

4. Queering School Culture — 49
School Climate	49
Traditions	51
Laws and Policies	54
National and International Events	62
Discussion Questions	66
Key Terms	67

5. Queering Clubs and Extracurriculars — 68
History and Purposes of GSAs	69
Starting or Developing a GSA	72
Know Your Rights: The Equal Access Act	76
Building Bridges and Networks	79
Conclusion	83
Discussion Questions	83
Key Terms	83

6. Express Yourself — 84
Student Expression	85
School-Sponsored Speech	91
Staff Expression and Government Speech	93
Other Speech Issues	95
Conclusion	99
Discussion Questions	100
Key Terms	100

7.	**Busting Binaries**	**101**
	Roots of Cisheteronormativity	102
	Know Your Rights: Title IX	104
	Names and Pronouns	107
	Bathrooms and Locker Rooms	111
	Athletics	114
	Nonbinary Students	116
	Gender Support Plans	116
	Conclusion	117
	Discussion Questions	118
	Key Terms	118
8.	**Strategies for Action**	**119**
	Creating the Context for Change	120
	Amplifying Student Voice: Ideas for Action	125
	Sustaining Your Spirit	129
	Conclusion	134
	Discussion Questions	135
	Key Terms	135
Appendix: Glossary		**137**
References		**149**
Index		**165**
About the Author		**171**

Preface

I miss being a high school teacher. I loved working with teenagers and seeing them learn and grow. Teaching was especially meaningful when we were working together on something that felt important—something that really mattered. I guess I started researching this book my first year teaching in 1993 when I got involved with the organization that came to be known as GLSEN. I got inspired to take on this book project in the fall of 2022 when I started interviewing educators who actively supported students working for LGBTQIA+ equity. This book shares some of what I learned from these interviews, but it is more of a response to what they repeatedly asked for: more resources, accessible research, support, ideas, and information about how to do this kind of work with their students. Over my long career in education, I have amassed knowledge about tools, activities, organizations, policies, and practices that I wanted to share with these committed educators and students around the world. I have done this in an ongoing way since I started my blog on *Psychology Today* in 2009, but it felt more important now to put it all together in a format that could be read with students, in a way that was accessible to teenagers and written specifically for them as well as the adults in their lives.

Queer Justice at School is a practical guide designed to answer common questions and provide useful ideas, information, and activities for young people working to improve their school community's culture regarding gender and sexual diversity (GSD). This might be a student club such as a gender and sexuality alliance (GSA) or feminism club. It might be in a leadership or social justice class. It might be an after-school youth group at a community organization designed to support LGBTQIA+ young people. It might be a small group of friends who read it together and take actions on their own or an informal book group that meets at your school library. It could also be read by school district–level equity committee members working to improve the overall experience with and for students in their district. It could also be read by a local chapter of GLSEN or PFLAG (Parents and Friends of Lesbains and Gays) looking to better support efforts for LGBTQIA+ equity in their community. It includes a glossary of terms to help explain important concepts as well as a companion website with links to additional resources and interactive activities including recommended podcasts, blogs, and downloadable lessons. Each chapter ends with a set of discussion questions and key terms to spark ideas for conversations related to each chapter. The book is also filled with images and activities that you can flip to 5 minutes before a meeting and get an idea for an engaging group session. I learned that many educators and mentors want to better support youth doing this work but don't have the time to extensively research, plan, and prepare for every meeting. If any of these suggestions feel familiar, this book is for you.

Chapter 1 sets the stage for understanding the context of youth activism related to gender and sexuality in schools. It shares profiles of important youth change-makers over the past 50 years as well as a brief history of activism for LGBTQIA+ equity in the United States. It continues by sharing ideas about effective partnerships between youth and adults and suggested activities to develop these valuable connections. The first chapter concludes with specific ideas on how to build strong coalitions with other groups interested in equity and justice.

The second chapter offers an overview of current research to provide evidence to convince anyone you need to about the importance of LGBTQIA+ equity work in schools. It shares both the harms that occur due to hostile school climates and the features of more positive climates that enable all students to thrive. It then offers a series of activity ideas to collect and analyze data from your own school, district, or state. This can help ensure your information is local, specific, and current to reflect the needs and experiences of youth in your community.

Chapter 3 provides ideas and information about how to support efforts to make curriculum and classroom interactions more affirming of gender and sexual diversity. It specifically addresses social-emotional learning and character education programs as well as the importance of visual displays that support LGBTQIA+ communities. This chapter also includes additional resources for lesson plans and class content. Chapter 4 talks about school culture and traditions that often exclude, erase, and harm LGBTQIA+ people and ways to make them more inclusive. This chapter addresses issues such as homecoming, prom, graduation, and yearbooks as well as national and international events to help generate support and awareness of LGBTQIA+ history and people.

Chapter 5 focuses on the history and current context for extracurricular clubs such GSAs and provides examples of ways to start such a club or to make your current club more successful. This section includes a discussion of the Equal Access Act, a federal law that establishes the right for extracurricular clubs to meet at school. Chapter 6 addresses free speech in schools and the rights and limits that exist for student and employee expression. This chapter talks about different forms of student expression including dress codes, petitions, and protests. It also addresses school-sponsored speech, which includes plays, assemblies, sporting events, and the like. Staff expression, which counts as a form of "government speech," is also addressed.

Chapter 7 speaks to the unique challenges experienced by trans and nonbinary students due to the binary structures that exist and can be challenged in schools. It presents the important federal law, Title IX, and how it can be used to better support trans and nonbinary students and then addresses specific challenges such as names and pronouns, bathrooms and locker rooms, sports participation, and gender support plans. The last chapter, Chapter 8, provides information and resources for planning successful advocacy work and activist projects that draws from my research with the educators who inspired this book. It presents a detailed discussion of how to think strategically about forms of advocacy and activism as well as how to sustain your spirit and ensure long-term changes are implemented and maintained.

It seems like every day that I worked on this book there was another news story about backlash against LGBTQIA+ youth and their rights at school. As of May 2024, the American Civil Liberties Union (ACLU) has documented 513 bills attacking LGBTQIA+ rights and 203 bills that are designed specifically to restrict the rights of LGBTQIA+ people in public education institutions. The most commonly occurring proposed bills include those restricting the ability to talk about LGBTQIA+ people in the curriculum (54), excluding transgender students from participating in school sports (48), requiring the outing of students (59), and limiting access to school facilities (36). Others provide religious exemptions from respecting LGBTQIA+ rights, ban drag performances in schools, and attempt to redefine "sex" to exclude protections for transgender and nonbinary people (ACLU, 2024). These bills have been steadily on the rise since 2018. CNN reported that in 2023 there was a high of 510 bills proposed compared to 180 in 2022 and only 42 in 2018 (Choi, 2024). They also noted that the number of anti-LGBTQIA+ education–related bills more than doubled from 2022 to 2023 (from 123 to 314). In this political context, the work of advocating with and for LGBTQIA+ youth in schools has become increasingly complex and critically important for educators, school leaders, community members, and researchers to understand. I hope this book provides you with the information and inspiration to create the affirming school community that all students deserve.

Acknowledgments

I want to thank my spouse, Micah, and my son, Cartier, for their continued love and support as well as my brother, Rob; sister, Cherie; and my mom and dad. I am also grateful to all the colleagues, friends, and current and former students who took time to give me feedback on early drafts of these chapters, including Alex Boeding, Lee Iskander, John Spear, Tracy Stegall, Tiffany Wright, Emily B. Wakefield, Robyn Tomiko, Jordan Paterson, Carly Smoot, Sean Costello, and Lane Juntunen. I also want to thank the Spencer Transgender Studies in Education Learning Community for your ongoing engagement and support as I developed the concept for this project: Melinda Mangin, Mollie McQuillan, Lance McCready, Mario Suarez, Page Regan, Harper Keenan, and Lee Iskander.

I am also grateful to all the teachers who participated in the research project that inspired this book and my colleagues working in the field of queer and trans studies in education whose work is so valuable to advancing our understanding of these issues in schools, including Lee Airton, Mollie Blackburn, Ed Brockenbrough, Mary Bryson, Emily Greytak, Jill Herman-Wilmarth, Joe Kosciw, Kevin Kumashiro, Bethy Leonardi, Bettina Love, Catherine Lugg, Kimberly Manning, Caitlin Law Ryan, Karleen Pendleton-Jiménez, Annie Pullen Sansfaçon, Sara Staley, Catherine Taylor, Susan Wooley, and members of the Queer Studies Special Interest Group of the American Educational Research Association.

It is also important to name a few of the national organizations that provide research, resources, and tangible supports to anyone aiming to support activism and advocacy for LGBTQIA+ equity in schools: the ACLU, Education Deans for Justice and Equity, Egale Canada, FAIR Education Act Implementation Coalition, Gender Spectrum, GLSEN, GSA Network, Welcoming Schools (part of the Human Rights Campaign), Learning for Justice (part of the Southern Poverty Law Center), National Center for Lesbian Rights, P-FLAG, and the Transgender Law Center.

Finally, I want to thank all the local activists and committed educators and community members who engage in this work and have helped me in my own understandings of successful coalition work and advocacy projects. I want to specifically name Gender Creative Kids—Canada, EGALE Canada Education Subcommittee, GLSEN Research Advisory Council, the Central

Coast Coalition for Inclusive Schools (California), the Boulder Valley Title IX Stakeholder Council (Colorado), and A Queer Endeavor. My relationship with each of these groups deeply shaped my understanding of creating and sustaining successful coalitions and building conditions that can lead to lasting and impactful changes.

Queer Justice at School

CHAPTER 1

Queering Your School
Youth-Led Change

> We need, in every community, a group of angelic troublemakers.
> —Bayard Rustin

INTRODUCTION

Queering your school? Yes, please! I am excited that you found this topic interesting enough to open this book! What does it mean to queer your school, and why is it important? If you are reading this, you probably already know why it is important, and Chapter 2 will provide even more evidence to that point. What does *queering* mean? For starters, it means questioning the ways that heterosexuality and gender binaries work together to produce *cisheteronormativity* by being presented as "normal" or "natural." It also means disrupting the ways schools have acted as sites of pain, exclusion, and erasure for lesbian, gay, bisexual, transgender, *queer*, intersex, and asexual (*LGBTQIA+*) people. Queering helps us think outside of *normative* categories that shape hierarchies of popularity and who has power in schools and society. It provides ways to take action to challenge and change ways of speaking, learning, and being that are restrictive and harmful for anyone who doesn't fit the dominant mold created by White colonial cisheteropatriachy.

This book explicitly acknowledges the diversity of the LGBTQIA+ community and will talk about working in coalitions to address related forms of injustice that impact LGBTQIA+ communities, including racism and White supremacy, ableism, colonialism, and classism, as well as other structural oppressions that exist based on religion, immigration status, language, and culture. It means asking questions about the ways things have always been done and generating creative and new ways to build supportive learning communities. It means connecting with and amplifying voices that have been marginalized and excluded in our society to ensure all people can feel safe, valued, and respected at school. It means listening to students and centering their knowledge and expertise while providing supports and resources to help them create and maintain the school communities they want and deserve.

Young people have always been on the front lines of social change. LGBTQIA+ students have also been leaders in improving K–12 school environments by naming and resisting exclusionary and harmful practices that are grounded in *homophobia, transphobia*, and cisheteronormativity. This book is written to share these stories and provide youth and the adults who support them with ideas, tools, resources, and inspiration to continue doing this important work. I start by sharing the success stories of activism for LGBTQIA+ justice led by youth to set the context of possibility for the readers of this book. Change is possible, and you can be the spark that shifts a practice, a policy, or a tradition at your school to make your community less toxic and more affirming for gender and sexual diversity as well as LGBTQIA+ students, staff, and families.

Gender and sexual diversity are all around us; however, the traditional ways of doing things in schools have been built around outdated stereotypes and binary structures. While LGBTQIA+ people are often the most visible and vocal ones speaking out against cisheteronormativity, these structures harm everyone. Making schools and classrooms more inclusive and affirming of gender and sexual diversity not only benefits LGBTQIA+ students, staff, and families but also makes more space for everyone to be free from rigid gender and sexuality norms. This chapter will share some stories of youth activists to provide some historical context and inspiration. These stories are followed by sections that will talk about youth and adult partnerships for change and building coalitions around justice-oriented goals and will conclude with an overview of the remaining chapters in the book. Now for some stories from inspiring youth who queered their schools.

EARLY ACTIVISTS: 1980s AND 1990s

One of the earliest and well-documented cases of LGBTQIA+ students making change was the story of Aaron Fricke, a gay student attending high school in Rhode Island. After coming out at school, he decided he wanted to bring his boyfriend to prom. In 1979, the year before, another gay student had been denied the opportunity to attend prom with the date of his choice by the school principal, Richard Lynch. When Aaron's request was also denied, he filed a federal lawsuit asserting his *First Amendment* right to express himself at school and *Fourteenth Amendment* right to equal protection (*Equal Protection Clause*). The court agreed with Fricke and his lawyers and granted what is called a preliminary *injunction* that would allow him to attend with his male date. The lawsuit, *Fricke v. Lynch* (1980), helped pave the way for students around the country to participate in school-sponsored events while honoring their LGBTQIA+ identities and relationships. However, as recently as 2010, a school in Mississippi cancelled its prom rather than allowing Constance McMillen to attend in a tuxedo with her girlfriend as her date (*McMillen v. Itawamba County School District*, 2010).

Marc Hall from Ontario, Canada, led a similar change in 2002 when his public school, affiliated with the Catholic Church, tried to prevent him from attending prom with his boyfriend. In the decision for *Hall v. Durham Catholic District School Board* (2005), the court granted an interlocutory injunction allowing him to attend the prom. Marc Hall then dropped the case so no similar legal precedent was decided for Canadian students. However, the media coverage generated by the case raised awareness and generally showed strong support for Hall and his date. This public attention alone had a tangible impact on other students and schools facing similar issues. It helped make same-sex dates a more well-known and acceptable aspect of these widespread school traditions.

In addition to controversies over prom, other forms of LGBTQIA+ activism in the 1980s and 1990s centered around bullying and student-led clubs, also known as *GSAs* for Gay-Straight Alliance. In 1995, Kelli Peterson was trying to find ways to make school better for her and other gay and lesbian teens (Lane, 2019). She and a friend decided to start a GSA club much like other schools had around the country. However, at her school in Salt Lake City, Utah, her request was denied and led to a high-profile lawsuit against the school board. The case, *East High GSA v. Salt Lake City Board of Education* (1999), was the first of many lawsuits that applied the Equal Access Act to ensure schools must allow GSAs to meet if they allow any extracurricular clubs to meet (Lane, 2019). While the controversy and legal battle lasted after Kelli had graduated from East High, she persisted along with other current students also named as plaintiffs to ensure other students wouldn't have to face the same challenges.

It has been well documented that many LGBTQIA+ students do not feel safe at school. Part of this is due to pervasive homophobic and transphobic bullying that many students experience. One student, Jamie Nabozny, was subjected to extreme forms of antigay violence for many years during middle and high school in Wisconsin. The bullying and harassment were so severe that he had been hospitalized, run away from home, dropped out of school, and attempted suicide. He decided to sue his school district to ensure no other students experienced such trauma at school. In 1995 he filed a federal lawsuit that claimed the school violated his Fourteenth Amendment right to equal protection under the law, and in 1996 he won. Additionally, he was awarded $962,000 in damages (*Nabozny v. Podlesny*, 1996). This price tag and the decision were groundbreaking and sent a clear message that schools could be held responsible for failing to prevent and address antigay bullying. A similar case was decided in 2005 in Canada after Azmi Jubran sued the North Vancouver School District for failing to effectively intervene to stop antigay bullying directed at him although he didn't identify as gay. The Supreme Court of Canada applied federal human rights protections to determine that schools have a duty to provide educational environments free from discriminatory harassment, and they must address root causes of homophobia and heterosexism in schools (Howard, 2002; Meyer, 2007b). These early lawsuits led by strong young activists helped pave the way for additional actions and changes in the new millennium.

MILLENNIAL CHANGE-MAKERS

In the new millennium, more and more students have been proudly claiming an identity in the LGBTQIA+ community in larger numbers and at younger ages. This new generation of young people have continued to push for important changes in schools, including rights and supports for transgender youth and incorporating information about LGBTQIA+ people in curriculum. Several lawsuits have been filed by transgender students when their schools failed to recognize their gender identity and support appropriate access to activities and facilities as a result. Ash Whitaker and Gavin Grimm are two students who led public fights against their schools because of the anti-transgender discrimination they experienced. In 2017, a federal court ruled in *Whitaker v. Kenosha Unified School District* (2017) that *Title IX* protects transgender students from discrimination. This includes providing them access to bathrooms consistent with their gender. Ash's case did not get appealed to the Supreme Court; however, Gavin Grimm's did. This resulted in more national attention and media coverage, including a mention by Laverne Cox at the 2017 Grammy Awards (Reynolds, 2017). Gavin had filed a similar case against his Virginia school district that spent years in courts due to changing interpretations of Title IX under the Trump administration. The lawsuit finally ended in 2021 when the Supreme Court declined to hear the appeal, which left the lower court's decision—consistent with the Whitaker decision—in place. His school district also agreed to pay a $1.3 million settlement to Grimm (ACLU staff, 2021). During this time, Gavin became the public face for the challenges trans youth face in schools, and even though he was done with high school in 2016, he remained engaged in the litigation and public information campaigns connected to the lawsuit. These efforts and the visibility of this decision sent clear messages to people around the country about what they should expect from their schools. Many school districts have since worked to proactively adopt trans-affirming policies and guidance to better support transgender and nonbinary students (Meyer & Keenan, 2018).

Another major issue students are taking on in the new millennium is the exclusion of LGBTQIA+ people and topics from the curriculum. For example, KC Miller, a Pennsylvania high school student. created an organization called Keystone Coalition for Advancing Sex Education to advocate for more comprehensive and inclusive sex education in schools. He started this work as a sophomore in high school in 2015 and led statewide education and activist activities until 2019, when he announced the end of the nonprofit organization since he started a job in the Philadelphia Department of Health (Miller, 2019). In his blog, he documents many of the organizing and public information activities he engaged in, including a TED talk, social media, and outreach at Pride celebrations in New York and Pennsylvania, as well as building strategic connections with organizers in California, Georgia, New York, and Virginia. While he did not yet change the sex education curriculum for the state, his efforts and energies have had a lasting impact.

The issue of sexist and racist dress codes in schools has also been taken on by young people. Deanna and Mya Cook are African American twin sisters who were banned from extracurricular activities at their charter school because they violated hair and makeup policies. They were given detention and threatened with suspension unless they removed the braided extensions in their hair. The school's trustees temporarily lifted the ban in response to the public pressure generated when the sisters went public with their experience. The extensive media coverage and letter of support signed by over 30 civil rights organizations helped ensure the school paid careful attention to the issue. The school did not permanently rescind the policy, so the sisters, with the support of the National Association for the Advancement of Colored People (NAACP) and the American Civil Liberties Union (ACLU), filed a civil rights complaint against their school (ACLU staff, 2017). The following school year, the policy was removed from the student handbook (Shaffer, 2017). Their story and resistance to these policies led to widespread actions in Massachusetts, including the passage of a new state law. The Create a Respectful and Open Workplace for Natural Hair (CROWN) Act was passed in July 2022 and explicitly prohibited race-based hair discrimination; it has also been passed in a total of 24 states as of May 2024 (Payne-Patterson, 2023). Other students have worked against gendered dress codes that limit the expression of female, trans and nonbinary students, as well as Native students whose cultures often value long hair in boys and men (Nittle, 2022).

Schools have also unfairly censored and edited images of students in yearbooks to make photos more reflective of gender and sexuality norms. One student, Riley O'Keefe, ran for student council after having her yearbook photo edited without her knowledge; a black bar was put over her chest to conceal her cleavage. She created an online petition that generated over 7,000 signatures. After her story went viral, her school adopted a gender-neutral dress code policy, much like the one created by Oregon's chapter of the National Organization for Women (Oregon N.O.W., 2016).

Most recently, students in Florida have been organizing and challenging the Parental Rights in Education Act, commonly referred to as the Don't Say Gay law, passed in May 2022 (Diaz, 2022). For example, Javier Gomez is among the youth activists who are leading resistance efforts against laws restricting what can be taught in schools. Javier, who was president of his school's GSA, traveled from Miami to Tallahassee to lobby against the bill at the statehouse as part of a group organized by Safe Schools South Florida. He also led a walkout at his school, where he was joined by approximately 100 peers (Ruiz, 2022). While the Don't Say Gay Law passed by a slim margin of only five votes, teachers in Florida are now having to work under its restrictive mandate, which excludes discussion of gender and sexual diversity in all grades. Students and community activists continue to organize to find ways to support LGBTQIA+ students in Florida and limit the harmful impacts of this law.

To put these stories of activism in context, it is important to understand a bit more about the history of LGBTQIA+ activism in the United States. Figure 1.1 provides some key dates and figures and can be a useful starting point for student groups to learn more about the history of LGBTQIA+ activism in the United States. You can plan an activity where pairs of students work together to choose events from the timeline to research and then can take turns presenting to each other in class or your student club. Other related activities are available on the companion website (www.elizabethjmeyer.com/queer-justice.html), including podcasts, interactive timelines, and printable cards that you can cut up and distribute as a starting point to learn more about key people and moments in the LGBTQIA+ rights movement.

PARTNERSHIPS: ADULTS AND YOUTH TOGETHER FOR CHANGE

Adults and youth working together can create strong networks of support and lead to more long-term, grassroots changes than if one of these groups worked alone. The challenge is that youth and adults often have different needs, interests, motivations, skills, and capacities that can lead to conflict, frustration, miscommunications, and burnout. These tensions can doom well-designed and important equity efforts if youth and adults don't consciously work to name and understand these tensions so that they can resolve them and focus on the changes they want to make happen.

For example, one GSA advisor explained to me the difficulty he had in continuing to advise the club because the students were more interested in socializing and goofing around together than talking about and planning efforts to change problems in their school community. While the advisor wanted very much to maintain a safe and supportive community for his students, the misalignment between the students' needs and the teacher's vision and hopes for the club almost led to its demise. Finally, the advisor had a formal discussion with the club about his capacity to advise them if their focus remained on exclusively having a social space. This frank conversation led the group to arrive at an agreement to have a balance between social time and activist work time in the club. This restructuring based on open and clear communication led to the students focusing on addressing a

Figure 1.1. Brief History of LGBTQIA+ Rights and Activism in the United States

- 1924: Society for Human Rights founded by Henry Gerber in Chicago.
- 1948: Alfred Kinsey publishes *Sexual Behavior in the Human Male*.
- 1950: Mattachine Society founded in Los Angeles by Harry Hay with the aim to "eliminate discrimination and bigotry" and to assimilate "homosexuals" into mainstream society.
- 1955: Daughters of Bilitis founded in Los Angeles, the first documented organization focused on lesbian rights.
- 1966: Compton Cafeteria Riot: resistance to unjust police action against transgender people in San Francisco. Activists then established the National Transsexual Counseling Unit, which is noted as the first peer-run support and advocacy organization in the world.
- 1969: Stonewall Riots: resistance to unjust police action against the gay, lesbian, and transgender community in New York City.
- 1970: Gay Youth was established on the East Coast as a group of under-21 activists associated with the Gay Liberation Front.
- 1971: Street Transvestite Action Revolutionaries (STAR) founded by Sylvia Rivera and Marsha P. Johnson.
- 1972: Students at George Washington High School in New York City established a club for gay students called the "Third World" club. Their first meeting included a presentation by the "Gay Activists Alliance."
- 1979: National March on Washington for Lesbian and Gay Rights.
- 1987: AIDS Coalition to Unleash Power (ACTUP) is formed in New York City. Other direct-action groups organized in this era include Queer Nation, The Lesbian Avengers, and the Transsexual Menace.
- 1988: First Gay-Straight Alliance is formed at Concord Academy in Massachusetts by Kevin Jennings and his students.
- 1990: The Gay and Lesbian Independent School Teachers Network (GLISTN) is formed in Boston. This group will become the national advocacy organization now known as GLSEN.
- 1993: *"Don't Ask, Don't Tell" (DADT)* directive passed by Department of Defense prohibiting military service by openly gay, lesbian, and bisexual people.
- 1996: President Clinton signs the Defense of Marriage Act (DOMA) into law, which defined marriage as only between one man and one woman.
- 2000: Vermont is the first state to legalize civil unions and domestic partnerships between same-sex couples.
- 2004: Massachusetts is the first state to legalize same-sex marriage.
- 2010: "Don't Ask, Don't Tell" repealed by the U.S. Senate.
- 2015: *Obergefell v. Hodges* decision by the Supreme Court requires all states to recognize same-sex marriages
- 2020: *Bostock v. Clayton County* decision by the Supreme Court that extends the prohibition of discrimination "on the basis of sex" to also include sexual orientation and gender identity.

Sources: Bronski, 2019; Cohen, 2005; GLSEN staff, n.d.; Lane, 2019.

Figure 1.2. Tips for Youth and Adult Collaborations

Tips for Youth

1. Communicate openly.
2. Be honest.
3. Establish clear and tangible goals.
4. Understand where adults are coming from.
5. Challenge the idea and not the person.
6. Ask questions.
7. Acknowledge your capacity.
8. Remember that there are always lessons to be learned.
9. Offer skills. Everyone has their strengths.

Tips for Adult Allies

1. Be honored.
2. Expect success.
3. Walk your talk.
4. Do your part.
5. Encourage decision-making.
6. Help ask tough questions.
7. Encourage inclusiveness.
8. Share your roadmap.
9. Maintain interest.
10. Give credit.
11. Help define success.
12. Debrief.
13. Support yourself.

---

problem impacting many students in their school: access to gender-inclusive bathrooms. That year, they wrote and prepared 2-minute presentations to give at a school board meeting that led to the district changing signs on single-user staff bathroom spaces and creating several gender-inclusive bathrooms for student use at the high school.

Advocates for Youth, a national organization that supports youth activism related to sexual health, rights, and justice, compiled nine tips on working with adult allies. A summary of these tips for youth activists as well as tips for adult allies developed by Learning for Justice is provided in Figure 1.2. Links to these original documents are also available on the companion website: www.elizabethjmeyer.com/queer-justice.html.

SOLIDARITY WORK: BUILDING COALITIONS FOR JUSTICE

Working with a small group of committed activists on a shared problem can be inspiring, motivating, and exhausting. One way to avoid the exhaustion is to find ways to connect with other groups that have shared commitments to equity and justice on related topics of concern. These coalitions can amplify your voices and build on the diverse strengths that members from different organizations and communities bring. One example of a successful coalition is one that I helped start in San Luis Obispo, California: the Central Coast Coalition for Inclusive Schools (CCC4IS). I helped start this coalition with community partners who worked in and with local schools to specifically support local school districts to implement three newly passed state laws: Seth's Law (AB9), the FAIR Education Act (SB48), and the School Success and Opportunity Act (AB1266). Each of these laws was written and passed to address issues faced by LGBTQIA+ youth: bullying and harassment, curricular inclusion, and access to sex-segregated facilities based on gender identity. I reached out to local organizations that focused on issues such as sexual health, social and emotional learning, violence prevention, and antidiscrimination. The structure and format for this partnership were informed by training on the self-directed groupwork–social action research (SDG-SAR) methodology (Mullender & Ward, 1991) that was offered to interested academics and community members in San Luis Obispo in March 2013. This 16-hour training focused on principles of antioppressive organizing inspired by Paulo Freire's concepts of *critical pedagogy, praxis,* and consciousness-raising or *conscientização*. Through ongoing meetings with stakeholders who are impacted by a shared social problem, groups are guided in activities to help them collectively identify root causes for the problem and develop solutions that are grounded in the knowledge and experiences of those most impacted.

This led to the creation of a community advisory board (CAB) to inform an action research project I was leading and had grant funding to initiate. Representatives from the following organizations were present at the first meeting in June 2013 of the CAB: Cal Poly Pride Center, Cal Poly School of Education, Community Action Partnership of SLO, Gay and Lesbian Association (GALA), Q-youth group, PFLAG, SLO County Community Foundation, SLO County Office of Education, "Teaching FAIR" (Santa Barbara, CA), and Tranz Central Coast. At subsequent quarterly meetings we had the participation of additional organizations, including the ACLU of Southern California, Gay Straight Alliance Network, People of Faith for Justice, California Teachers Association, Anti-Defamation League, Cal Poly's Women's and Gender Studies Department, and Cal Poly's Disability Resource Center. During the first year we worked to develop a name, a logo, and a mission statement. These collective identity-building activities helped establish a shared vision and processes for exchanging ideas and honoring the contributions, priorities, and interests of each represented organization.

Though many of the high schools in San Luis Obispo County had campus clubs known as Queer or Gender and Sexuality Alliances (GSAs) to support LGBTQIA+ youth, the effectiveness of these clubs varied from year to year based on faculty support, student leadership, and participation. The

GSAs mostly operated in isolation and thus lacked connection to a larger community. Using a community grant, I hired some college students to attend GSA meetings on local high school campuses for the purposes of networking, sharing information, and providing support. These efforts resulted in the coordination and planning of Harvey Milk Day picnics in May 2015 and 2016. These events attracted students from all the local GSAs and teen allies from youth-serving clubs in the county for a day of celebration, games, fun, food, and networking. The most notable outcome of Harvey Milk Day events was a reported decrease in the sense of isolation and the creation of feelings of community among LGBTQIA+ youth and educator-allies who participated.

Another annual event supported by the CCC4IS was participation at a conference hosted by the local university. Change the Status Quo (CSQ) is an annual social justice conference organized by undergraduate student staff and volunteers. Participants (presenters and attendees) typically include college students and faculty/staff, community members, and a growing number of participants from California and, in some cases, other states. As described on its website, "The conference aims to challenge social norms to make lasting changes in our community and around the world. The mission of CSQ is to empower students to challenge stereotypes, demand solutions, and use education to make a lasting change." This youth-led conference created an opportunity to further support networking and youth leadership development.

Members of the CCC4IS attended as a group and organized workshops connected with the coalition in 2015 and 2016. Participation in CSQ served five primary purposes:

1. Connecting LGBTQI and allied youth in local high schools throughout the county with each other in workshops and via participation in informal networking and socializing
2. Connecting LGBTQI and allied youth in local high schools throughout the county with coalition members and with Cal Poly students, faculty, and staff working to create a more just and equitable world
3. Providing leadership development for LGBTQI and allied youth in local high schools throughout the county
4. Educating CSQ participants on the challenges faced by LGBTQI and allied youth in local high schools
5. Empowering students and allies to challenge stereotypes, demand solutions, and use education to make a lasting change (per the goal of CSQ)

At the 2015 conference, 30 students from the GSAs of five different high schools gathered with a few college students to attend a workshop entitled "Creating LGBTQ-Inclusive Schools: Empowering Youth Leaders." During this workshop, students were asked to come up with ideas about what they would like to accomplish by the end of the current academic year and what resources CCC4IS could provide for their club. When asked what activities they would like to have accomplished by June 2015, most GSAs focused on securing gender-neutral bathrooms for their campus and educating their high school's faculty on *microaggressions*, the daily hostilities they face as LGBTQIA+ students in their schools. Other common goals included selling merchandise, advertising the club, and developing an LGBTQIA+-inclusive health/sex education course for students. The most common resources requested by local GSA members were funding, help with networking between clubs, and support for giving presentations to faculty.

Students also participated in an activity where they each wrote down two things they would like to see change in their schools that would make the lives of LGBTQIA+ students better. Each idea was written down on a sticky note. These were then collected and shared, sparking a discussion about how we can improve our communities. As of 2023, the CCC4IS group continues to come together on a regular basis to address topics of shared concern and to plan events to support youth in the Central Coast region of California.

Other more well-known examples of student-led coalitions that have had long-term national impacts include the "March for Our Lives" organized by the students in Parkland, Florida, against gun violence ("How the parkland students pulled off a massive national protest in only 5 weeks," 2016) and the #BlackLivesMatter at School movement, which is a national coalition that focuses on organizing for racial justice in education (2024). I encourage you to read more about these other youth-led coalitions and identify ways in which their steps and strategies could be applied to your community to motivate change on the current challenges you are seeing in your schools.

One lesson that is important to learn from early mistakes in the feminist movement and the gay and lesbian rights movement is the failure to include and honor the voices, needs, and priorities of diverse members of your community. For example, in the early women's rights movement, the organizers primarily focused on the needs and interests of White middle-class women and ignored the realities of women of color, lesbians, and trans women (hooks, 1984). In the early gay rights movement, the emphasis was on securing rights for White gay men, with little attention paid to the experiences of gay men of color, lesbians, trans people, and people with disabilities. For example, the Lesbian Avengers was formed after lesbian activists in the AIDS Coalition to Unleash Power (ACT UP) got frustrated that the needs and voices of lesbians with AIDS were not being heard or addressed by the primarily White, gay, male leadership of the organization (McCabe, 2022). Several studies of GSAs and other similar student groups have shown that these groups often center the priorities of a small clique of students who are often White women and that students of color and trans or nonbinary students don't feel welcome (McCready, 2004; Poteat et al., 2018). Student groups need to work consistently on remaining open to new members, welcoming to youth of diverse backgrounds and experiences, and making efforts to establish and maintain connections with other student groups that focus on equity, diversity, and justice-oriented issues. This type of organizing work might be uncomfortable at first, as it will require you to reach out to peers you don't know that well or that you don't normally interact with outside of class. I encourage you to move out of your comfort zone and ask hard questions to ensure that your student group and your organizing efforts aren't repeating these mistakes from the past.

CONCLUSION

Now let's get started! The rest of this book is organized to provide you with the tools and knowledge to identify issues in your school that need attention and to develop activism and advocacy activities that will create sustainable changes. I hope the stories of successful student activists and the historical context provided in this introduction help you see how much is possible when young people focus on an unjust issue that they want to change and work with supportive adults to plan and implement their actions. As Margaret Mead reminds us, "a small group of committed citizens can change the world." Now let's get to it!

DISCUSSION QUESTIONS

1. What youth change-maker's story in this chapter most resonated with you? Why?
2. Reviewing the history of some LGBTQIA+ activism in Figure 1.1, what events did you find surprising or want to learn more about?
3. Have you ever participated in a coalition or an LGBTQIA+-serving community organization? What was it focused on, and what did you get out of that experience?
4. What forms of activism have you witnessed or supported in your community? What made them successful?
5. What experience do you have with youth and adult collaborations? Which of the suggestions from this chapter do you think would be helpful to focus on?

KEY TERMS

- cisheteronormativity
- *conscientização*

- critical pedagogy
- Don't Ask, Don't Tell (DADT)
- Equal Protection Clause
- First Amendment
- Fourteenth Amendment
- GSA
- homophobia
- LGBTQIA+
- injunction
- microaggression
- normative
- praxis
- queer (n.)
- queering (v.)
- Title IX
- transphobia

CHAPTER 2

Making Your Case
Evidence to Support LGBTQIA+ Equity Work

> Research is formalized curiosity. It is poking and prying with a purpose. It is a seeking that he who wishes may know the cosmic secrets of the world and they that dwell therein.
>
> —Zora Neale Hurston

Now that you have (hopefully) been inspired by some stories of successful youth activists who have organized and advocated for changes in their schools and districts, this chapter will help you learn more about the diverse experiences of LGBTQIA+ youth in schools to identify areas you want to focus on improving in your school and region. When doing activist work, it is important to recognize that a variety of stakeholders are involved who need to be included in change efforts. A *stakeholder* is a person or group of people who have a "stake" or are invested in a particular community. In a public school, some key stakeholders include school board members, district leaders (superintendent, other district office personnel), principals, teachers and other educational staff (librarians, counselors, paraeducators, social workers), students, parents, and other community members. In charter and private schools, there are different stakeholders to consider including charter network leaders, board members, heads of school, alumni associations, and sometime religious leaders as well. Each one of these stakeholders has different priorities, knowledge of the issue, and values shaping their positions on matters related to LGBTQIA+ equity in schools. In order to successfully engage stakeholders to support your cause, one important strategy is to use research and relevant information to educate your community about why change is necessary.

In many cases noted in Chapter 1, the students involved testified at school board meetings or the state legislature or shared their personal experiences via social media or mainstream news outlets. In addition to sharing details of personal incidents that were difficult or impactful, sharing research collected by reliable sources that provides context and more general information about the issue can also be persuasive. This chapter will offer a summary of research about the experiences of LGBTQIA+ youth in schools and is divided into two main sections: impacts of a negative school climate and features of a positive school climate. While much of the data in the first section present a dismal picture of the impacts of cisheteronormativity, homophobia, and transphobia on youth, the second section focuses on the positive impacts a supportive school climate can have. Many scholars rightly critique the reliance on *risk narratives* that circulate about depression, homelessness, and suicide rates for LGBTQIA+ youth to advocate for change in schools. This critique is important to underline that LGBTQIA+ youth are not damaged or in need of rescuing and that they are strong, brilliant, and creative despite some of the hostile climates they have to navigate. However, it is important to be able to educate parents, educators, and community members about the harmful impacts that pervasive *cisheternormativity*, *homophobia*, and *transphobia* have on youth while also sharing how affirmation, support, and creating spaces for *queer joy* can help counteract those negative messages.

In each section I will share evidence that paints a picture of how diverse LGBTQIA+ youth have experienced schools over a span of the past two decades. This chapter also includes activity ideas that you can do in a class or group meeting to identify and collect updated information about schools like yours or in your same general geographic region and/or grade level(s). The more current and relevant your evidence is, the more persuasive it is likely to be for your intended audience.

IMPACTS OF A NEGATIVE SCHOOL CLIMATE

Early studies that examined the experiences of LGBTQIA+ youth in schools focused mostly on students who identified as gay or lesbian. In the late 1980s and early 1990s, there was a growing awareness that gay and lesbian youth were at risk for suicide in rates three to four times higher than youth who did not identify as gay or lesbian (D'Augelli & Hershberger, 1993; Gibson, 1989; *Massachusetts High School Students and Sexual Orientation: Results of the 1999 Youth Risk Behavior Survey*, 1999). This initial focus on suicidality and other harmful behaviors (like drug and alcohol abuse and other forms of self-harm) led to a dominant risk narrative for gay and lesbian youth (Hillier et al., 2020; Meyer, Leonardi, & Keenan, 2022). While the use of this information was intended to motivate changes to make schools and society safer for gay and lesbian youth, it also had the consequence of linking gay and lesbian identities to stigmatizing concepts of danger, risk, and harm. This initial focus on safety and harm reduction did have some success in improving antibullying initiatives and motivating some states and districts to develop supports for gay and lesbian youth; however, it also built a narrow understanding of youth experiences and painted a grim picture of the lives of gays and lesbians. This early era of research also missed out on the diversity of experiences among LGBTQIA+ youth since these early studies did not explore the distinct experiences of transgender and nonbinary or bisexual and pansexual youth, nor did these studies attend to variations based on race, disability, or geographic location. More recent research has begun to address these gaps, and this chapter will present details that will hopefully resonate with the diversity of identities, experiences, and communities in your club or school.

Safety and Well-Being

One of the most compelling arguments for addressing LGBTQIA+ equity in schools is that of student safety and well-being. It is difficult for anyone to argue that they don't want students to be safe, healthy, and successful. As such, sharing evidence about the ways in which schools are unsafe or cause certain students to feel isolated, depressed, or in danger has been an effective strategy to persuade audiences to make important changes to state laws, district policies, and school practices. This section of the chapter will address some of the evidence that illustrates how schools can be unsafe and toxic places for many LGBTQIA+ youth. From the most recent national data available at the time of this writing, we know that 50.6% of LGBTQ students felt unsafe at school because of their sexual orientation, 43.2% because of their gender expression, 42.1% due to body size, and 40.3% because of their gender identity. LGBTQ students also reported feeling unsafe due to their mental health or emotional disability (61.6%), academic ability (25.9%), religion (11%), or race or ethnicity (9.3%) (Kosciw et al., 2022, p. 10–11). Furthermore, 70% of undocumented LGBTQ students reported feeling unsafe at school due to their citizenship status (Kosciw et al., 2020, p. 17). One student shared, "I don't feel very safe or accepted at my school at all. I feel like if I were to come out to my friends/classmates, I would be hated for just being who I am" (Kosciw et al., 2020, p. 18). Much of the data shared in this chapter are from the 2021 GLSEN *National School Climate Survey* and are based on responses from over 22,000 LGBTQ+ students ages 13–21 from across all 50 states as well as the District of Columbia, Puerto Rico, U.S. Virgin Islands, Northern Mariana Islands, and Guam (Kosciw et al., 2022). A second important source of information is shared from a national survey of 1,300 students age 13–18 and 1,015 secondary teachers (Greytak et al., 2016).

This section begins with information about bullying and harassment and then addresses safety and mental health. If you or someone you care about has experienced any of these harms firsthand, this section may be difficult to read. Please feel free to skip to other parts of this section if you prefer not to read the detailed evidence of how toxic school climates impact LGBTQIA+ students. If you do keep reading and are feeling as if it is making you terribly sad or hopeless, please reach out to a friend or trusted adult so you can get some support. You can also contact a confidential and free hotline service with trained peer or professional counselors. Four different free services are described in Figure 2.1.

Making Your Case 17

Figure 2.1. Youth Hotlines

The Trevor Project. The Trevor Project is an international hotline created to provide confidential and free crisis counseling for LGBTQIA+ youth in the United States and Mexico. Support is available 24/7, 365 days a year via online chat; text START to (678-678), or phone (1-866-488-7386). This organization also provides a moderated online community for youth ages 13–24 and reliable information about topics including sexual orientation, gender identity, mental health, suicide, and diversity: www.thetrevorproject.org

Youthline. Youthline is a peer support hotline for LGBTQIA+ youth in Canada. Support is available via online chat, text (647-694-4275), email (askus@youthlin.ca), or phone (1-800-268-9688) from 4:00 to 9:30 p.m. EST. This website also can direct you to local LGBTQIA+ organizations in your region: www.youthline.ca

Trans Lifeline. This organization "connects trans people to community support and resources to survive and thrive" and is fully run by trans people for trans people. You can call from the United States (1-877-565-8860) and Canada (1-877-330-6366). This website also has resources for coming out, crisis support, ID change, and how to support a trans loved one: www.translifeline.org

It Gets Better Project. This international network of supports and services for LGBTQIA+ provides links and information to additional hotlines and organizations around the world: www.itgetsbetter.org/get-help

---

Bullying and Harassment. The problem of bullying and harassment grounded in homophobia and transphobia is one of the everyday challenges many youth face at school, especially LGBTQIA+ and gender-nonconforming students. A majority of LGBTQ+ students (68%) in the GLSEN study reported hearing the word "gay" used in a negative way (e.g., "that's so gay") at school, and 93.7% were distressed because of this language (Kosciw et al., 2022, p. 14). Students also hear negative comments related to gender expression: 56% of LGBTQ+ students heard negative remarks about gender expression (not acting "masculine enough" or "feminine enough"), and 83.4% of LGBTQ+ students heard negative remarks specifically about transgender people, like "tranny" or "he/she" (Kosciw et al., 2022, p. 14). Furthermore, students reported hearing homophobic remarks (58%) and negative remarks about gender expression (72%) from their teachers or other school staff. Sadly, less than one-fifth of LGBTQ+ students (12.3%) reported that school staff intervened most of the time or always when overhearing homophobic remarks at school, and only 8.7% of LGBTQ+ students reported that school staff intervened most of the time or always when overhearing negative remarks about gender expression (Kosciw et al., 2022, pp. 14–16). Students also reported hearing other biased remarks frequently or often. This includes sexist remarks (75.7%), ableist remarks ("spaz" or "retarded") (72.6%), comments about weight or body size (60%), and racist language (54.7%) (Kosciw et al., 2022, p. 18).

Figure 2.2. 2021 National School Climate Survey excerpts: Bullying (Kosciw et al., 2022)

- 60.7% of LGBTQ students experienced in-person verbal harassment (e.g., called names or threatened) at school based on sexual orientation, 20.6% based on gender expression, and 20.5% based on gender (p. xvi).
- 31.2% of LGBTQ students were physically harassed (e.g., pushed or shoved) in the past year based on sexual orientation, gender expression, or gender; 22.4% based on sexual orientation; 20.6% based on gender expression; and 20.5% based on gender (p. xvi).
- 12.5% of LGBTQ students were physically assaulted (e.g., punched, kicked, injured with a weapon) in the past year based on sexual orientation, gender expression, or gender; 8.8% based on sexual orientation; 8.2% based on gender expression; and 8.3% based on gender (p. xvii).
- LGBTQ students were also bullied or harassed at school for other reasons: 34.4% based on actual or perceived disability, 29% based on actual or perceived religion, and 23.3% based on actual or perceived race or ethnicity (p. xvii).

You can access more reports from GLSEN's research at www.glsen.org/research.

In addition to experiencing the everyday homophobic and transphobic speech from peers and educators that fills school halls, LGBTQIA+ students are also targets for verbal and physical assaults. Most LGBTQ+ students (83.1%) experienced harassment or assault due to their sexual orientation, gender expression, gender, actual or perceived religion, actual or perceived race and ethnicity, and actual or perceived disability (Kosciw et al., 2022, p. xvi). They also reported experiencing online harassment (36.6%) and sexual harassment (53.7%) (unwanted touching or sexual remarks) (Kosciw et al., 2022, p. xvi). Students who experienced higher rates of victimization also reported being subjected to more school discipline sanctions (Kosciw et al., 2022, p. xix), and other studies have also shown a relationship between victimization and school discipline; that is, students who report experiencing higher rates of victimization (bullying and harassment) also report higher rates of discipline (detention, suspension, expulsion) (GLSEN, 2016). For additional results from GLSEN's 2021 survey, see Figure 2.2.

While these data alone are disturbing, it is also important to compare these experiences to students who don't identify as LGBTQ. Overall, LGBTQ students experience a more hostile school climate than their *cisgender* and heterosexual peers. Compared to non-LGBTQ students, they were more likely to be bullied or harassed based on actual or perceived sexual orientation (67.0% vs. 13.5%), gender expression (59.7% vs. 17.6%), gender (39.9% vs. 17.0%), appearance/body size (68.4% vs. 50.3%), and ability (26.7% vs. 12.2%). LGBTQ students were also more likely to experience sexual harassment (43.6% vs. 26.4%), having rumors and lies spread about them (67.2% vs. 52.7%), property damage (44.1% vs. 38.1%), and cyberbullying (40.2% vs. 32.8%) than non-LGBTQ students (Greytak et al., 2016, p. xiv).

Safety and Mental Health. While mental health has been a growing concern in adolescents—particularly since the COVID-19 pandemic—LGBTQIA+ youth report experiencing higher rates of depression and anxiety that are related to higher rates of victimization (Kosciw et al., 2014). LGBTQ+ students who experienced more homophobia and transphobia at school also had lower self-esteem and higher levels of depression than those who experienced lower levels of victimization (Kosciw et al., 2022, p. xix). Another negative result associated with homophobia and transphobia in schools is substance abuse, self-harm, and suicidal ideation. Students reporting more severe levels of in-person victimization were two times more likely to have seriously considered suicide in the past year than those who reported less severe victimization (Kosciw et al., 2022, p. 40), and those experiencing online victimization were more than three times more likely to have seriously considered suicide (Kosciw et al., 2022, p. 43). Higher rates of substance abuse and self-harm by youth who identify as LGBTQ+ have also been documented (De Pedro et al., 2017; Jordan, 2000; Taliaferro et al., 2019), and studies have reported that LGBT youth with higher levels of family acceptance are less likely to engage in such behaviors (Ryan et al., 2010). These experiences of discrimination at school also impact students' academic performance and future plans.

Academics and Attendance

In addition to one's overall safety and well-being, school climate shapes how well students can learn and engage in scholarly activities. Research shows that experiences with discrimination and harassment impact students' grade point averages (GPAs), attendance, and plans for postsecondary education. Students who were targeted for harassment due to their sexual orientation or gender expression were three times more likely to miss school in the past month, have lower GPAs (2.83 vs. 3.15), and were less likely to pursue any form of postsecondary education (Kosciw et al., 2022, pp. xviii–xiv). While most students (93.8%) in the GLSEN study planned to graduate from high school, 5.3% said they did not plan to graduate or were unsure. Of this group of students, 92.3% reported mental health reasons (depression, anxiety, stress) and 51.5% said it was due to a hostile school climate (Kosciw et al., 2022, p. 34). The rates of victimization due to sexual orientation or gender expression were related to students' plans to pursue any postsecondary education: higher rates of victimization at school were related to higher rates of students not continuing their education beyond high school (9.4% low victimization and 16.6% higher victimization) (Kosciw et al., 2022, p. 35). When compared to their cisgender and heterosexual peers, LGBTQ students were more likely to say that they did not plan to complete high school (2.7% vs. 0.8% of non-LGBTQ students) or to continue their education past high school (9.6% vs. 5.7%) (Greytak et al., 2016, p. xiv).

The impacts of a negative school climate also shape students' willingness and ability to be present at school and school-related events. In the GLSEN study, 32.7% of LGBTQ students missed at least one entire day of school in the past month because they felt unsafe or uncomfortable, and 8.6% missed four or more days in the past month. Many also skip school functions (31% frequently or often) and extracurricular activities (25% frequently or often) because they felt unsafe or uncomfortable. Nearly a fifth of LGBTQ students (17.1%) reported having changed schools due to feeling unsafe or uncomfortable at school (Kosciw et al., 2020, p. 19). We know that changing schools causes a significant disruption to one's learning and daily routines and is only done as a last resort (McGuire et al., 2010; Meyer et al., 2016). A second study also reported that LGBTQ students had higher rates of absenteeism, lower grades, and lower educational intentions and that higher rates of victimization were related to more negative outcomes (Aragon et al., 2014).

Variation in Schools and Student Experiences

While some consistent trends are noted in this chapter about the negative impacts many LGBTQIA+ students experience in school, there are some distinct differences in degree and impact based on where and what kind of school you attend, as well as other identity categories that shape the forms of bias and discrimination students may experience in addition to the cisheteronormativity, homophobia, and transphobia noted earlier.

LGBTQ Students of Color. The information presented earlier reflects that of the 22,000+ students who responded to the survey, over 60% of these students are White and reported different experiences than did students of color. Many diversity and equity initiatives in schools focus on inequalities based on race, disability, and language learning status. However, what these initiatives often fail to acknowledge is that LGBTQIA+ students have multiply marginalized identities. This means they are also students of color, students with disabilities, and students who are emerging bilinguals (Meyer, Quantz, & Regan, 2022). To help others recognize the diversity of the LGBTQIA+ community and the different experiences some students have based on multiply marginalized identities, we need to talk explicitly about the experiences of these students as well. For example, in GLSEN's study, all students of color experienced similar levels of victimization based on race/ethnicity, although Black and Asian American–Pacific Islander (AAPI) students were less likely to report feeling unsafe due to their sexual orientation and gender than Latinx, Native and Indigenous, Middle Eastern and North African (MENA), multiracial, and White students (Kosciw et al., 2022). Native and Indigenous LGBTQIA+ students were generally more likely than other racial/ethnic groups to experience anti-LGBTQIA+ victimization and discrimination (Kosciw et al., 2022,

p. 96). The majority of LGBTQIA+ students of color experienced victimization based on both their race/ethnicity and their LGBTQIA+ identities. The percentages of students of color experiencing these multiple forms of victimization were similar across racial/ethnic groups (Kosciw et al., 2022, p. 96).

Many LGBTQIA+ youth of color experience higher rates of exclusionary punishment (suspensions and expulsions) as well (7.2% MENA; 7.4% multiracial; 8.8% Black; 9% Native American, American Indian, and Alaska Native vs. 2.8% AAPI; 4.6% White) (Kosciw et al., 2020). Finally, access to culturally responsive social supports is more limited for trans youth of color (Garofalo et al., 2006; Singh, 2013). This is why it is essential that gender and sexuality alliances (GSAs) explicitly address racial justice issues and that other student groups focused on racial equity address topics related to queer justice. For more detailed data on various racial and ethnic groups, I recommend reviewing a series of GLSEN reports titled, "Erasure and Resilience: The Experiences of LGBTQ Students of Color," which share data based on the information shared by Black, Native and Indigenous, and Latinx LGBTQIA+ youth (Truong et al., 2020, Zongrone et al., 2020a, 2020b).

Transgender and Nonbinary Students. In addition to the widespread negative experiences reported by most LGBTQIA+ youth in schools, we know that transgender and nonbinary students tend to have more frequent and more severe experiences with harassment, exclusion, and negativity at school. In a 2021 research brief on trans and nonbinary (TNB) students, GLSEN found that TNB students were more likely to feel unsafe at school due to their gender (84% transgender, 52% nonbinary, 20% cisgender students) and miss school because they felt unsafe or uncomfortable (43.6% transgender, 38.1% nonbinary, 24.9% cisgender students) (Kosciw, 2022). TNB students also reported having fewer LGBTQ-supportive educators and were less likely to have access to LGBTQ-inclusive curricula (Kosciw, 2022). Students with access to such supports had much higher levels of school belonging. Additionally, discriminatory school policies are a bigger problem for TNB students than their cisgender peers. TNB students were prevented from accessing appropriate bathrooms and locker rooms, wearing certain clothing deemed "inappropriate" for their gender, and using their chosen names and pronouns at much higher rates than cisgender LGB students (Kosciw, 2022).

In school-based research, little attention is paid to the complexity of transness. A recent study found that trans students who embodied aspects of femininity seemed to be the most heavily targeted (Leonardi et al., 2021). While studies that attended to this complexity revealed conflicting results (e.g., no differences) (Greytak et al., 2009) and more hostility toward trans male students (Kosciw et al., 2016) and nonbinary students assigned female at birth (Murchison et al., 2019), most found important differences. This perspective urges all of us to consciously consider the nuanced distinctions across the diverse category of individuals who can be described as "transgender" when thinking about school communities and how students of diverse genders experience various spaces at school (Labuski & Keo-Meier, 2015).

Students With Disabilities. Sixty-one percent of LGBTQ+ students felt unsafe at school due to their mental health or emotional disability. This was the second most rated reason for feeling unsafe at school after sexual orientation and gender (68%). The rate was much lower for students reporting feeling unsafe due to a developmental or physical disability (9.3%) (Kosciw, 2022). Students also reported hearing negative remarks about students' ability/disability quite regularly (72.6% hearing them "often" or "frequently"). This was the second most common form of biased remarks students heard (Kosciw, 2022). Over one-third (34.4%) of LGBTQ students were verbally or physically harassed at school due to their actual or perceived disability (Kosciw, 2022).

Geography and School Type. GLSEN's National School Climate Surveys have consistently found significant differences in the experiences of students in different types of schools: public, private, religious, or charter, as well as locale (urban, suburban, rural) and region of the country. For example, LGBTQ students in rural schools reported experiencing more hostile school climates than students in urban and suburban schools. They heard higher rates of biased language and experiences more victimization and anti-LGBTQ discriminatory school policies and practices. LGBTQ students in rural schools were also the least likely to have related school resources or supports as compared to students in urban and suburban schools (Kosciw et al., 2022, p. 107). Some regional differences noted in this study were that LGBTQ students in the South had more negative school experiences overall than students in all other regions, including higher rates of biased language, victimization, and anti-LGBTQ discriminatory school policies and practices. They also found that LGBTQ youth in the Midwest had more negative experiences overall than those in the Northeast and West (Kosciw et al., 2022, p. 107). In the "From Teasing to Torment" study, Greytak and colleagues (2016) found that students in rural schools (as compared to suburban and rural schools) reported higher rates of bullying based on sexual orientation, and students in the West were less likely to report bullying and harassment based on sexual orientation compared to students in other regions.

Additionally, GLSEN reports that LGBTQ students in private nonreligious schools had fewer hostile school experiences than those in public schools and those in religious schools, whereas students in religious schools were the most likely to report anti-LGBTQ discriminatory school policies and practices. Among students in public schools, those in charter schools had similar experiences to those in regular public schools regarding anti-LGBTQ experiences and resources and supports. However, charter school students were more likely to say that they had access to the following: inclusive curriculum, supportive policies for transgender and nonbinary students, and a supportive administration. Students in regular (noncharter) public schools were more likely to have LGBTQIA+-inclusive school library resources (Kosciw et al., 2022, pp. xxviii–xxiv).

This section aimed to focus on the variety of experiences students can have based on their identities and school characteristics. The data shared here indicate that multiple aspects of student identities and school contexts will shape how students experience safety, support, and belonging at school. We also know some LGBTQIA+ students are? emerging bilinguals, from immigrant and refugee families, and come from diverse spiritual and religious traditions. As of this writing there is limited information on the specific experiences of LGBTQIA+ students in these groups; however, it is important to be aware of these aspects of diversity in your school community and to recognize that gender and sexual diversity is present within all communities, cultures, and demographic groups. The next section suggests some activities your school can pursue to generate more specific evidence about the experiences of students in your community.

Finding Updated Evidence

Depending on when and where you are reading this, some of the data presented here might not feel current or reflective of your school community. One way this chapter can help you build your case is to offer ideas and resources to create fact sheets, posters, graphs, or other data displays that can tell the story that feels most relevant and impactful in your community for the changes you, other students, and educator-allies want to make. In Figures 2.3a–2.3c, I suggest several different data sources along with some tips for accessing these resources so that anyone with time and curiosity can make use of this evidence to learn more about particular issues impacting youth in your community.

Other publicly available studies that have valuable information related to this topic include the U.S. Trans Survey (https://www.ustranssurvey.org/) conducted in 2015 and again in 2022 (forthcoming) and the American Association of University Women (AAUW) study on sexual harassment in schools conducted in 1993 (Harris & Associates, 1993) and 2011 (Hill & Kearl, 2011). For Canadian students and educators, consider using the EGALE Canada reports on teachers' (Taylor et al., 2015) and students' experiences with homophobia, biphobia, and transphobia in schools (Peter et al., 2021; Taylor & Peter, 2011).

FEATURES OF A POSITIVE SCHOOL CLIMATE

In the face of the harms and challenges related to negative school climates, it is important to note what aspects of schools can be addressed to help all

Figure 2.3a. Activity: Finding Updated Evidence

Several large-scale surveys are conducted on a regular basis (every 2–3 years) and are focused on understanding the experiences of youth nationally or statewide on public health measures including substance use, sexual behaviors, bullying, and mental health. Consider choosing the database that is the most recent or most likely to reflect the experiences of youth in schools in your region.

Centers for Disease Control Youth Risk Behavior Surveillance System (CDC-YRBSS). https://www.cdc.gov/healthyyouth/data/yrbs/index.htm

One way to begin exploring this data set is by accessing the "Youth Data Analysis Tool," where you can select a state (or school district) and topic and then select by gender and sexual orientation to see what data are available on that topic. For example:

1. Select the "other health topics" box in the menu on the right of the screen.
2. On the next screen click on "school connectedness."
3. When the new screen loads, filter your results using the radio buttons in the left menu. I chose "gay, lesbian, and bisexual" and left the others on "all."
4. Choosing the "Graph" tab at the top of the page makes the results easier to see and understand.
5. My results from the 2021 data set show that 45.6% disagree/strongly disagree that they feel close to people at their school.
6. To compare subgroups by sexual identity, leave the "all" radio button selected for all categories and then use the drop-down menu at the top to "view data by subgroup" and then select "sexual identity." This approach generated Figure 2.3b that shows straight students are less likely (34.9%) than GLB or questioning students (45–51%) to feel disconnected from people at school. This means straight students generally have more positive connections with people at school.

---

students—especially LGBTQIA+ students—to be supported and successful. From decades of research, we know that students feel safer and report higher levels of belonging at school when they have (1) supportive adults, (2) access to LGBTQIA+-inclusive curriculum, (3) explicit policy protections, and (4) access to GSAs or other similar clubs (Kosciw, 2020; Kosciw et al., 2008; Szlacha, 2003). While many schools have one or two of these elements, there are opportunities to expand these supports for students. One way to take action is to choose one of these four elements and focus your efforts on one specific element to change. Being involved in such change efforts can be empowering for students (Elliott, 2016; Mayberry, 2006; Russell et al., 2009) and have lasting positive impacts on the community.

Supportive Adults

For students to engage in learning and consistently attend school, positive relationships with adults at school are important. If teachers can't get your pronouns right, respect your identity, or support your development as a whole person, then it is more challenging to be present, take on challenges,

Figure 2.3b. CDC-YRBSS 2021 Data Output Example

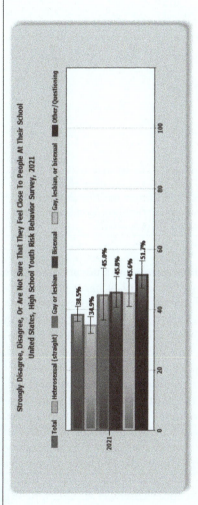

California Healthy Kids Survey (CHKS). https://www.cde.ca.gov/ls/he/at/chks.asp

From the landing page you can select the "Data dashboard" and then select "secondary student." On this screen you can select the filters and topics by using the drop-down menus labeled "Step 1," "Step 2," etc., on the left. For example, I selected:

Step 1: state
Step 2: social and emotional health
Step 3: chronic sadness/hopelessness
Step 4: gender identity

These steps created a series of bar graphs that indicated transgender students reported experiencing these feelings at two times the rate (60%) of cisgender students (30%) across all grades (7, 9, and 11).

Healthy Kids Colorado Survey (HKCS). https://cdphe.colorado.gov/hkcs

On this page you can scroll down and choose from existing reports or select "open dashboard." On the next page select "dashboard" and select data from the drop-down menus. I chose:

Step 1: Survey Year 2021
Step 2: Health Topic: Consent
Step 3: Percentage of students who touch, grab, or pinch in a sexual way when unwanted

This generated a visualization (Figure 2.3c) that showed these data broken down by age, grade, race, gender, and sexual orientation. In Colorado, straight (2.3%) and cisgender (2.7%) students reported this behavior at much lower rates compared to gay/lesbian (6.3%) and transgender (8.9%) youth.

25

Figure 2.3c. HKCS 2021 Data Output Example

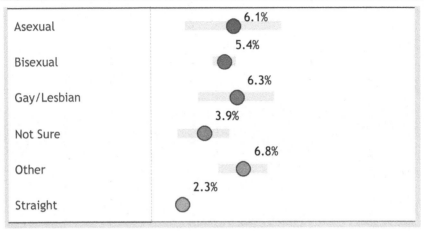

GLSEN State Snapshots. https://www.glsen.org/research/state-by-state-research-2019-state-snapshots-national-school-climate-survey. These are two- to three-page PDFs that present infographics and short summaries of the data from the 40 states that had large enough response rates to share in this format. These fact sheets don't require any additional analyses or preparation and can be helpful advocacy tools.

and focus on academic and personal development. When students have more than a few supportive staff they can identify at school, it has a positive impact on their academic performance, attendance, and aspirations after high school. GLSEN's research tells us that compared to LGBTQIA+ students with no or few supportive school staff (0–5), students with many (11 or more) supportive staff at their school felt safer, had higher GPAs (3.34 vs. 3.14), were more likely to plan on pursuing postsecondary education, and felt greater belonging to their school community. Educators can show their support through their welcome routines at the start of the school year, classroom decorations and displays, and curriculum choices and language use. For example, students who report seeing a Safe Space sticker or poster in their school were more likely to identify school staff who were supportive of LGBTQIA+ students (Kosciw et al., 2020, p. xxiii). The more supportive school staff students can identify, the less likely students are to report feeling unsafe, miss school, or not complete high school (Kosciw et al., 2020, p. 76).

Inclusive Curriculum

The question of including LGBTQIA+ people and families in the curriculum has been a hotly debated discussion in recent years. In 2023, seven states (California, Colorado, Connecticut, Illinois, New Jersey, Nevada, and Oregon) had enacted laws requiring LGBTQ inclusion in the curriculum, and seven states had laws preventing the inclusion of LGBTQ topics in the curriculum

Figure 2.4. 2021 National School Climate Survey: Curriculum (Kosciw et al., 2022, pp. xxi–xxii)

As compared to LGBTQ students in schools without an LGBTQ-inclusive curriculum, LGBTQ students in schools with an LGBTQ-inclusive curriculum were less likely to:
- Hear "gay" used in a negative way often or frequently (48.7% vs. 72%)
- Hear homophobic remarks such as "fag" or "dyke" often or frequently (26.7% vs. 47.8%)
- Hear negative remarks about gender expression often or frequently (42.8% vs. 58.9%) and about transgender people often or frequently (23.6% vs. 42.7%)
- Feel unsafe because of their sexual orientation (23.4% vs. 34%) and gender expression (34% vs. 54%)
- Miss school in the past month because they felt unsafe/uncomfortable (54.7% vs. 67.1%)

(Alabama, Arkansas, Indiana, Iowa, Florida, Kentucky, and North Carolina) (Movement Advancement Project, 2023b). In spite of the political nature of this issue, the research on including the history and literature by and about LGBTQ people is clear: LGBTQ students in schools with an LGBTQ-inclusive curriculum experience a whole host of benefits, including hearing fewer negative remarks about gender and sexual orientation. They also performed better academically in school (3.32 vs. 3.23 average GPA), were more likely to plan on pursuing postsecondary education, and report that their classmates were somewhat or very accepting of LGBTQ people (66.9% vs. 37.9%) (Kosciw et al., 2020, p. xxiii). For additional data on benefits of an inclusive curriculum, see Figure 2.4.

LGBTQIA+-Affirming Policies

Schools that have policies that are comprehensive and *enumerated* (a list of protected categories like race, gender, ability, sexual orientation, etc.) had fewer students reporting negative experiences. Some policies that can support LGBTQIA+ students are (1) nondiscrimination policies that specifically name gender and sexual orientation, (2) comprehensive and enumerated antibullying and harassment policies, and (3) policies that explain how the schools will support transgender students—especially regarding access to sex-segregated spaces and name or pronoun usage. Such policies provide guidance and procedures for school staff to follow and provide a clear statement of support to the school community. Such policies and formal statements of affirmation create more positive environments for LGBTQIA+ students.

Students in schools with supportive policies reported lower rates of biased remarks and experiences with victimization as well as higher rates of intervention by school staff. Policies that are clearly enumerated and comprehensive had more positive impacts on LGBTQ student experiences. Students in schools with no such policies fared worse than students in schools with generic policies. Students in schools with a comprehensive antibullying policy were less likely to hear all forms antigay language and were more likely to report staff intervention in anti-LGBTQ+ remarks (24.5% vs. 11.6%). Students in schools with comprehensive antibullying policies were less likely to miss school due to safety reasons (30% vs. 38% missed one day for safety) and were more likely to report higher levels of school belonging (69% vs. 42%) (Kosciw et al, 2022, pp. xxiii–xiv).

GSAs and Student Clubs

The presence of a GSA or other similarly themed club has been shown to have an overall positive impact on school climate for LGBTQIA+ youth—whether they actively participate in the club or not. It seems that just knowing that there is a space, a supportive adult, and an active group of peers can change a school community for the better. For example, students in schools with GSAs reported lower rates of biased remarks like "no homo" and "gay" in a negative way. They were less likely to feel unsafe due to their sexual orientation (41% with GSAs vs. 55% without GSAs) and gender expression (36% with GSAs vs. 46% without GSAs) and reported lower levels of in-person victimization (Kosciw et al., 2022, p. xx). There were also links between the presence of a GSA and students' connections to supportive staff. It is not surprising that students in schools with a GSA could identify more supportive staff members than those without a GSA: 67.9% could name six or more supportive staff versus 32% in schools with no GSA (Kosciw et al., 2022, pp. 60–62). Simply having a GSA at school was related to more students saying that they felt accepted by their peers (55.4% vs. 32.4%) and students reporting higher rates of active intervention by staff and students when negative remarks were made about gender or sexual orientation. Having access to an active GSA can also provide students with valuable leadership and community engagement opportunities. Student clubs are addressed more fully in Chapter 5.

COLLECTING EVIDENCE FROM YOUR COMMUNITY

The first activity idea in Figure 2.3a of this chapter explained ways that you can access data collected by external organizations. Another idea would be to collect data to capture the stories and experiences of students in your community right now. Five ideas for how you can do this are presented in the following sections: digital photo essay, mapping project, art show, microaggression journals, or a local climate survey. These are each described so you can choose a project or combination of projects that seem most interesting and rewarding for your current needs and goals.

Digital Photo Essay

This form of evidence combines visuals and text to share experiences surrounding a guiding question or theme. This project draws from traditions of photojournalism and photo voice research methods (Mackenzie & Talbott, 2018), also known as "photo elicitation" (Walton & Niblett, 2013). This project can be done over a fixed time period determined by your class or club: a semester, a month, or an awareness week. Students who want to participate can take photos and post images that respond to a focused question such as: "Where do you feel safe and supported at school?," "Where do you feel unsafe?," "Where do you feel like you belong?," or "What are examples of queer joy in your day?" Students involved can choose a hashtag, website, app, or physical time and place to post and share these images (with or without captions) that are most accessible for the audience they want to view and learn from this project.

Mapping Project

Creating maps of buildings, campuses, neighborhoods, or communities is another way to collect and share data about how students experience safety and belonging at school. This project involves either drawing or printing out a map of the space students are interested in collecting and sharing data about. Once you have the basic map of the location you are focusing on (building diagram, campus map, etc.), you can use stickers, crayons, or markers to indicate how students feel in certain locations. One way would be to use a traffic light color scheme to indicate places students feel safe (green), unsafe (red), or neutral/unsure (amber). You might use a grayscale if you want to print it out on a black and white printer: safe (white), unsafe (black), neutral/unsure (gray). You could even add emojis or symbols to indicate places where students feel belonging and joy or come up with your own icons based on the experiences you want to learn about and share. This map could then be discussed with the student council or school administration, presented at a school board meeting, or posted on a bulletin board (after photographing it in case it is defaced or taken down). For more tech-savvy students, you could imagine ways of doing this in your community using Google Maps or other digital tools. For more on mapping projects, I suggest starting with an article titled, "Identity Safety and Relational Health in Youth Spaces: A Needs Assessment with LGBTQ Youth of Color" (Gamarel et al., 2014).

Art Show

For students who are creative and have visual arts interests, you could develop a community-wide art show built around a guiding theme or question such as "What does being a part of the LGBTQIA+ community mean to you?" or "experiences of LGBTQIA+ youth in our town." Contributions could be poems, music, drawings, collages, paintings, or sculptures to encourage a wide variety of perspectives and contributions. One school district in Colorado had an art show in 2023 on the theme of "consent" that generated a wide array of powerful pieces that shared with the community how current students felt about and experienced consent. This could also be an engaging project for out-of-school youth groups and community organizations to collaborate on with school art programs (Furman et al., 2019; Wells, 2007).

Microaggression Journals

For students who struggle to understand the impacts of cisheteronormativity and related *intersectional* forms of oppression such as racism, ableism, and bias against immigrant communities, one idea from a school in Oregon is to keep a microaggression journal (Pascoe, 2023). Participating students keep a log in a notebook or notes app on their phone for a set period of time (5–7 days is a good start) where they write down every interaction they witness or experience that feels like a microaggression. *Microaggressions* are smaller, harder-to-notice forms of exclusion and oppression that can be verbal or nonverbal (Nadal et al., 2011; Solarzano & Perez Huber, 2020). Some examples of microaggressions are "wow, I didn't know you were in the honors program" to a Black athlete, or "you are surprisingly well-spoken" to a bilingual student, or "you must have a crush on somebody" to a student who is asexual and aromantic. Examples of nonverbal microaggressions include eye-rolling when someone else is speaking about a difficult experience, physically excluding someone from a lunch table or gathering space, or bumping into/pushing past someone intentionally (Sue, 2010). Once these journals have been completed, students can share their results verbally in a meeting or can choose to create a visual display such as a poster, word cloud, collage, or bulletin board to share the results and educate others.

Local Climate Survey

This is the most traditional form of data collection suggested here. One well-developed tool that requires minimal knowledge about survey creation and distribution is to use GLSEN's Local School Climate Survey (LSCS). This digital tool enables users to create an account, select from a list of prewritten topics and questions, and then distribute the survey on paper or digitally to collect results. The tool will also generate summaries of the data that are easy to read and share with others. To create an account and start using the LSCS tool, visit localsurvey.glsen.org.

CONCLUSION

We know from the research shared in this chapter as well as a large body of evidence on school climate in general that feelings of belonging and safety, as well as academic and overall well-being at school, are essential for student success. Despite this knowledge, the safety and well-being of certain groups of students have not been prioritized in many programs aimed at improving school climate. When asking if your school is safe or if students feel like they belong, it is important to reframe the questions to consider "safe for whom" or "who belongs here." In one study of Canadian teachers, we asked that exact question. Initially the responses to the question of if their school was "somewhat" or "very" safe were quite high (96.9% agree). However, when we asked the follow-up question: "Is your school safe for LGB youth/transgender students?" the positive responses decreased significantly to 71% and 52% agreeing, respectively (Meyer et al., 2014). To support diverse LGBTQIA+ students, school programs and leaders need to intentionally focus on improving policies, practices, and programs to create schools that affirm gender and sexual diversity while attending to ongoing efforts to address racial bias and other related forms of inequity in schools. Collecting data and talking about your own experiences at school are important ways to help others understand what needs to change to make your community safer and more welcoming for all students—especially those in the LGBTQIA+ community.

DISCUSSION QUESTIONS

1. Which of the harms noted in this chapter seem like the biggest problem in your school? Which ones should we focus on trying to address first?
2. Which of the supports do you experience in school? Which ones could we try and improve?
3. What else do you wonder about? What information and evidence should we try and collect to share the experiences of students here?

KEY TERMS

- cisgender
- cisheteronormativity
- enumerated
- homophobia
- intersectional [oppression]
- microaggression
- National School Climate Survey (NSCS)
- queer joy
- risk narrative
- stakeholder
- transphobia

CHAPTER 3

Queering Learning and Classrooms

> Learning is about disruption and opening up to further learning, not closure and satisfaction.
>
> —Kevin Kumashiro

What is normal? What is natural? What is cool or popular? Who decides? Why does it matter? Has it always been this way? When did things change? Why? Who benefits? Who is harmed? Which of our answers are right or wrong? How many right answers can we find? Whose stories and perspectives are we learning from? Which voices and ideas are missing?

These questions are here to warm you up and get you ready to ask more since this chapter aims to provoke curiosities while pointing to some starting places for answers; to inspire a new way to think about teaching, learning, and how classrooms and schools are organized. This chapter starts by introducing the guiding concept of queer pedagogy, which offers ideas for teachers and students on how to reshape how we learn and what is taught. We will then explore questions and approaches to discussion that promote critical thinking and make space for learning about any content area in new and creative ways. I will then suggest some ideas on how to engage in an ongoing process of "queering" the curriculum related to commonly taught subjects including social studies, language arts, math, science, health, and sexuality education. The chapter will conclude with information about some ideas for how to queer your classrooms and school. Let's queer it up!

QUEER PEDAGOGY

Pedagogy is just a fancy word to talk about how we design spaces for teaching and learning, so when we add "queer" to pedagogy, it helps us think about new and creative ways to go about what happens in classrooms and other learning spaces. When using the word "queer" in this context, I am using it in the most expansive way: It is not just about including LGBTQIA+ topics and stories in the curriculum. It is more about questioning what has been defined as normal, natural, or "common sense" (Kumashiro, 2004) and pushing at the boundaries of the ways things have always been done. It encourages us to question assumptions and to be like curious children who keep asking "why"? Queer pedagogy invites us to rethink how we approach everything related to teaching and learning environments and makes space for innovative, creative, and critical ideas to emerge instead of following dominant patterns of the ways things have always been done. It may mean making classrooms more student-centered or flipping the way you think about assessing learning or demonstrating a new skill. It can mean asking questions that invite others to consider topics and information from a new angle. It also encourages learning that disrupts normalcy (Bryson & De Castell, 1993) and centers the ideas and knowledge of people and communities that have been historically excluded or marginalized by traditional texts, lessons, and curricula. This starts with expanding our ways of thinking, talking, and interacting beyond White, Western, colonial, patriarchal, cisheterornormative binaries of right/wrong, good/bad, Black/White, male/female. This also includes explicitly and consistently talking about *gender and sexual diversity (GSD)* (Meyer, 2009a) and not just people who identify as LGBTQIA+. Talking about GSD goes beyond naming people who are part of the LGBTQIA+ community and recognizes that regardless of your identity, gender and sexuality are much more expansive and creative than the narrow stereotypes and scripts (Keenan, 2017) that are part of dominant culture.

Queer pedagogies also invite us to focus on joy, pleasure, and desire or *eros,* in learning (Britzman, 1995). How can we make learning more fun, playful, and connected to issues that matter to us in our everyday lives? We know that for deep learning to happen there needs to be some sort of relationship of trust, mutual respect, and even love between teacher and student, not a romantic love, but an ethic of *radical love* (hooks, 1994a) that is grounded in shared commitments to justice, equity, and liberation. This love and pleasure for learning and working together inspire more committed and engaged work and allow all those involved in the learning process to feel supported, challenged, and rewarded by the work together.

It also helps us to learn how to handle working with partial knowledge—often carefully selected pieces of a puzzle—as well as with uncomfortable information and not always knowing or having "the" right answer. Drawing from *critical pedagogy* (Freire, 1970/2000), queer pedagogies move away from "banking" styles of education. *Banking education* is a term that describes traditional approaches to schooling where the teacher deposits facts and knowledge in the minds of students, who are seen as passive receptacles. Critical and queer pedagogies encourage us to sit with discomfort, to recognize there may not always be one correct answer, and to explore questions that inspire curiosity and further inquiry (Staley & Leonardi, 2020) rather than ones with answers written upside down in the back of the textbook.

Learning is more than just being able to apply a new concept, repeat certain facts, or perform new skills. It is also about disrupting knowledge that we take for granted and opening ourselves up to more questions, not just seeking the right answer to move on to the next topic or to secure a certain grade (Kumashiro, 2002). This chapter does not offer simple how-tos, checklists, or a binder of activities that teachers can open and deliver. What I hope to do is pique your curiosity to find ways to disrupt and queer existing classroom structures, routines, lessons, assignments, assessments, grades—everything! Drawing from queer pedagogy, this section will help you rethink what is "normal" and how we can encourage students to ask engaging questions about the way the world works. Some of these questions could be about dominant gender norms, disrupting binaries, and heteronormativity, but other questions might include: What are grades for? What kinds of assignments expand our curiosity? What kinds of activities and questions help students think more critically? How can we develop skills to understand and act in ways that center equity and justice? How can we create learning spaces that elevate and draw from historically silenced and excluded voices? What are the hidden expectations in the school or each classroom, and should these be made explicit? Why or why not?

Why is this "queer"? Because it disrupts binary power structures and can playfully call attention to contradictions as well as empower us as we

---

Figure 3.1. Queering Questions

Materials: paper and pens, newsprint and markers or Google Docs/JamBoard

1. Start by having students read the beginning of this chapter or by presenting a brief overview of the concept of queer pedagogy.
2. Ask students to work in small groups to generate a list of binaries they have been taught or have noticed in their everyday lives such as good/bad, Black/White, gay/straight, normal/abnormal, weak/strong, etc.
3. Have the whole class come together and generate a list on paper, whiteboard, or Google Docs of the binaries they noticed. Add any other examples you would like to use to generate queering questions.
4. Review the list of binaries and invite students to think of questions they have about them. You can start the brainstorming with examples like these: Where did these binaries come from? Where did you first notice them? Is there one part of each pair that is more valued than the other? Why? How did you learn that? In what ways are these binaries useful? In what ways are they harmful? What are ways we can reshape or rethink these binaries?
5. Facilitate a discussion about what these binaries and questions mean and how this changes how you think about your community or your school. *Note*: There is no right answer. The goal is to have the conversation to support and develop more creative, critical, and expansive thinking.
6. Conclude by inviting students to think about how they can bring queer questions into other learning spaces via a free-write, "exit ticket," or discussing their ideas with a partner.

address injustices. Queer pedagogy helps expand how we think about identity, families, relationships, bodies, pleasure, power structures, and intimacy. I invite you to brainstorm questions about what you are teaching and learning. What are new ways to queer the learning at your school? See the suggested activity on "queering questions" in Figure 3.1 for ideas to engage in a collective brainstorming activity. The next section will introduce ideas for how to queer commonly taught subjects to stimulate your own creativity.

QUEERING THE CURRICULUM

In addition to adopting a queer pedagogy, there are ways to queer the content in your classes to make it more inclusive of GSD and LGBTQIA+ people, stories, and topics. This section is not intended to provide lesson plans or teaching strategies; rather, the goal is to provide ideas that could stimulate your own creativity to queer existing units, topics, or texts that you already use. In 2011, California passed SB 48, also known as the FAIR (Fair, Accurate, Inclusive, and Respectful) Education Act, which amended the state education code to require the inclusion of LGBTQIA+ people, Pacific Islanders, and people with disabilities in the K–12 social sciences curriculum. More recently, in November 2022, the Colorado State Board of Education approved revised social studies standards that had been updated to align with a 2019 law passed to make the standards inclusive of African American, Latino, American Indian, Asian Americans, and LGBTQIA+ people and history (Brundin, 2022). As of this writing seven states have laws requiring the inclusion of LGBTQIA+ people in social studies curriculum: California, Colorado, Connecticut, Illinois, New Jersey, Nevada, and Oregon. On the other hand, 10 states have laws prohibiting the discussion of LGBTQIA+ people or topics in schools and 5 more states have parental notification laws that allow families to opt out of LGBTQIA+-inclusive lessons (Movement Advancement Project, 2023b). For the most updated information on this topic, I recommend visiting the website for the Movement Advancement Project (lgbtmap.org), a nonprofit organization that keeps updated maps and policy information on the United States.

Social Studies

Since the focus of this book is on queer justice, starting with social studies makes sense with its focus on civic engagement, history, government, law, and democracy. It is also the content area that has seen the most official expansion to include the history and contributions of people from the LGBTQIA+ community through state laws and updated curriculum standards. If you live in a state like California or Colorado, you already have laws and revised standards in place to provide guidance and support to queer your curriculum. If you live in other states like Iowa or Florida that have prohibited certain discussions of gender and sexuality in the official curriculum, then teachers may need to be more strategic in their choices.

First, it is possible to queer your classroom while adhering to the letter of such exclusionary "don't say gay" and "parental rights" laws. First, many of these laws are focused on prohibiting the discussion of gender identity and sexual orientation in elementary schools (North Carolina, Alabama, Iowa) or only address sex education (Indiana, Kentucky), so be sure to educate yourself on the actual restrictions in your state. If restrictions on teaching about gender identity and sexual orientation apply to your grade level, then you can't design lessons or assign texts that explicitly teach about "gender identity" and "sexual orientation." However, one way is to be ready for teachable moments when queer questions arise organically from students during class discussions. Another is to be in the habit of asking expansive questions about existing curricular content with your students such as: Whose stories are missing? What perspectives do we need to work harder to learn about? How can we expand our knowledge beyond what is presented here? A third way is to design a unit on research skills that culminates in independent research projects. The guiding questions of these projects could be to explore hidden histories from a chosen era or region that haven't been presented in their school assigned texts. Students could create final products (slideshow, podcast, short video, research paper) to share in oral presentations, digital repositories, gallery walks, or library displays.

If you are able to explicitly name and discuss GSD in your curriculum, some commonly taught social studies lessons that can be expanded to include LGBTQIA+ people and topics are as follows:

1. Colonization and westward expansion: This includes impacts of contact with missionaries on *gender roles* and family structures in Indigenous communities of North America and the story of Charley Parkhurst, a transgender stagecoach driver during the California Gold Rush.
2. Civil disobedience and free speech: Examples include how protests and the First Amendment are central elements of democracy and civic engagement for LGBTQIA+ people's rights.
3. World War II: The pink triangle was used to identify gay men in concentration camps and the black triangle to label people as "asocial" (which included alcoholics, homeless people, Roma, lesbians, and prostitutes).
4. Civil Rights Movement: Marsha P. Johnson, Audre Lorde, Harvey Milk, and Bayard Rustin are important leaders to name from this era, as well as the Stonewall Riots of 1969.

These are just a few ideas to help stimulate your own creativity and curiosity as you think about your experiences teaching and learning about history, government, and democracy. I have offered a few more websites with resources and information to dive more deeply into this work on the book's companion website: www.elizabethjmeyer.com/queer-justice.html.

Language Arts

A second critical area in the curriculum is language arts. The use of oral and written language to understand laws, policies, stories, and related advocacy and action we can take is important to community organizing and activism. There are four general ways I think about queering this content area: selecting queer texts (by LGBTQIA+ authors and with LGBTQIA+ main characters), queering discussions about traditional texts, discussing censorship and book bans targeting LGBTQIA+-themed texts, and using written and oral expression to engage in advocacy activities.

Finding and selecting queer texts for your class may feel overwhelming. Don't worry—there are a wealth of ideas and resources to support you. You can consider starting with making books available for independent reading, or a brief poetry or short story unit can be a great place to start if you have difficulties getting class sets of newer novels. Several professional associations curate reading lists that include books with LGBTQIA+ characters, themes, and authors. I have included some resources and booklists at the end of this chapter and on the companion website. I also highly recommend the book *Reading the Rainbow* (Ryan & Hermann-Wilmarth, 2018).

Queering discussions of canonical texts is another way to start this process by using content that you are already comfortable and familiar with. One idea comes from a middle school teacher who used a unit on *Animal Farm* (Orwell, 1945) to talk about propaganda and government persecution of minorities, which led into a persuasive writing unit that was introduced with a speech given by Harvey Milk. Another high school English teacher I know opened the school year with first-person narratives to help students explore their own identities and link them to experiences of privilege or oppression in their communities using a tool called the "Social Identity Wheel." She designed this activity to set the tone and build community. By modeling her own identities as a bisexual Latina, she demonstrated how her identities impact the ways she reads and understands texts and her place in the world. Finally, the article "Already on the Shelf: Queer Readings of Award-Winning Children's Literature" (Ryan & Hermann-Wilmarth, 2013) offers valuable questions and reading strategies that queer representations of gender, relationships, and families in canonical texts. Along this theme, Paula Ressler has written about queering Shakespeare and how to teach *Romeo & Juliet* in a way that helps students read queerly and explore "non-normative sex and gender identities" (Ressler, 2005).

A third approach is to discuss the ways books have been banned across history and discuss recent news articles and other nonfiction texts to explore which topics and stories are subject to such bans. Starting in 2020, more and more of the texts targeted for censorship have had LGBTQIA+ characters and themes (Feingold & Weishart, 2023). Discussing the titles and excerpts from the news stories can offer students opportunities to engage in critical thinking and learn about current events related to their own identities and experiences.

Studying book bans and censorship can build into the fourth idea of using language arts classes to learn about and engage in persuasive writing, public speaking, or other advocacy activities related to LGBTQIA+ equity in schools or the community at large. You can analyze texts and speeches made over the years by public figures on all sides of the issue. What arguments have been commonly used? Which points seem to be the most persuasive? To whom? What sources of evidence are often cited? Students could also write and give speeches, compose letters to the school or local paper, or even write comments to share at student council or school board meetings about current topics or debates related to the topic. Helping students learn to critically evaluate arguments and evidence and convey their ideas is an essential goal of language arts classrooms. If we can connect these skills to topics that are timely and important to our students, they can be so much more engaging and meaningful. This same principle can also inform lessons in the discipline of mathematics.

Math

The ability to use numbers to tell stories is one essential skill in secondary math classrooms. To be able to understand quantities and percentages and what those numbers mean using graphic displays of data is another core skill of quantitative reasoning. Queering math instruction can be a tool for social justice. Queering helps us to ask questions about data that explore student experiences and identities. These queer questions can also help students use data to tell a story about LGBTQIA+ people in their school or community. For example, in the edited book, *Teaching about Gender Diversity: Teacher-Tested Lesson Plans for K-12 Classrooms*, Suarez and Wright (2020) share a middle-grades lesson on teaching data management and analysis categories. The lesson builds skills and knowledge to help students interpret and apply data collected from a variety of national surveys, including the U.S. Transgender Survey and Canada's TransPULSE Survey. You can use the lesson principles and apply them to other data sources presented in Chapter 2, Figure 2.3a–2.3c. In that same book, Gardner (2020b) shares ways to build a school climate audit to understand students' experiences in your school and then analyze and share your findings. This could be an interdisciplinary lesson in cooperation with advisory/health or social studies lessons. A guide for creating local surveys as well as a survey generator are available at https://www

.glsen.org/school-climate-survey#snt--2/. As Chapter 2 points out, it is important to be able to use data in meaningful ways to make your case for change.

A third approach comes from the work of Kai Rands, a trans-identified scholar of math education. In Rands's 2013 article, "Supporting Transgender and Gender-Nonconforming Youth Through Teaching Mathematics for Social Justice," they present a middle-grades lesson on proportional reasoning and developing "graph sense" using a gender-complex approach to math instruction (Rands, 2013). Rands proposes using data from GLSEN's National School Climate Survey to help students connect their experiences with gender bias and harassment in school to national data on the topic. Students can interpret charts and graphs in the report or even build their own with statistical statements from the executive summary. Rands's article offers various extension activities and ideas to deepen students' understandings of these mathematical concepts and ways to represent similar survey data.

Finally, in the spirit of queering the math classroom, math educators of all ages can trouble the notion of a single right answer by encouraging students to find multiple possible solutions to a problem or demonstrate their quantitative reasoning in various ways: words, images, numbers, and so on. Helping students see that math can be more creative and complex than it has often been taught can be exciting and offer learners new opportunities to express themselves and challenge binaries in this content area. These math lessons offer just a few ideas of ways to support students' development of quantitative reasoning skills that can help them advocate for more equitable and just schools. A few additional resources are listed on the companion website.

Sciences

Another overlooked content area for supporting efforts toward queer justice is the science classroom. Life sciences or biology lessons are the most obvious place to help students learn more about sex hormones, reproduction, same-sex pairings in the animal kingdom, and natural variation of sexual diversity in the animal kingdom. Allison Gonsalves and her colleagues (2020) share a model lesson titled, "Are There Really Only Two Sexes?" that uses model-based inquiry (Windschitl et al., 2008) to develop a more nuanced understanding of sex chromosomes and meiosis in order to explore natural variations beyond XX and XY. Nehm and Young (2008) also share ways to discuss how sex hormones are presented in biology texts. This article shares with readers how sex hormones are often oversimplified as "male" and "female" hormones even while most bodies have varying levels of estrogen and testosterone and suggests teachers use the more accurate term "steroid" hormone. This inquiry could be paired with discussions about the arguments to exclude trans women from girls' sports and about examining data related to hormone-level tests for athletes in certain athletic associations but not others.

In his book, *Against Common Sense: Teaching and Learning Toward Social Justice*, Kumashiro (2004) offers ways to teach about embryonic development that helps expand our understanding about sex differentiation in human bodies. This lesson could be paired with discussions about "gender reveal" parties and how genitals are used to predefine a child's gender. This can be paired with a short blog I wrote for *Psychology Today* on gender reveal parties (Meyer, 2014).

Gardner (2020a) also designed an elementary science lesson called "Sex-Shifting Fish as Reproductive Strategy" to talk about sexual fluidity in the animal kingdom. This lesson uses clownfish to explore how social and environmental factors impact the survival of animal populations and introduces scientific language including ichthyologist, allele, protandrous, protogynous, sequential hermaphrodite, and serial hermaphrodite (p. 60). Using graphic organizers and videos, students are taught about how clownfish adapt to the needs in their environment and may change their sex due to various factors.

The use of evidence from current scientific and medical research can be exciting and empowering for activists. Helping students see the ways in which science can help them advance knowledge and arguments for justice is one way to deepen engagement in concepts that don't always feel important or exciting to the average high school student. I conclude this section with a lesson idea on same-sex coupling in the natural world that uses a combination of books, podcasts, and accessible science articles to help students explore how the presence of same-sex couples in the animal kingdom has been documented in hundreds of species but was prevented from getting published and widely disseminated for many years due to institutional barriers related to homophobia (see Figure 3.2).

Sexuality and Health Education

Another very clear connection for lessons about GSD is in sexuality and health education. In lessons about relationships, sexuality, and bodies, it is important to talk expansively to ensure accurate and inclusive information is available to students of all genders and sexualities about puberty, reproduction, and safer sex practices. While some states have laws prohibiting sexuality education that speaks about LGBTQIA+ people in positive ways, there is a clear shift in this field away from abstinence-only perspectives toward "inclusive and comprehensive" sex education. This means that instruction addresses more than just pregnancy and disease prevention to talk about healthy relationships, GSD, consent, and pleasure. One excellent source of information is SIECUS (SIECUS.org), a national nonprofit organization whose motto is "sex ed for positive change." Another helpful guide, *Full Spectrum: Educators' Guide to Implementing LGBTQ+ Inclusive Sex Ed*

Figure 3.2. Same-Sex Coupling in the Natural World

This lesson idea was inspired by a podcast I listen to called *You're Wrong About* that unpacks common media myths and misconceptions. I heard the original podcast in June 2023, and it explored how the field of science suppressed knowledge of same-sex coupling in animals for centuries. It also explains how a 1977 study on seagulls opened up that field of research while simultaneously contradicting the popular antigay rhetoric claiming that homosexuality was "unnatural" with their landmark article published in *Science*.

Foundational Texts:

- *Queer Ducks (and Other Animals): The Natural World of Animal Sexuality*, Eliot Schrefer (2023) Harper Collins Publishers
- May 24, 2022, NPR interview with Eliot Schrefer (8 minutes) (https://www.npr.org/2022/05/24/1101040207/animal-sexuality-may-not-be-as-binary-as-were-led-to-believe-according-to-new-bo)
- June 12, 2023, episode of podcast *You're Wrong About*, "Lesbian Seagulls with Lulu Miller" (1 hour)
- June 2, 2023, episode of podcast *Radiolab*, "The Seagulls" (35 minutes)
- "Same-Sex Behavior Seen in Nearly All Animals, Review Finds" (June 17, 2009) *Science Daily* https://www.sciencedaily.com/releases/2009/06/090616122106.htm
- *Biological Exuberance: Animal Homosexuality and Natural Diversity* (1999) Bruce Bagemihl
- George L. Hunt, & Hunt, M. W. (1977). "Female-Female Pairing in Western Gulls (Larus occidentalis) in Southern California." *Science*, 196(4297), 1466–1467. https://doi.org/10.2307/1744394

Activity Ideas

Teachers can use these resources to (1) design a 1-week unit, (2) offer an extension or extra credit activity for students needing more challenge, (3) as an interdisciplinary lesson on the history of science and how research findings have been managed or politicized over time, or (4) as one option in a set of inquiry activities in a unit on animal behavior, biodiversity, or the history of science. I recommend starting with the *You're Wrong About* podcast, as it provides an engaging and entertaining context for the history and science shared in these materials and is sure to pique students' curiosity—especially the section that shares how this knowledge was systematically suppressed and erased from the historical and scientific record. Students can share what they learn via (1) a brief oral presentation, (2) a poster display, (3) a written research paper, or (4) making their own website on the topic. If you try any of these activities at your school, please email me: Elizabeth.j.meyer@colorado.edu—I'd love to hear what you did with it and how it went!

---

produced by the state of Vermont (Vermont Agency of Education, 2018), offers a set of best practices such as using gender-neutral language (people, partners, students, they/them pronouns), using body-first language (people with uteruses, having vaginal sex, external or internal condoms), and including queer and trans representation in images, scenarios, and names during lessons and other class activities.

For more specific lesson ideas, I recommend looking at benjamin lee hicks's lesson called "The Festival of Puberty" (hicks, 2020). As a trans middle school teacher who developed this lesson with his 6th-grade students, he offers brilliant trans- and queer-informed perspectives to have safe, positive, and inclusive conversations about puberty. He shares a two-part lesson where the first part, "Most Me," invites students to bring items to class that represent who they are and discuss what they like about themselves. In the second part, "Puberty Pledge," students are invited to think collectively and intentionally about how to respect oneself and others during a time of significant changes to bodies and relationships in the social context of peer pressure and sometimes hostile school and community contexts. He writes, "It is a symbolic action that invites everyone involved to remember this moment when they promised themselves that they are worthy of love and care" (hicks, 2020, p. 154). The pledge that his class wrote together reads as follows: "I believe in the inherent worth and dignity of each and every person, including myself. I believe that each person is special and unique. There is no such thing as 'normal'" (hicks, 2020, p. 157).

Another great activity that engages students around gender norms and stereotypes presented by Karleen Pendleton Jimenez in her book, *Tomboys and Other Gender Heroes* (Pendleton Jimenez, 2016), invites students to reflect on their own experiences being taught about "boy" things and "girl" things after watching a short film about a tomboy. Students were asked to write short examples on sticky notes about "any event, observation, rule, anecdotes, question or idea that they have witnessed or thought with regard to nonconforming gender expression" (Pendleton Jimenez, 2016, p. 26). Pendleton Jimenez then describes having students place sticky notes on a public rubric with the following headings: 1: Gender destroyer; 2: Gender police; 3: Gender bystander; 4: Gender bender/defender (Pendleton Jimenez 2016, p. 26) and then leading a discussion about what they notice and what they'd like to change about what they see and experience. She reports using this activity with students ages 9–18 with great success and rich learning outcomes every time. Students can advocate for the use of these practices by sharing their request with some specific ideas and resources with their teachers individually or working with your gender and sexuality alliance (GSA) or other student equity group to write a letter to your principal or school board requesting more inclusive sex education and including websites or PDFs of some of the resources on the companion website.

For any content area, when designing such lessons, it is always strategic and important to align with existing state standards when queering your curriculum. While standards aren't particularly "queer" since they are fixed and often reflect dominant norms, these standards are still valuable tools to help guide your decisions about texts, lessons, assessments, skills, and topics to discuss in class. Having clear alignment to standards provides important support for your pedagogical choices—particularly if you anticipate pushback or resistance from parents, colleagues, administration, or community groups outside your school. Another site for discussion and learning about healthy relationships and safety at school is social-emotional learning (SEL) and character education initiatives.

SOCIAL-EMOTIONAL LEARNING AND CHARACTER EDUCATION

An often-overlooked element of the curriculum includes school and district initiatives related to SEL and/or character education. While many of these programs have been criticized for failing to honor the knowledge and experiences of Black, Indigenous, and People of Color (BIPOC) youth (Love, 2019), in terms of focusing on individual coping strategies to manage behaviors that are often related to social injustices, there is potential to use these learning spaces for positive change. What we do know about effective SEL programs is that they can reduce bullying and social isolation and improve bystander intervention and student overall well-being (Espelage, 2015; Espelage et al., 2013; Swearer & Espelage, 2009). For minoritized youth, having access to SEL programs that are "transformative" (Jagers et al., 2019), which means they are designed to promote "equity and excellence," is essential to addressing biases and climate related to multiple forms of equity and justice in schools. While the current emphasis in *transformative SEL* literature is on more effectively addressing racial bias and inequality in schools, the framework also lends itself to addressing safety and well-being for LGBTQIA+ and other marginalized youth.

Jagers et al.'s (2019) framework for transformative SEL builds on the Collaborative for Academic, Social, and Emotional Learning (CASEL)'s existing five competencies of self-awareness, self-management, social awareness, relationship skills, and responsible decision-making. The goal is to align SEL frameworks with transformative and justice-oriented notions of citizenship (Westheimer & Kahne, 2004) by integrating four new elements: identity, agency, belonging, and engagement (p. 167). Jagers and colleagues emphasize that since they view SEL as a civic enterprise, political agency or "efficacy" is an important element in SEL—specifically within the second competency of self-management. They argue that "although it is important to limit or inhibit one's self in some instance[s], it is equally important to be agentic—to participate in or actively change an interaction or context" and that "collective efficacy is an essential transformational SEL competence" (Jagers et al., 2019, p. 170). For the new criterion of belonging, they explain that "belonging implies not only recognition but also full involvement in meaning making and the building of relationships and institutions" (p. 171). They advocate for more student-centered activities that promote inquiry and agency such as culturally relevant education (CRE, which is also related to culturally responsive and culturally sustaining pedagogies)

(Ladson-Billings, 2014), problem-based learning (PBL), and youth participatory action research (YPAR) to help integrate these four transformative SEL principles more effectively throughout a school community.

SEL programs are common in most elementary schools but, unfortunately, are usually phased out during middle school and are virtually nonexistent in most high schools. However, if your school has some initiative or program related to SEL and/or character education, I encourage you to explore the lessons and learning objectives to see if they contain elements of transformative SEL. If they don't, consider thinking together with leaders at your district about ways you can update your programs to include some of the elements noted earlier. You may also work with parents' groups or other interested parties to advocate for the school district to consider investigating new SEL programs that include these four elements of transformational SEL. The "What Works Clearinghouse" (https://ies.ed.gov/ncee/wwc/) is a searchable database of evidence-based educational programs and is one place to start researching SEL and character education programs that have evidence of promising effects in schools. Outside of the formal curriculum, there are other ways teachers and students can help LGBTQIA+ students feel welcome and supported at school. The next section shares ideas to support various forms of visible displays of LGBTQIA+ pride and support.

FLAGS, STICKERS, AND OTHER DISPLAYS: VISIBILITY MATTERS

Teachers and districts around the country have experienced public backlash for having symbols of LGBTQIA+ support in their classrooms and school buildings. For example, in August 2023, Florida school districts ordered the removal of such stickers in response to the newly passed "Don't Say Gay" bill (Skinner, 2022). Their argument was that the "safe space" sticker "distracts from our goals of creating a school-wide and districtwide safe environment." There have also been several stories of schools in places like Missouri (Associated Press, 2022), Connecticut (Álvarez, 2023), and Pennsylvania (Rizzo, 2023) asking teachers to remove Pride flags from their classrooms. What's the concern about a Pride flag or safe space sticker, and what reasons are there for teachers to display them? To help understand the research that supports positive symbols of support in schools, this section aims to help refute the more common arguments I have seen against these symbols to help advocate for the value and importance of having them at your school. There are five common arguments I have heard:

1. School safety: "Safe space" stickers indicate that only some spaces are welcoming for LGBTQIA+ students and prove that not all spaces are safe for all students. By removing the stickers, we can proclaim the whole school "safe" for all students.

2. Turning gay: Pride flags show support for LGBTQIA+ people. Saying it's "OK to be gay will make more students come out. Seeing a Pride flag will make kids "turn" LGBTQIA+, which is seen as an undesirable outcome or something schools should discourage.
3. Parents' rights: Discussing gender and sexuality should happen in the privacy of the family unit. Displaying safe space stickers and Pride flags violates parents' rights to raise their children with their worldview that does not include LGBTQIA+ people and families.
4. Student learning: Schools should focus on teaching students the official curriculum: math, history, science, English, and so on. Showing support for the LGBTQIA+ community distracts from the academic purpose of schools.
5. Teacher speech and political statements: Teachers should not display political symbols or express personally held political viewpoints in the classroom.

School Safety

To address the school safety argument, as Chapter 2 showed, there is ample evidence that clearly shows that LGBTQIA+ youth are not safe in many schools. They experience higher rates of bullying and harassment and dropping out and lower feelings of school safety and belonging. School climate research indicates that for students to be successful at school, they need to feel safe, feel like they belong, and have positive student–teacher relationships. If these elements aren't present, students are more likely to struggle academically, skip school, or drop out (Thapa et al., 2013). Teachers understand this and try to build positive relationships with their students. LGBTQIA+-affirming symbols are one way to signal support and visibility for students who often don't feel seen and respected at home or at school.

"Turning Gay" (or Trans)

There is no evidence that seeing a Pride flag or safe space sticker will "turn" a person gay. What it might do is make them feel supported enough that they are willing to "come out" or share that aspect of their identity with you. However, this argument is inherently homophobic and transphobic. It assumes that having an LGBTQIA+ identity is a bad thing that is to be avoided and schools should discourage the healthy development of such identities. This framing is harmful. If more kids come out as LGBTQIA+, that should be viewed as a good thing: It means they feel seen, safe, and supported and can lead healthier lives because of having pride and confidence in their developing identities. The reasons someone identifies as LGBTQIA+ are not settled in the research community, nor are the reasons one comes to identify as cisgender or heterosexual, but there is no evidence that seeing a Pride flag is a factor in causing someone to feel LGBTQIA+ (Halley, 2014).

Parents' Rights

This argument is growing in popularity as "transparency" and "parents' rights" laws have spread around the United States, famously led by the state of Florida in 2022, which passed House Bill 1557, "Parental Rights in Education," popularly referred to as the "Don't Say Gay" law. As of December 2023, FutureEd reported 85 parental-rights bills had been introduced in 24 states, mostly by Republican lawmakers (Dimarco, 2023). As of this writing, Florida, Arizona, Georgia, North Carolina, Iowa, and Louisiana have signed such bills into law. These state laws are harmful and undermine the public schools in a diverse democratic society, as they either offer parents the ability to "opt out" of any part of the curriculum they personally disagree with or require parental notification and permission to teach their child about topics related to race, gender, and sexuality. The Supreme Court has already decided that parents don't have a right to dictate the curriculum in public schools (Mead & Lewis, 2016); however, these state laws can deprive students of meaningful learning about many topics including racial inequality and LGBTQIA+ people. Public schools are a public good (Labaree, 1997), and the education professionals who are experts in content, child development, school safety, and equity should be allowed to make these decisions without the overinvolvement of extreme factions of their community.

Student Learning

We know that students will refuse to learn and disengage from adults who don't see and respect them (Watson & Russell, 2016). We know that students will stop attending school if they aren't safe and supported (Kosciw, 2022). If we want students to learn and teachers to support their overall success, then we need to be able to ensure their safety, both physically and emotionally. Posting stickers and Pride flags helps promote student safety, learning, and engagement and should not be framed as a distraction or contradiction to the goals and purposes of school.

Teacher Speech and Political Viewpoints

Finally, there is the teacher speech and political viewpoint argument. Chapter 6 explores the tensions of navigating competing elements of religious freedom and freedom of expression in public schools with more detail and nuance. For now, I simply share the argument that the LGBTQIA+ Pride flag is not an explicitly political symbol. Displaying it is much like having posters of diverse authors or flags from different countries; it displays support for the values of diversity, equity, and inclusion so all students can feel a sense of belonging to learn and thrive. It is a symbol of support for students' lives, families, and identities, which shouldn't be seen as political.

CONCLUSION

I hope this chapter has offered you some new questions, ideas, resources, and inspiration to help you bring queer pedagogy to teaching and learning at your school. By building on the ideas from queer theory and queer pedagogy, teachers and students can work together to disrupt harmful *normative* patterns in school and expand their abilities to think critically and act collectively to improve the school climate for everyone. By learning to ask queering questions, by incorporating more LGBTQIA+ content throughout the curriculum, and by having visible displays of support for the LGBTQIA+ community, you can slowly help change the culture of your school.

When teachers and students work together and focus on justice and equity as a larger intersectional project focused on collective liberation that includes support for various marginalized groups, you can imagine new and unique ways that respond to local challenges and build coalitions of support. Think about what other student groups and community organizations are invested in justice work in your community such as disability rights groups, Black Lives Matter and other racial justice organizations, the National Organization for Women, the American Association for University Women, and other feminist organizations. The American Civil Liberties Union, Southern Poverty Law Center, P-FLAG, and GLSEN are other national organizations engaged in social change and education efforts. By building broad coalitions for your efforts to implement some of the ideas shared here, you can create networks that support you and your students as you take action and spark changes at your school.

DISCUSSION QUESTIONS

1. Think of a time when you felt curious and excited about something you were learning. Where did that joy and curiosity come from? How can that be transferred into something you are currently teaching or learning?
2. What are some examples of binary thinking you have experienced? What new words, concepts, or questions might help reframe these binaries to move away from this style of thinking?
3. What are some concerns you have about integrating queer pedagogy in your school? Or about asking queer questions in your classes? How might you get support to work through these

concerns and improve the climate for queer pedagogies at your school?
4. Who makes the decisions about curriculum in your school district? Teachers? Department heads? District leaders? In what ways can you educate and persuade them to consider adopting some of the ideas shared here?

KEY TERMS

- banking education
- critical pedagogy
- gender and sexual diversity (GSD)
- gender roles
- normative
- queer pedagogy
- radical love
- transformative SEL (social-emotional learning)

CHAPTER 4

Queering School Culture

> To teach in a manner that respects and cares for the souls of our students is essential if we are to provide the necessary conditions where learning can most deeply and intimately begin.
>
> —bell hooks

What we learn and experience at school go way beyond what happens in classrooms. The overall environment of the school, referred to as *school climate*, also teaches lessons and impacts our experiences of our time there. The culture of the school community helps shape the climate, so these concepts are related but slightly different, and both are discussed in this chapter. In addition to the official curriculum of what is taught in classrooms and through assigned texts and activities, there is also the "hidden" curriculum, or the unofficial and informal values and messages communicated by the structures, systems, and leaders in a school community. This chapter first presents information about the importance of school climate on student engagement and success and then moves to talk about common traditions and practices that you may consider queering if they haven't already been updated to be more inclusive. We will talk about traditions including homecoming and prom, yearbooks, and graduation. Then we get into information about diversity in terms of laws and policies, nondiscrimination, *bullying*, and *harassment* as well as the *Equal Protection Clause* of the Fourteenth Amendment. This chapter concludes with a detailed list of nationally and internationally recognized events that your school could participate in to help queer various aspects of your school culture.

SCHOOL CLIMATE

How safe do you feel at school? How welcome? Is your school building in good shape? Are rules enforced consistently and fairly? Do students have a strong sense of community or belonging at school? Some students more than others? These questions are just a few that can help give you a sense of the climate at your school. The culture of the school community helps shape the climate and reflects the norms and values of the community, so these concepts are related but slightly different. The concept of school climate has been studied since the 1980s and grew out of the field of industrial and organizational research. Early researchers showed that "the distinctive culture of a school affects the life and learning of its students" (Thapa et al., 2013). One definition that is widely used is "School climate is based on patterns of people's experiences of school life and reflects norms, goals, values, interpersonal relationships, teaching and learning practices, and organizational structures" (Thapa et al., 2013, p. 358). According to the National School Climate Center, school climate has five main elements that can be studied and addressed directly: safety, teaching and learning, interpersonal relationships, institutional environment, and leadership and efficacy (Thapa et al., 2013). As the research presented in Chapter 2 shows us, school climate is experienced by LGBTQIA+ youth and youth of color differently than other students at school. Two important aspects of school climate are relationships with adults and consistent and equitable enforcement of school rules. Research shows that authoritative school environments characterized by consistently enforced rules, high expectations for behavior, clear structures, and highly responsive educators have much better climates. This is as compared to authoritarian environments, which have high structure (very strict rules and enforcement) but low support and responsiveness from adults, or permissive environments, which have low expectations (flexible and inconsistently enforced rules) and high levels of support from adults (Bear, 2020).

Authoritative school climates—which I remember as different from authoritarian because authoritative reminds me of tough love—generally have fewer suspensions and behavior problems, less bullying, less student aggression and truancy, and overall higher levels of student engagement and academic achievement (Bear, 2020). What does your school feel like? Strict? Strict only for certain kinds of students? Do you feel like rules are enforced consistently to maintain safety? Or does it feel arbitrary? Or focused only on certain kinds of students? Do you experience high levels of support from adults? Or do you feel lower levels of trusting relationships with adults? The way you feel reflects your school climate. Your school climate is also a reflection of the school culture: who is valued, who has influence, who gets celebrated, who gets excluded, and how.

When we think about school safety and belonging, it is important to think about "safe for whom." In one study of Canadian educators, we found that 97% of teachers reported that they felt their schools were "somewhat" or "very" safe. However, when we asked about safety for LGBTQIA+ and gender-nonconforming youth, their responses dropped significantly to as low as 51% of teachers reporting their school is "somewhat" or "very" safe for transgender students. Even fewer teachers who identified as LGBTQIA+ reported their schools as safe than straight teachers (Meyer et al., 2014). This is another example that shows how different groups of individuals experience school climate and culture differently. This tells us that most teachers are unaware of the negative experiences many LGBTQIA+ youth have at school—and thus don't take action to improve it. One way to improve students' sense of belonging at school is to ensure that they feel seen, welcome, and celebrated at important school events and traditions. Unfortunately, many school traditions are designed around a cisheteronormative binary culture and so often leave LGBTQIA+ students feeling invisible, excluded, and devalued. Let's take a look at some of those traditions and think about what they look like at your school.

TRADITIONS

During rituals and rites of passage in the school year, LGBTQIA+ youth are often put in impossible situations where they must display their gender or sexuality in ways defined by their school but that don't always reflect their identities. Common examples of these rituals include homecoming, prom, yearbooks, and graduation.

Homecoming and Prom

In 2010 a controversy was covered in the national media surrounding a prom in Mississippi. The school cancelled their annual event rather than give permission to Constance McMillen to bring her girlfriend. They also did not want to allow her request to arrive in a tuxedo instead of a ball gown and told her if she arrived separately from her date and they slow danced together, they would be thrown out (*McMillen v. Itawamba County School District*, 2010). Constance won the right to attend prom, and her district was required to update their nondiscrimination policies to include gender and sexual orientation. She was also invited to be the grand marshal of New York City Pride that year! She was supported in this cause by her mom and grandmother, so having affirming adults while taking on these challenges makes a big difference. As noted in Chapter 1, these controversies over prom go back to at least the 1980s and yet continue today (Smith, 2011). What can be done to queer up your prom and make it more inclusive for everyone who wants to participate? I will share a story from back in 2001 when I was teaching high school in rural New Hampshire.

That year, I had the good fortune of supporting the first ever youth-organized prom for gay and lesbian youth in that state. This event had students arriving in same-sex and mixed-sex couples wearing formal and costume attire that made them look and feel fantastic. There was a drag show, and two prom kings and two prom queens were selected (two kings, one assigned male at birth [AMAB] and one assigned female at birth [AFAB], and two queens, an AMAB and AFAB). Over 200 students attended, and it was so inspiring to witness the joy in their faces and see them all dancing together. I was particularly moved to see one student who had been consistently bullied at school get elected prom king. We could feel the joy and pride glowing from him all night; it was powerful. This end-of-year dance celebrated individuality, and respected and recognized all the youth for presenting themselves the way they wanted to be seen. All youth should be able to celebrate themselves with their peers and shouldn't have to organize a special separate event to be included.

Yearbooks

Ceara Sturgis didn't want her graduation photo taken in the traditional black drape that all females were expected to wear at her school. Instead, and with her mother's support, she tried on a tuxedo and decided that she would feel more confident in her photo dressed in the button-down shirt, jacket, and bow tie historically worn by males at her school. The school officials did not agree with this decision and sent a letter home explaining that only boys could wear tuxedos and her photo would not be included in the yearbook. Although the school did not cite any specific policy violation, the superintendent Ricky Clopton reported that the school district had consulted its lawyers and was "within its rights" to exclude the photo (Joyner, 2009). According to her mother, Ceara identified as gay and generally prefers to wear androgynous clothing. The American Civil Liberties Union (ACLU) in Mississippi contacted the school district to inform them that they were "violating Sturgis' constitutionally protected freedom of expression"; however, the superintendent and principal were unwilling to reverse their decision. The yearbooks were printed and distributed without Ceara's photo or name in them. Consequently, the ACLU filed a complaint against the school for sex discrimination and unlawful sex stereotyping, citing Title IX and the Equal Protection Clause of the Fourteenth Amendment (*Sturgis v. Copiah County School District*, 2010). In November 2011, the school district settled the lawsuit with Ceara and made the following changes: posted her photo on the wall of senior photos at the school, changed their yearbook photo policy so that all students wear a gender-neutral graduation gown, and updated their nondiscrimination policy with language affirming its support of the Equal Protection Clause of the U.S. Constitution (ACLU, 2011).

In a second case of yearbook censorship, Andre Jackson spent $150 to purchase a yearbook page to include personal photos and quotations to commemorate his last year of high school. On this page, he included a photo of him kissing his boyfriend. When school officials in his New Jersey district saw the final printed version of the yearbook, they took action to remove a photo that the superintendent, Marion Bolden, felt was "suggestive," "provocative," and "illicit" (Fernandez, 2007, June 24). Since the yearbooks were already printed and ready to be distributed, the principal and teachers who were handing out the yearbooks were instructed to use a black marker to manually block out the photo in question in each of the 250 copies of the yearbook. On the page facing Jackson's there reportedly was a photo of a male–female couple kissing that was not redacted. Ms. Bolden did not cite any school district policy upon which she based her decision and actions but did admit that perhaps she acted too quickly. Andre did not pursue further action against the school, but the facts of Ceara's case are helpful and relevant to this one. The application of Title IX, sex stereotyping, and inclusion/exclusion from official school events and publications would apply to this case as well. These issues will be addressed in the second section of this chapter.

More recently in 2018, a student at a Louisiana high school was told by her principal that the school wouldn't print her yearbook photo and she wouldn't be able to participate in graduation (ACLU of Louisiana, 2018). Why? Kami Pham, who identifies as transgender, wore a pink polo shirt and jeans in her photo and did her hair and makeup in way that was seen as too "feminine" for the school principal. Fortunately, due to grassroots activism (and a bit of legal education by the district's lawyers, I'm sure), the community persuaded the school board to reverse the principal's decision and allow her to fully participate in the end-of-year celebrations.

Have you heard of your school censoring or editing yearbook photos without student consent? If so, what policies and procedures did the school mention? Is this an issue you want to take up at your school? When school leaders apply unwritten policies that reflect their own biases and beliefs, it can create a hostile and discriminatory school climate. This is not only problematic for the students whose lives and identities have been erased from their school yearbooks but also for the other students and teachers who are expected to follow unwritten rules that they only learn about when they have unknowingly violated them.

Graduation

When the end of the school year approaches, graduation celebration plans take center stage. For some students this time of year is complicated due to gendered dress codes and other restrictions schools place on student expression at graduation. Many schools have graduations robes that reflect the school colors and assign one color to boys and one color to girls; what do nonbinary, genderfluid, or agender youth do? I consulted with a school in Indiana that required female students to wear white dresses and male students to wear a jacket and tie. In 2014, they changed this policy to allow students to wear pants regardless of their gender. More recently, in 2023, one trans girl had been consistently presenting at school as a young woman and was told by the principal of Harrison Central High School that she had to attend graduation in "boy clothes" under her graduation robe, a white shirt and black pants, instead of the dress and heels she had already purchased (Rosales et al., 2023). The school policy stated that "a high school graduation ceremony is a sacred and inspirational ritual which is intended to be surrounded with decorum of dignity, grace, solemnity, reverence, pomp and circumstance," and "students whose attire does not meet the minimum dress requirements may not be allowed to participate in the graduation exercises." She was invited to walk across the stage in her dress, heels, and graduation robe at a local Pride celebration later that June (Mitchell, 2023). Not every student gets such attention and celebrations. Some may opt not to participate at all since the choice between celebrating their accomplishments with their peers or having their identities fully expressed and affirmed is a difficult one—one we shouldn't be forcing students to make. As such, I recommend that you consider asking your school about their graduation dress code policies and see if they need queering up! If you face resistance, sharing this chapter about prior lawsuits (also referred to as "legal precedent") and other relevant laws and policies discussed in the next section might help persuade your school leaders to get moving and update their policies.

LAWS AND POLICIES

Laws and policies exist to ensure safety and fairness in our society. This also applies to school communities. Several categories of laws and policies are important to understand when trying to improve safety and fairness at school. The three areas of law and policy this section will address are nondiscrimination laws and policies, including the Fourteenth Amendment of the U.S. Constitution's Equal Protection Clause, and bullying and harassment laws and policies. But first let's start out with a basic overview of law and policy and how they are different.

Laws are written and passed at various levels of government: federal (which apply to the whole country), state (which only apply to people and businesses located in that state), and county and city ordinances. These laws act like a set of nested bowls or concentric circles that contain narrowing degrees of specificity and application. Federal laws are the biggest, outside basket which contains the foundation or the "floor" of basic rights and expectations for the country. Each smaller level's laws are contained within the larger baskets and must not contradict the laws at the higher levels. This network of laws and jurisdictions (the geographic region that is covered by a certain law) can be very confusing—especially when states pass laws that appear to go against federal laws. This is where the federal court systems come in—including the Supreme Court of the United States (SCOTUS)—to make decisions about whether state laws violate federal laws, including the constitution. State courts exist to resolve disputes about the laws within each state. See Figure 4.1 for a diagram illustrating these concentric circles of justice.

Figure 4.1. Nested Bowls of Legal Jurisdiction

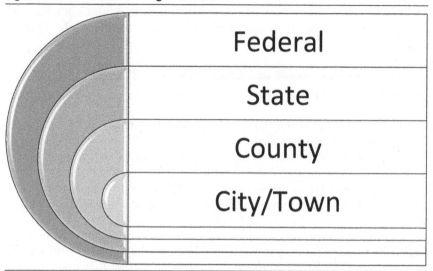

So how do laws and policies differ? Policies are like laws but instead of covering a geographic political territory (country, state, county), they govern organizations like universities, school districts, hospitals, religious organizations and so on. Policies are written by leaders in an organization and then approved and formalized by their governing bodies, such as the school board. Policies are generally used to help implement laws and provide guidance to individuals on how to interpret and apply the mission and values of an organization throughout its practices. In the following sections I will provide some sample language of various laws and policies to help illustrate how they work together and can be used to shape and improve school climate.

Nondiscrimination Protections

Laws and policies addressing nondiscrimination date back to the end of the Civil War when the country was rebuilding itself and needed to ensure formerly enslaved people were treated as full citizens. Three amendments to the Constitution were passed between 1865 and 1870, which are now referred to as the Reconstruction Amendments. The Thirteenth Amendment abolished slavery (U.S. Const. Amend. XIII), the Fourteenth Amendment granted citizenship to formerly enslaved people and guaranteed all citizens due process and equal protection under the law (U.S. Const. Amend. XIV), and the Fifteenth Amendment extended voting rights to formerly enslaved men (U.S. Const. Amend. XV). Women were not granted the right to vote until 1920 when the Nineteenth Amendment was ratified (U.S. Const. Amend. XIX). The Fourteenth Amendment is the one that is most relevant to our discussion of school climate, and the clause most relevant to discrimination is referred to as the "Equal Protection Clause."

Fourteenth Amendment and Equal Protection. The full text of the Fourteenth Amendment states:

> All persons born or naturalized in the United States, and subject to the jurisdiction thereof, are citizens of the United States and of the State wherein they reside. No State shall make or enforce any law which shall abridge the privileges or immunities of citizens of the United States; nor shall any State deprive any person of life, liberty, or property, without due process of law; *nor deny to any person within its jurisdiction the equal protection of the laws.* (U.S. Const. Amend. XIV)

The Equal Protection Clause of the Fourteenth Amendment is the final section in italics. This clause was at the heart of the Supreme Court decision in *Brown v. Board of Education of Topeka* (1954) that desegregated schools by concluding that "separate educational facilities are inherently unequal" and that the plaintiffs in the case were "deprived of the equal protection of the laws guaranteed by the Fourteenth Amendment." The Equal Protection Clause was also used in a groundbreaking case in 1996 where a gay student sued his school for failing to protect him from severe, pervasive, and violent antigay bullying and harassment over many years. The case, *Nabozny v. Podlesny* (1996), helped establish the effectiveness of the *Fourteenth Amendment* to prevent severe anti-LGBTQIA+ discrimination in the absence of state and local protections. Many states now have clear antidiscrimination laws, which will be addressed in the next section. But first let's talk briefly about the modern era of federal nondiscrimination laws that emerged during the Civil Rights Movement.

Civil Rights-Era Protections. During the Civil Rights Movement of the 1950s and 1960s the federal government passed a wave of new laws to ensure nondiscrimination was enacted in public services. The first of these laws was the Civil Rights Act of 1964, which includes Title VI that states, "No person in the United States shall, on the grounds of race, color, or national origin, be excluded from participation in, be denied the benefits of, or be subjected to discrimination under any program or activity receiving Federal financial assistance" ("Civil Rights Act of 1964," 1964). Eight years later, in 1972, Title IX of the Educational Amendments was passed and reads as follows, "No person in the United States shall, *on the basis of sex*, be excluded from participation in, be denied the benefits of, or be subjected to discrimination under any education program or activity receiving Federal financial assistance" (Title IX, Educational Amendments of 1972, italics added). You should notice that the wording is almost identical to the Civil Rights Act language, which was intentionally copied to ensure the spirit and intent of the laws were applied consistently. These antidiscrimination laws were established to help the government proactively enforce the principles of equal protection spelled out in the Fourteenth Amendment (Imber & Van Geel, 2010, pp. 270–271).

Until the Supreme Court decision *Bostock v. Clayton County, Georgia* (2020), there were no protections at the federal level against discrimination on the basis of gender and sexual orientation. This groundbreaking decision applied the language of Title VII of the Civil Rights Act "on the basis of sex" to include gender and sexual orientation. In 2021, the Biden administration issued an executive order that extended the *Bostock* decision to include all federal government agencies (Executive Order 13988, 2021). This is an improvement, but without a federal law, executive orders can be removed when a new president takes office. In the absence of federal laws, some states have taken the lead to provide certain protections to their residents. Laws passed at the state level often go further than the floor of basic protections provided by the federal government but only apply in that state, which leads to very different experiences for students and teachers around the country.

State Nondiscrimination Protections. As a result of regional variations and attitudes about addressing discrimination, states began passing their own nondiscrimination laws and creating enforcement agencies. As of this writing in 2024, 21 states, the District of Columbia, and one territory (U.S. Virgin Islands) have statewide nondiscrimination protections that explicitly name gender and sexual orientation, and 5 more states interpret existing protections based on sex discrimination to extend to sexual orientation and gender (Movement Advancement Project, 2024). For example, my home state of Colorado has the Colorado Anti-Discrimination Act (CADA), which prohibits discrimination based on the following protected classes: disability, race, creed, color, sex, sexual orientation, gender identity, gender expression, marital status, national origin, or ancestry (CRS 24-34-601 et seq.). Sexual orientation and gender expression were added to this state code in 2008. Denver had led the way in Colorado by passing a city ordinance protecting workers from discrimination due to their sexual orientation in 1990. You can get updated information on the laws in your state by exploring the resources presented in Figure 4.2.

Now that you have a better understanding of nondiscrimination laws, let's zoom into the school district level. What do the nondiscrimination policies of your school district say? Do they go beyond protections offered by the state? In what ways? In addition to nondiscrimination protections, school safety policies also impact school climate. The next section takes up the issue of bullying and harassment laws and policies.

Figure 4.2. Nondiscrimination Protection Matrix

Do you know what the nondiscrimination laws are in your state? What about your school district? This activity is one you can complete in about 30 minutes during a class or a club meeting—or you can divide it up across three sessions if you have fewer students sharing the research tasks. You will need an Internet-connected device and a piece of paper or shared digital document where you can track your findings.

Guiding questions: What are the current nondiscrimination protections for LGBTQIA+ people in my state? What policies exist in my school district to support LGBTQIA+ students and teachers?

Activity: In pairs or small groups visit the websites listed in the resources section and note which laws and policies are present in your state and school district. You can use the grid provided as a guide for how to track whether your state and district have the relevant antidiscrimination protections. Put a green (+) or (√) in each box if there is a law/policy that is supportive of people based on their sexual orientation or gender identity and a red (–) or (x) if there is a law/policy that is harmful or exclusionary of people based on their sexual orientation or gender identity. If you believe the existing law or policy is neither supportive nor harmful, you can put a gray (0) or (n) for neutral. Keep in mind that the absence of named or *enumerated protections* is not necessarily neutral. Without explicit protections, vulnerable groups are left exposed to historical and ongoing stigma and discrimination. Once you have completed the grid, discuss your results and consider comparing them with a neighboring state or district.

Topic	Sexual Orientation (+/N/-)	Gender Identity (+/N/-)	Notes
Antibullying			
Bathroom use—State law			
Bathroom use—School policy			
LGBTQIA+ topics in the curriculum			
Nondiscrimination: Public accommodation—State law			
Nondiscrimination—Local ordinance (city/town)			
Nondiscrimination—School policy			
Trans students—State law			
Trans students—School policy			
Trans youth medical care			

Figure 4.2. (*continued*)

Discussion questions:
1. In reviewing the data you collected, would you say LGBTQIA+ students in your school have adequate legal and policy protections?
2. Which missing protections would make the most difference in your life if they were improved?
3. What ideas do you have to advocate for updating a particular law or policy? Who could provide support and guidance to you in that process?
4. Were you surprised by what you found? Why/why not?
5. In what ways could you share this information with your school? Students? Teachers? School board?
6. What questions do you still wonder about?

Resources:
- Movement Advancement Project: https://www.lgbtmap.org/equality-maps/equality-maps
- GLSEN Policy Maps: https://maps.glsen.org/
- U.S. Department of Education: Stop bullying https://www.stopbullying.gov/resources/laws/key-components
- Your local school district website: district policies, school board meeting documents, student handbooks, etc.

Bullying and Harassment

The relationships between peers at school has a significant impact on shaping if students feel safe or welcome at school. Whether the school climate is filled with positive peer interactions and shared feelings of belonging or whether it is more common to see acts of bullying and harassment will clearly affect how students feel about coming to school. As Chapter 2 showed, LGBTQIA+ youth are targeted more often and experience more severe and enduring psychological harm due to bullying and harassment.

The terms "bullying" and "harassment" get used a lot, and as a result we may be desensitized to them and may have an oversimplified understanding of what they mean, how they are similar, and how they are different. Dan Olweus started the study of bullying in Norway in 1978 and established the following commonly used definition of bullying:

> A student is being bullied or victimized when he or she is exposed, repeatedly and over time, to negative actions on the part of one or more other students . . . it is a negative action when someone intentionally inflicts, or [attempts] to inflict, injury or discomfort on another. . . . Negative actions can be carried out by words (verbally), for instance, by threatening, taunting, teasing, and calling names. It is a negative action when somebody hits, pushes, kicks, pinches or restrains another—by physical contact. It is also possible to carry out negative actions without the use of words or physical contact, such as by making faces

or dirty gestures, intentionally excluding someone from a group, or refusing to comply with another person's wishes. (1993, p. 9)

Bullying studies report between 9% (Olweus, 1993), 33% (Bond et al., 2001), and 58% (Adair et al., 2000) of students are victims of bullying at school. The wide variation in reported rates of bullying may be due to how survey questions were phrased, what period of time was being studied (entire school career, the past year, the past month), and how the data were analyzed and reported. Researchers report negative impacts associated with being the victim of bullying including symptoms of anxiety, depression, stress, hopelessness, and low self-esteem and higher likelihood of self-harming behaviors and suicide (Bond et al., 2001; Coggan et al., 2003). The problem with the majority of bullying research and related antibullying programs is that they rarely identify or examine social group memberships (race, class, gender, ethnicity, sexual orientation), biased attitudes, and how they may interact with the bully–victim phenomenon (Meyer, 2007a, 2014). This is where definitions of harassment come in.

Harassment shares much with the definition of bullying except for two major differences: (1) the actions can be unintentionally biased (whereas bullying is intentional) and (2) they harm not just a targeted individual (like in bullying), but an entire social group due to the bias in the language and the behavior (sexist, homophobic, racist, ableist, transphobic, etc.) (Meyer, 2009b, Meyer, 2020). *Microaggressions* are a good example of unintended harassment since they are seemingly small harms, but they build up over time to create a consistently negative or toxic environment. Solórzano and Huber (2020) define racial microaggressions as "verbal and nonverbal assaults . . . carried out in subtle automatic or unconscious forms; layered assaults that are based on a Person of Color's race, gender, class, sexuality, language, immigration status, phenotype, accent, or surname and cumulative assaults that take a physiological, psychological, and academic toll on People of Color" (Introduction, e-book). While the focus of this definition is on people of color, this concept can also be applied to other marginalized groups such as LGBTQIA+ people, people with disabilities, women and gender minorities, and so on. Examples Solórzano and Huber provide of racial microaggressions include being told to speak English, that they couldn't be cast in a school play due to their ethnicity, being called the name of the one other student of color in class, given a racist nickname (like "Chief"), told to go back to their country, or asked where they are "really from" (Solórzano & Huber, 2020, chp1). These are all examples of racial microaggressions that also fit the definition of verbal harassment. Harassment, like bullying, can also be nonverbal or physical in nature, but the distinguishing factor between bullying and harassment is that harassing behaviors have bias at their root and have negative impacts on an entire social group as well as any specific individuals who may be targeted.

Antibullying and antiharassment laws and policies have become prevalent in the United States, but there is significant variation in the quality and enforcement of such laws depending on your state and school. Some states have very detailed and clear antibullying laws that can be used to ensure student safety, and effective intervention and prevention programs support widespread understanding of the law. As of this writing in 2024, there is no federal law against bullying in schools, but there are several civil rights laws that address harassment based on race, sex, disability, and religion that might be relevant if those forms of bias are present. However, most states have antibullying laws that cover other harmful behaviors that may or may not be discriminatory in nature. The federal Department of Education has helpful information on bullying policies and programs on their website stopbullying.gov. This website includes a matrix (see Figure 4.3) that illustrates the elements commonly found in state antibullying laws. This tally shows that every U.S. state and territory has a law that addresses bullying, but only 25 states have laws that include an *enumerated* list of groups protected by the policy. According to GLSEN, only 20 of those states include gender identity and sexual orientation in their list. Some state laws also require prevention education and staff training and that school districts adopt an antibullying policy that conforms with state law.

One state that has a very comprehensive set of laws is California. After the Columbine school shooting in Colorado in 1999, states started to give the problem of bullying and social exclusion more attention and began passing laws requiring schools to address the issue. California was one of the first states to pass antibullying legislation in 2000 with AB 537: Student Safety and Violence Protection Act. This law also protected students from discrimination and harassment based on sexual orientation, gender identity, and gender expression. In 2008 California passed AB 2845: Safe Place to Learn Act, which mandated that the California Department of Education monitor how schools are addressing discrimination and harassment. Then in 2012, AB 9: Seth's Law took effect, which required school employees to intervene immediately when witnessing discrimination or harassment and it is safe to do so. This set of laws works together to ensure that students' rights to learn in a safe environment are protected, that the state is monitoring local district efforts, and that teachers and other school staff consistently intervene. When these laws, policies, and prevention efforts fail, students suffer. One case of a student who experienced horrific antigay bullying at school was Jamie Nabozny. To learn more about his story and how this helped change how schools around the country responded to homophobic harassment, check out the suggested activities in Figure 4.3.

What are the bullying and harassment laws and policies like in your state? Your school? Do you feel like adults in your school are doing enough to intervene and prevent it from happening? Are certain kinds of harassment more tolerated than others? These are important issues to share with school

Figure 4.3. *Bullied: The Jamie Nabozny Story*

This activity will give you an opportunity to learn more about an extreme case of antigay bullying in school that was targeted at a young boy living in Wisconsin in the 1990s. This film was produced in 2010 by Teaching Tolerance (now called Learning for Justice) which is the educational arm of the Southern Poverty Law Center. The film is 40 minutes long and available to order for free with a discussion guide from the website: learningforjustice.org. It also may be available on Vimeo or YouTube.

Pre-viewing activities:

1. Discuss your own experiences with anti-LGBTQIA+ bullying at school. Some questions to start with include: What does it look like? What does it feel like? Where is it most common? Where is it least common? Why do you think that is?
2. Create a group collage with pictures, drawings, and words that help answer the prompt: What does antiqueer bullying look like at our school?
3. Build a word cloud using polleverywhere.com or wordclouds.com where students can anonymously submit antiqueer jokes, slurs, and other language they have heard at school. The word cloud will generate an image that shows the most commonly heard terms larger than others.

Post-viewing activities:

1. Have a discussion using the prompts in the discussion guide or others such as: This film is based on events from the 1990s; how much has changed since then? What feels familiar now? Who else would you want to see this film? Why? What is our school doing to prevent antiqueer bullying? What do I wish teachers/admin would do differently?
2. Plan a public showing of this film with a panel of local youth and educators to discuss how it is still relevant today and in your community.
3. Read about other cases of anti-LGBTQIA+ bullying that have led to social change such as Seth Walsh (Tehachapi, California) and Seth's Law (2012) or the *Flores v. Morgan Hill* (2004) case.

---

leaders and school board members so they can work to improve the climate at your school. You can use some of the climate data from Chapter 2 activities to help share this information and make your case. You can also help plan ongoing education and awareness events at your school. The final section offers some ideas to get started.

NATIONAL AND INTERNATIONAL EVENTS

What can you do to shift these cultures and traditions at your school? In addition to some of the ideas mentioned earlier, there are several events led by national and international organizations that you can plan and implement in your school community. Most of these events have free planning guides, social media materials, and other resources to help make your planning

Queering School Culture 63

smoother and more supported. I present the activities in chronological order starting in September to help you plan based on the traditional school calendar observed in most North American schools.

Anytime

1. *Mix It Up at Lunch Day* (https://www.learningforjustice.org /classroom-resources/mix-it-up). This event doesn't have a particular date or time frame but is one way to try and help students connect with peers outside of their immediate friendship group. It can be a great community-building activity to use at the beginning of the school year. While it is common for students to develop friendships with peers that they share common backgrounds with (language, culture, social class, athletic team, etc.), these social groups can become cliques that result in some students feeling excluded and can reinforce harmful social hierarchies in school. The idea behind Mix It Up at Lunch is to structure the activity such that students sit with new people and can engage in a fun activity to create new friendships and social connections. You could assign seats, have students draw numbers or colored ribbons when they enter, or have students sit in tables organized alphabetically by last name. Having teachers and adults support the interactions can be valuable as well. This activity might be better suited to students in grades 6–9 and in schools that have an indoor cafeteria space where everyone gathers during lunch period. You also might consider planning one every month or as a regular part of a "spirit week."

October

1. *LGBTQIA+ History Month*. Much like Black History Month or Women's History Month, LGBTQIA+ History Month is designed to help highlight contributions of LGBTQIA+ people to our culture. There are so many resources to consider when planning lessons, assemblies, bulletin boards, and other school events, so I will highlight just a few here.
    a. *LGBTQ+ History Cards* (https://www.glsen.org/activity /lgbtq-history-cards). You can purchase a deck of cards or download a free set from GLSEN to engage in a list of suggested games and learning activities about queer leaders and events in history.
    b. *31 Days: 31 Icons and Event Ideas* (https://lgbthistorymonth .com/ideas). This website lists 31 individuals to learn about as well as 14 ideas for activities including poster displays, film

screenings, inviting speakers, making daily announcements, and writing an article for the school paper.
    c. *Civics Renewal Network* (https://www.civicsrenewalnetwork.org/resources/pride-month-and-lgbtq-history-month-lesson-plans-resources/). This site provides lesson plans for all grades for social studies classes. Pick one and email it to your history teacher.
    d. *FAIR Education Act Implementation Coalition* (https://lgbtqhistory.org/lgbtq-educational-resources/). This California-based resource provides links to primary source documents, suggested books you can ask your school library to purchase and display, and LGBTQIA+ history timeline activities.
2. *National Coming Out Day, October 11.* This national event can be highlighted during LGBTQIA+ History Month activities. Coming out is a complex, personal, and always evolving process. Providing education and awareness about the diversity of ways LGBTQIA+ people can come out—or not—and are always having to think about coming out—or not—can be an important way to mark this day. Some resources include:
    a. *Human Rights Campaign* (https://www.hrc.org/resources/national-coming-out-day)
    b. *American Psychological Association* (https://www.apa.org/pi/lgbt/resources/coming-out-day)
    c. *P-FLAG coming out books* (https://pflag.org/resource/comingoutbooks/)
3. *Spirit Day* (https://glaad.org/spiritday/). This national antibullying awareness day that occurs at the end of October encourages people to wear purple to make a visible statement against anti-LGBTQIA+ harassment and violence. The Gay and Lesbian Alliance Against Defamation is the national organization that endorses and promotes this event. #SpiritDay, #GoPurple, and @GLAAD were some hashtags and profiles to follow on social media during the October 20, 2022, event.

November

1. *Transgender Day of Remembrance (TDOR), November 20.* This day is observed each year to honor the memories of trans people who lost their lives to violence. Guiding principles for events include:
    » "Those who cannot remember the past are doomed to repeat it." (Santayana)
    » All who die due to anti-transgender violence are to be remembered.

» It's up to us to remember them, since their killers, law enforcement, and media often seek to erase their existence.
» We can make a difference by being visible, speaking out, educating, and organizing around anti-transgender violence.
» Transgender lives are affirmed as valuable.

GSA Network resources (https://gsanetwork.org/resources/transgender-day-of-remembrance/)

January

1. *No Name Calling Week (NNCW)* (https://www.glsen.org/no-name-calling-week). This is an event primarily geared toward the middle grades and often paired with reading an anchor text such as *The Misfits* by James Howe. Related activities might include a poster design contest, button-making day, and a Mix It Up at Lunch activity. One educator wrote a blog about how she incorporated lessons about the Civil Rights Movement, Martin Luther King, Jr., and his gay colleague Bayard Rustin into events related to NNCW: https://www.glsen.org/blog/4-tips-glsens-no-name-calling-week. In 2022 GLSEN announced that they are phasing out their support for this national event; however, it might still be an activity your school or club might want to plan on your own.

February

1. *Pink Shirt Day (Canada), fourth Wednesday in February* (https://www.pinkshirtday.ca/ or https://www.alberta.ca/pink-shirt-day-alberta.aspx). This event grew out of an organic show of solidarity for a 9th-grader who was targeted by antigay bullies for wearing a pink shirt to school. Older students at his school in Nova Scotia led a movement to wear pink at school to stand up against such harmful behavior. This is now a national event in Canada to wear pink to stand up against bullying.

April

1. *Day of Silence* (https://www.glsen.org/dayofsilence). This national event started at the University of Virginia and has spread to schools across the United States. People participating take a vow of silence for the day and usually wear some symbol to show their participation (t-shirt, sticker, button, armband, etc.). This day is often followed by after-school events such as the "Night of Noise" or "Break the Silence" rallies.

May

1. *International Day Against Homophobia, Biphobia, and Transphobia (IDAHOBIT), May 17* (https://may17.org/ or https://www.unfpa.org/events/international-day-against-homophobia-transphobia-and-biphobia). This worldwide event is another opportunity to plan speakers, announcements, lessons, or activities that specifically address the harms caused by homophobia, biphobia, and transphobia.

June

1. *Pride Month.* If your school is still in session in June, this can be a great opportunity to look back on the accomplishments of the past year and end with a big celebration and setting of goals for the next year. Pride celebrations nationwide generally culminate at the end of June to mark the anniversary of the Stonewall Riots on June 28, 1969. Here are a few suggested resources to support Pride Month activities at your school:
    a. *History.com* (https://www.history.com/topics/gay-rights/the-stonewall-riots)
    b. *Anti-Defamation League* (https://www.adl.org/resources/tools-and-strategies/lgbtq-pride-month-and-education-resources)
    c. *GLSEN Pride Month Educator Guide* (https://www.glsen.org/activity/lgbtq-pride-month-guide-educators#:~:text=June%20is%20LGBTQ%20Pride%20Month,and%20communities%20around%20the%20world)

DISCUSSION QUESTIONS

1. How would you describe the climate at your school in general? How about for LGBTQIA+ students? How about trans students? LGBTQIA+ students of color? Students with disabilities? Is it the same or different? Why do you think so?
2. Who has the most control over the climate at school? Students? Teachers? Administrators? Are there groups of students who impact your experience at school positively? Negatively? What ways might you leverage their influence to improve school culture?
3. What is the difference between law and policy, and why does it matter?
4. Do you see how laws and policies impact your own experiences at school? Which ones might you change to improve the climate at your school?

5. What events seem like they might be fun or exciting to plan at your school? What is interesting to you about the one(s) you chose?

KEY TERMS

- AFAB
- AMAB
- Fourteenth Amendment
- bullying
- enumerated protections
- Equal Protection Clause
- harassment
- microaggressions
- school climate

CHAPTER 5

Queering Clubs and Extracurriculars

> How wonderful it is that nobody need wait a single moment before starting to improve the world.
>
> —Anne Frank

So many of the reasons we are able find joy at school are due to the relationships and community we find and create there. One important part of this community is created through extracurricular activities: clubs and organizations that are not directly tied to academic content or the official curriculum of the school. While athletic teams are an important set of extracurriculars, they will be addressed separately in Chapter 7 due to the sex-segregated nature of most school-sanctioned athletic programs. This chapter is written to help think about the clubs that currently exist or that you hope to create that could be involved in supporting queer justice projects in your community. The most common club that takes up this kind of work is often referred to as a GSA. This abbreviation initially stood for "gay/straight alliance" and more recently "gender and sexuality alliance." Some groups have added "activist" to the name instead of alliance or called themselves something else such as PRIDE, Prism, Rainbow Club, Social Justice Club, etc. Regardless of the specific name, if the club has a central focus on addressing topics related to gender and sexual diversity, then I mean to include it when I use the term GSA. For that reason, this chapter begins with what we know about queer youth organizing in general and then moves on to address GSAs in particular, including the history and purposes of GSAs, how to start a GSA, and ideas for creating a diverse and inclusive club experience. The second section of this chapter will address how to reach out and build bridges and networks with other clubs and organizations to strengthen the work and expand the reach of your GSA. The last section will provide basic legal information about the Equal Access Act, which is a federal law that guarantees students' rights to form clubs and meet on school grounds. Let's get started with a little walk through history: How did we get to where we are with student clubs today?

HISTORY AND PURPOSES OF GSAs

Queer youth programs have a long history that predates the emergence of GSAs in the late 1980s. Historian Stephan Cohen documented the emergence of queer youth groups in the late 1960s and early 1970s, including Gay Teenagers in San Francisco and the Sodom Radical Bisexual Free Communist Youth in Hayward, California, to the Young Peoples Group in Miami, Florida, and Chicago's Alternatives for Teenage Gays (Cohen, 2005). He shares rich examples of the contents of their newsletters, activities, and priorities of activist and support groups such as Vanguard in San Francisco; Gay Youth, a part of the national Gay Liberation Front designed for people under 21; and Street Transvestite Action Revolutionaries (S.T.A.R.) in New York City (pp. 74–75).

The first documented school-based club was at George Washington High School in New York City (NYC) in 1972. This "Third World" club included nine lesbians, six gay men, and five straight friends and worked to build a coalition of similar groups at other NYC high schools (Cohen, 2005, p. 75). In the late 1970s, other groups formed including Horizons Youth in Chicago in 1978 and the Hetrick-Martin Institute in NYC in 1979. In 1984, a Los Angeles high school counselor named Virginia Uribe created Project 10, which was designed as a confidential support group for gay teens in response to the harassment of a Black gay student at her school (Cohen, 2005, p. 78).

It was 1988 in a private school outside of Boston when a group of students and two teachers established the first documented school club that used the name "Gay-Straight Alliance." Kevin Jennings, who later become the first executive director of GLSEN, was one of those teachers (Jennings, 2016). The start of this club is described as follows:

> [A] young, straight student [who] approached Jennings with the idea of creating a group for gays and straights alike to advocate for LGBT students at Concord Academy and to be a vehicle for activism outside of school as well. Jennings, activist par excellence, the man widely credited with beginning the GSA movement, defers much credit to his students, not only for the founding of the club but for its agenda—first addressing homophobia, later advocating for the inclusion of sexual orientation in Concord Academy's nondiscrimination policy. (Lane, 2018, p. 113)

Massachusetts provided a fertile context for the growth of these groups. In 1992, Governor Weld, who had campaigned on addressing the problem of youth suicide, convened the Massachusetts Governor's Commission on Gay and Lesbian Youth (Perrotti & Westheimer, 2001). This commission was formed partially in response to a study released in 1989 by the U.S. Department of Health and Human Services that reported approximately one-third of youth suicides were being completed by gay, lesbian, and bisexual youth (Gibson, 1989). The Governor's Commission, which Jennings cochaired, made the following five recommendations to address this public health issue in schools. Schools should:

1) [Create school] policies protecting gay and lesbian[1] students from harassment, violence, and discrimination
2) [Offer training for] teachers/counselors/school staff in crisis intervention and violence prevention
3) [Create school-based] support groups for gay and straight students
4) [Provide information] in school libraries for gay and lesbian adolescents
5) [Implement curriculum] which includes gay and lesbian issues (The Governor's Commission on Gay and Lesbian Youth: Breaking the Silence in Schools and in Families, 1993)

The Massachusetts Board of Education unanimously adopted the first four recommendations but not the fifth addressing curriculum. Jennings later explained:

> The overwhelming majority of the commission rejected [the curriculum recommendations], saying they were simply politically impossible to advance in the wake of the controversy in New York City about its "children of the rainbow" curriculum (which had resulted in the chancellor losing his job). We ended up settling on a rather mild plea for curricular inclusion (with no specifics as to what that means), and sent the report to the governor in February 1993). (Jennings, 2016, p. viii–ix)

Governor Weld also created the Safe Schools Program for Gay and Lesbian Students in 1994 (Perotti and Westheimer, 2001, p. 3). An LGBTQIA+-inclusive curriculum was not created by the Massachusetts Department of Education until 2018, and it is still optional for schools to adopt (Belle, 2018). However, in 2023, Massachusetts did adopt new sex and health education standards that explicitly included the LGBTQIA+ community (Drysdale, 2023).

The third recommendation specifically called for "support groups," which was the initial goal behind most early GSAs. From this early start, through informal professional networks and then the formal organization that started as the Gay and Lesbian Independent School Teachers Network

---

1. The language at the time had shifted from "gay" to "gay and lesbian" and didn't yet reflect the full diversity now included in the LGBTQIA+ acronym in use at the time of this writing.

(GLISTEN), which became the national organization now known as GLSEN, GSAs expanded across the country.

Fast-forward to 1995 when a legal battle in Utah elevated the profile of GSAs to the national level. The case, *East High Gay/Straight Alliance v. Board of Education of Salt Lake City School District* (1999), was brought by a group of students who had requested to form a GSA and been denied by their school district. Kelli Peterson, profiled in Chapter 1, was one of those students. The GSA students ultimately won their right to start a club due to the Equal Access Act, but the school district then banned all clubs to prevent the GSA from meeting, which led to a mass student walk-out (Mayberry, 2006). In an interview study conducted with eight of the students involved, Mayberry (2006) reported that involvement in the GSA helped students build a community of support that also led to them each developing identities as activists. This "politicized identity community" (p. 27) helped counter narratives of gay and lesbian youth as "at risk" and strengthened their connections to each other and the broader community coalition that emerged to support their cause.

It is hard to track the number of active GSAs due to turnover in advisors and lack of centralized reporting of these clubs. GLSEN and the GSA Network both provide optional opportunities for groups to register on their websites to access resources from these organizations. In 2009, over 3,000 GSAs were registered with GLSEN (Meyer, 2009a), and in 2014 Cris Mayo (2014) reported that GSAs were in about 4,000 schools nationwide. GLSEN's (Truong et al., 2021) study of GSAs tells us that about 61% of students reported having a GSA at their school (up from only 25% in 2007) and that GSAs were more likely to be found in suburban, urban, and public schools and less likely to be found in religious schools or in the South (p. 3).

Early studies of GSAs explored the various reasons they were started in Massachusetts in the 1990s and included examples such as:

- An open lesbian asked and the principal was worried about lawsuits
- In response to a serious incident of antigay harassment against a teacher
- In response to student suicides
- In response to public resistance to an openly gay HIV/AIDS educational consultant working with the school
- After student surveys identified intolerance and harassment issues (Doppler 2000, cited in Perotti & Westheimer, 2001, p. 158)

In their book, *When the Drama Club Is Not Enough: Lessons from the Safe Schools Program for Gay and Lesbian Students,* Perotti and Westheimer (2001) identified the following three most common purposes of GSAs:

education, support, and social (p. 159). In the most recent national study of GSAs, students reported that their GSA engaged in the following activities:

1. Meet new people and socialize (90%)
2. Discuss or learn about LGBTQ topics (87.6%)
3. Provide emotional support (70%)
4. Work with school staff to create a safer school environment for LGBTQ students (47%)
5. Talk about my experiences with harassment and discrimination at school (47%) (Truong et al, 2021, p. 27).

More recently, some GSAs have become explicitly advocacy or activist oriented (Meyer & Kurtz, 2024), but this is not widespread. The GLSEN study found that only 30–37% of students reported their GSAs organizing awareness events and collaborating with other groups on advocacy work. Only 15% of students reported their GSA worked with district officials to advocate for inclusive policies or staff training (Truong et al., 2021, p. 27). What purposes does your GSA serve for you? For your school community? Are there any new purposes you would like it to address more? Less? If you don't have a GSA or yours needs to be re-energized, the next section can help with that.

STARTING OR DEVELOPING A GSA

If your school doesn't already have an active GSA, then Figure 5.1 is a great place to start. Maybe there once was one that met but the student leadership graduated and nobody took their place, the advisor retired, or the membership faded away. Ask some students or teachers who have been around longer than you and find out if you need to start from scratch or if you can reactivate an already-recognized club that has been in hibernation.

If you already have a student club that acts like a GSA, there are lots of ways to think about helping it grow and strengthen. Two main ways clubs can grow include (1) membership and leadership development and (2) strategic planning of activities and visibility.

Membership and Leadership Development

Membership development activities can include increasing your numbers by actively recruiting new members. Any such recruitment efforts should also consider diversifying the membership—which can be hard since small friendship groups often get such clubs started and then you may find it difficult to be open to students who aren't already in your social circle. Some research indicates that GSAs may not intentionally support or provide safe

Queering Clubs and Extracurriculars 73

Figure 5.1. Starting a GSA

There are some important steps that all student organizers need to take when starting a new club at your school. If your school doesn't currently have an active GSA and you want to create one, this activity will help get you started. The following list combines elements from the resources listed at the bottom of this section. I recommend consulting these as well since they provide additional information and resources for some of the steps along the way.

1. Ask a teacher or administrator about the process to start a club at your school.
2. Read some of the resources listed here to guide you.
3. Gather a few other peers who are also interested in your club idea.
4. Find an advisor who is willing and able to support your club.
5. Decide on a club name. You can change this later as part of the first few meetings; you might have an official name for district paperwork and an informal name that better reflects the interests and preferences of the members.
6. Complete required forms to become a recognized club.
7. Decide on a meeting time and place.
8. Advertise the club.
9. Plan activities for the first meeting.
10. Meet!

Resources:

Indicates links available on book website: www.elizabethjmeyer.com/queer-justice
- ACLU*
- GSA Network*
- GLSEN*
- Macgillivray, I. K. (2007). *Gay-Straight Alliances: A Handbook for Students, Educators, and Parents*. Harrington Park Press.

---

space for trans students and students of color (McCready, 2004; Poteat et al., 2018; Truong et al., 2021), so thinking about ways to make your club welcoming to these students is an important way to start.

Another valuable way to develop your membership is to provide leadership opportunities for members. Depending on the leadership structure of your club, you can consider the following: holding elections to choose a "president-elect" to shadow the current president for half the school year, forming committees for specific events that can be led by members, or inviting club leaders and other members to community-organized leadership events. For example, many states and cities offer GSA or student leadership conferences. These events might be affiliated with a local university or LGBTQIA+ community group. Studies of students in GSAs have shown that involvement in the club improves leaders' sense of empowerment: personal, relational, and strategic (Russell et al., 2009) as well as members' "sociopolitical efficacy," or their confidence in their ability to engage in social change (Poteat et al., 2020). This is important, as it challenges the common story told about LGBTQIA+ youth as being vulnerable, victimized, and at risk for suicide and depression. Showing strength, resilience, and leadership is also part of their experiences. All of these things can be true.

If you can't find local, in-person leadership development opportunities, virtual training resources are provided by the GSA Network that are free to access on the Web (see book website for links). One major national event to consider attending is called Creating Change. This is an annual conference planned by The Task Force (formerly known as the National LGBTQ Task Force) that focuses on leadership and skills-building for the LGBTQIA+ movement. You can find links to information about the event on the book's website. They also host year-round virtual events called "Creating Change 365," which are more affordable and worth checking out. You can learn more about what is available in your region by connecting with local experts and organizations such as P-FLAG or your local LGBTQIA+ community center and then see if you can get permission and support for some members to attend. As you develop your membership and leadership capacity, you also can focus on how you want to use the time and energy of your club.

Strategic Planning: Activities and Visibility

Strategic planning is just a fancy word for some long-term and short-term goals that fit the current size, scope, and capacity of your organization. Strategic planning for a GSA could include mapping out goals and activities for the school year as well as setting goals for activities, membership, and leadership development over the next 2–3 school years. While you are taking stock of what your group has done in the past, you can also brainstorm ideas about what you want to see happen for the club in the future. Do you want to have more events? More participation at existing events? Fewer events but higher quality? Do you want to increase the profile or awareness of your club and its activities? Do you want to partner with other clubs and organizations? Which ones? Who can help with these ideas? When do you want to accomplish them by? What resources do you need to be successful? Figure 5.2 offers a chart to help track your planning activities.

Successful examples of how clubs have worked to increase their visibility include making announcements, creating bulletin boards, writing school newspaper articles, presenting at school board meetings, posting on social media, and hosting bake sales or other short events that have broad appeal. Daily announcements can include details about when the club meets or educational information about LGBTQIA+ rights, historical figures, or birthdays of current LGBTQIA+ icons. You can design and create a bulletin board or display case that is in a central location at your school. The theme of the bulletin board can rotate and include LGBTQIA+ vocabulary, memes for humor, images reflecting famous members of the diverse LGBTQIA+ community, or popular media (books and movies) that reflect stories from the LGBTQIA+ community. Writing articles for the school newspaper is a

Figure 5.2. Strategic Planning

This chart is presented to help you organize the results of your discussion and brainstorming session. You can keep this on chart paper in your GSA advisor's classroom to refer to or create it as a Google Doc that everyone has access to. I recommend making reminders to revisit this plan each month and have the project lead share progress, challenges, and updates throughout the year. I entered a few sample ideas to help you see how you might use it.

Goal/activity	Lead person	Target date	Resources Needed (people, information, funds, materials, etc.)
1. Increase membership		Dec. 1	Draft announcement text to be read, write story for school paper, post flyers, social media posts
2. LGBTQIA+ History Month bulletin board		Oct. 1	Websites in Chapter 4, books in library, printouts of information, colorful paper, Pride flags
3. Establish partnership and plan an event with one other student club		Jan. 15	Time to meet and co-plan; find another club willing to work together
4. *your ideas here . . .*			

valuable way to integrate the experiences of LGBTQIA+ students into the public life of the school. You can share research from Chapter 2, or present personal stories, or address current controversies in schools such as curricular inclusion, equitable access to sex-segregated facilities, and participation on sports teams. Some GSA members have written and presented public comments at school board meetings about issues such as a district's "controversial topics" policy, requesting access to all-gender bathrooms, and supporting LGBTQIA+-inclusive curriculum bills. Student voices at public school board meetings are often picked up by local media, so you should be aware of the potential for much greater attention if you are interested in this level of activity.

In interviews with GSA advisors, I learned that there is often a struggle to find balance between the diverse needs of student members who are seeking a safe space—a place to socialize with queer friends and allies—while also working on peer and professional education, as well as other activities that are defined as advocacy and activism (Meyer & Kurtz, 2024). In GLSEN's

(Truong et al., 2021) nationwide study of students and teachers affiliated with GSAs, they reported that engaging in activism or advocacy was not a common experience. The most common activities reported were helping GSA members address incidents of harassment and discrimination (62.3%) and working with school staff to create safer school environments (57.5%). The least common activities were educating student members about LGBTQIA+ issues (8.6%), encouraging or assisting in advocacy work (8.4%), and developing student leadership (3.8%). This study also shared the types of information and resources students and advisors in GSAs wanted to see. The top three needs identified by both students and advisors were general meeting activity suggestions, ideas on how to bring up LGBTQIA+ problems to our school, and resources to help be more inclusive toward queer people with disabilities and people of color (Truong et al., 2021, p. 35). For additional activity ideas, see Figure 5.3. This book is designed to help fill this gap—I hope you are finding it helpful!

I recommend planning regular check-ins (at least once in mid-fall and once mid-spring) with members and the advisor about the balance of these activities over the course of a school year. For example, a sequence of monthly meeting themes and activities might go as follows:

- **September:** Socializing, getting to know one another, establishing group norms and expectations that encourage a diverse and inclusive club environment.
- **October:** Strategic planning about club purposes (see common ones earlier) and club activities and events for the coming year. You can get some ideas from Chapter 4.
- **November:** Group check-in on balance between unstructured social time and structured activities: Is it meeting student needs? If not, what should change?
- **December:** Adjust plans based on November discussions.
- **January:** Recruit new members, rebuild social environment, and plan additional activities and events for the rest of the year.
- **February:** Planned activities and events, leadership development.
- **March:** Group check-in on balance between unstructured social time and structured activity and planning time: Is it meeting student needs? If not, what should change?
- **April:** Planned activities and events, leadership development.
- **May:** Reflect on past year and set goals for next year.

KNOW YOUR RIGHTS: THE EQUAL ACCESS ACT

The idea of a school club that talks about gender and sexuality is not always met with support from students, teachers, administrators, parents,

Figure 5.3. Meeting Activity Ideas

indicates links available on book website: www.elizabethjmeyer.com/queer-justice

Minimal Preparation

- Ice-breakers.*
- Team-building activities.*
- Current events discussion: Bring in a news article or share a brief news video to discuss.
- Coloring, photography, or collage-making session. This can be a fun stress-reliever and can offer folks something creative to do together. You can suggest a theme or guiding question such as: Where do you feel safest at school? What brings you joy? What does love feel like to you? What do you feel like on the inside today?
- School climate discussion. Have students first talk in groups of two to three and then share their ideas with larger group. Some starter questions you can use are: (1) What makes you feel happy and connected to school? (2) What makes you feel stressed or anxious at school? (3) What ways do you hear LGBTQIA+ people talked about at school? Is it positive? Negative? Neutral? Not at all? (4) What would make our school a better place for LGBTQIA+ people?
- Mapping activity. Provide the students with a photocopied or digital map of the school building, and then they can each color the school to represent (1) where they feel safe or happy (green or blue), (2) where they feel unsafe or uncomfortable (red or orange), and (3) Where they have been bullied or harassed (black x's). Students can then talk about their maps and why they chose certain colors for certain areas and create a collective map that captures their shared experiences to possibly present to the administration.
- LGBTQIA+ Kahoot! If you use this digital learning game, you can pull up quizzes and activities prepared by others as a fun group game. Putting students in pairs or teams might also help them forge new relationships.

Some Preparation

- Invite a guest speaker from a local LGBTQIA+ organization to talk about what they do and careers in LGBTQIA+ advocacy and/or social justice.
- Choose and read a section of this book together and discuss how it is connected to your school and GSA's experiences.
- Try doing GLSEN's LGBTQ timeline lesson.*
- Invite the school or local librarian in to highlight a few LGBTQIA+-themed books in the school collection.
- Ask a local expert to come talk about your state's sexuality education policy and your district's curriculum through a queer lens. What is missing? What would you like to see changed?
- Ask an author to come talk with your GSA. You can ask me! I can't say yes to every inquiry, but I try to make time at least once a month to work with students and school groups at no cost to you. Email me, and we'll see what we can set up. Be sure to ask if you need permission to invite guests to join club meetings: Elizabeth.j.meyer@colorado.edu.

community members, and school boards. Earlier in this chapter I shared the example of the 1995 national controversy about the East High School GSA in Salt Lake City. The legal reason these students were able to meet was due to the Equal Access Act. The Equal Access Act is a federal law passed in 1984 to ensure that students' First Amendment rights of freedom of association were protected at school (Imber & Van Geel, 2010, p. 163). It was introduced by Republican senator Orrin Hatch from Utah to help ensure Bible study groups could meet in schools (Perotti & Westheimer, 2001, p. 35). I love this fact, since it was a law introduced by a Right-wing conservative, religious lawmaker that now ensures GSAs get to meet too! In part it states,

> It shall be unlawful for any public secondary school which receives Federal financial assistance and which has a limited open forum to deny equal access or a fair opportunity to, or discriminate against, any students who wish to conduct a meeting within that limited open forum on the bases of the religious, political, philosophical, or other content of the speech at such meetings.
>
> A public secondary school has a limited open forum whenever such school grants an offering to or opportunity for one or more noncurriculum-related student groups to meet on school premises during noninstructional time. (20 U.S.C. section 4071)

Many students and advisors are unaware of their legal right to form a club and meet on school grounds even though this law has been tested repeatedly in cases around the country. For example, in 2003, in Kentucky there was a student walk-out, "open hostility" from opponents, an acrimonious school board meeting, and a protest from local ministers when a student-initiated GSA petitioned the Boyd County High School (Canonsburg, Kentucky) to meet during noninstructional time. To try to stop the controversy surrounding the GSA, much like what happened in Utah, the principal proposed to ban all noncurricular clubs. However, several noncurricular clubs, including the drama club and a Bible club, continued to meet during noninstructional time and homeroom. The GSA petitioned the courts for the same access as other noncurricular groups (*Boyd County High School Gay Straight Alliance v. Board of Education of Boyd County, Ky.*, 2003). The federal district court determined that Boyd County High School continued to operate a "limited open forum" and that denying the GSA the same opportunities violated the Equal Access Act. The federal district court also considered the uproar surrounding the GSA. It acknowledged that schools could ban groups that created "material and substantial disruption" to the educational process (*Tinker v. Des Moines Independent School District*, 1969). However, in this case, the disruption was caused by GSA opponents, not GSA members. Other issues related to the First Amendment and expression at school will be addressed more in Chapter 6. Other courts have reached similar conclusions that school districts have violated the *Equal Access Act* when banning GSAs because of student, parent, and/or community protests while continuing to operate a limited open forum. See also *Straights and Gays for Equity v. Osseo Area Schools* (2006), reaffirmed in 2008, and *White County High School Peers in Diverse Education v. White County School District* (2006) for similar decisions from federal district courts (Minnesota and Georgia, respectively).

In one exception, a Texas federal district court sided with the school's decision to ban the GSA in *Caudillo v. Lubbock* (2004). This case differs from the previous cases in at least one significant way: The GSA aligned itself with a non-district-approved advocate whose website linked to information about safer sex practices. The school and the court viewed this information as "sexually explicit" and "obscene." Due to existing school policies that endorsed abstinence-only education and the state sodomy law (which had recently been ruled unconstitutional (see *Lawrence v. Texas*, 2003), the court sided with the school's decision to ban the GSA, even though the students removed the link to the website (Leonard, 2004).

Despite such community opposition, the Equal Access Act is clear, and now most school districts know that they have to allow GSAs and most other student groups to meet. For example, in a 2003 Texas case, Klein School District officials said that they would have fought the lawsuit brought by the GSA and American Civil Liberties Union (ACLU) if they thought they had a chance of winning the case. The superintendent stated: "The issue is that regardless of my personal feelings, the principal's personal feelings or the community's opinion it is a matter of law" (National Coalition to Support Sexuality Education, 2003, n.p.). When this decision was announced, a student from this GSA commented, "I definitely think that the effort was worth it. I had to give up a little bit of time, but now my school is going to be a whole lot safer because of it" (NCSSE, 2003, n.p.). I hope that you don't find yourself experiencing resistance to the existence of your GSA, but if you are, helpful downloadable letters are available from the ACLU that you can use to educate the people blocking your right to meet. These links are available on the book's website. We all experience resistance in different forms to being advocates and activists for LGBTQIA+ equity. Building bridges and networks with others is one way to generate support to help you continue this important work.

BUILDING BRIDGES AND NETWORKS

Change-oriented advocacy and activism can be draining, isolating, and exhausting. Doing this work in community with like-minded others can not only lend strength to your movement but also provide vital social support and personal connection beyond your immediate peer group. To sustain your spirit and protect your energy, this section offers ideas for building connections and support networks to help you and your club thrive for many years. The next sections address ideas specifically for students and then advisors, and additional ideas are offered in Chapter 8.

For Students

You may be very happy with the membership in your GSA right now. You may know everyone and feel a sense of trust and safety with them. Or not. Maybe your GSA has lost membership and needs some rethinking to get a new burst of energy. Or maybe there has been some drama, heartbreak, and hurt feelings and you need to spend some time on healing and repair. I have heard stories about students showing up at a GSA meeting and feeling like nobody greeted them or wanted them there or that the meeting they attended didn't make them feel welcome. Students of color and trans students often struggle to find support and community in some GSAs. Look around your club: Does it reflect the diversity of the student body of your school? If not, why do you think that is? What could you do to address that? How can you put the long-term health and goals of the club over individual hurts or past interactions?

I want you to think about how you want your GSA to feel for new and existing members—particularly students from groups who are already underrepresented at your school—and what might need to change to make more people feel welcome in your club. If your GSA is perceived by others to be "clique-y," then many potential new members may avoid the group for fear of not being welcomed. One easy strategy is to develop a routine greeting that acknowledges and welcomes everyone to a club meeting. This could be a welcome high five from the president, a "Hi, what's your name? We're glad you're here!" from the cochair, or a ritual opening activity where everyone gets 5 minutes to talk in randomly assigned pairs about their day. The way you make someone feel when they walk in the room is important, and being conscious about including new members in activities and inviting their ideas is how you build community and a sense of belonging.

If there has been some interpersonal drama or relationship fallout, you may need to seek help to do some *restorative justice* (RJ) activities to regain trust, rebuild damaged connections, and start fresh. Morrison and Vaandering (2012) share some specific ways communities can engage in restorative circles to name the harms, share feelings about the impacts of those harms, and then come together to make a path forward for the community to heal. They apply the concept of RJ that includes four elements: restitution (reparation of harm), resolution (by the parties involved), reconciliation (reason for emotions), and voluntary engagement (p. 141). RJ activities can be completed between two individuals regarding a specific incident or the whole club if others have been impacted by the behaviors. RJ can be a complex process that requires knowledgeable leaders to lead well. If not facilitated effectively, discussions can cause more harm than repair. Be sure to find people who understand RJ and are trained in it so you can implement it well. If you think members of your GSA would benefit from some restorative conferencing or peacemaking circles, work with your advisor to identify resources available in your district or community that can support this process.

If your club needs more support or wants to grow, you might also reach out to other student groups that are also interested in activism, education, or justice-oriented work. Such clubs might include feminist clubs that may be affiliated with groups like the National Abortion Rights League (NARAL) or the National Organization for Women (NOW), international justice clubs like Amnesty International or immigrants' rights groups, or antiracist organizations such as a Black Student Alliance or U.M.A.S. y M.E.Ch.A. (United Mexican American Students and *Movimiento Estudiantil Chicano de Aztlán*; "Chicano Student Movement of Aztlán"), as well as Indigenous and Asian student organizations. By building coalitions with other student groups and/or community organizations, you may be able to expand and diversify your membership while ensuring your club isn't replicating work already underway by others. Strength in numbers is a valuable principle to consider when establishing partnerships and working in tandem to improve your school. You might also plan activities that specifically educate about or address issues of shared concern such as unfair school discipline practices and the school-to-prison pipeline, dress codes and bodily autonomy, supports for refugee and asylum seekers, police violence, accessibility of bathrooms and buildings, or environmental justice (clean water, food deserts, etc.). These are all issues that impact our diverse LGBTQIA+ community.

For Advisors

Advising a GSA is often extra uncompensated work done by educators who are committed to supporting their students—whether it is part of their official duties or not. It has been described as "exhausting" or "draining" as well as "inspiring" and "motivating" (Meyer & Kurtz, 2024). To help advisors find some support, balance, and longevity in this role, I offer some ideas and information from research on advisors working with GSAs. As this book demonstrates, advocating for queer justice at school is both inspiring and challenging—especially for educators trying to support students and keep a healthy balance for their personal lives and responsibilities outside school.

In a study with 22 GSA advisors, Watson et al. (2010) reported several factors that acted as both barriers and facilitators to their work with the GSA, including parents, public policy or politics, "society in general," administrators, school personnel, students, and school policies. My 2022 study in Colorado found similar results as advisors talked about the various challenges and supports they experienced while advising the GSA. They rarely spoke of supports without also describing how they also had turned into barriers. For example, one supportive administrator left for a new school and was replaced with someone unsupportive. Working with students in the GSA was both inspiring and exhausting, as already mentioned. A district equity committee was a power space for queer student voices as well as a stage for parents to voice conservative backlash. One advisor spoke about having an administration that was supportive of the GSA in general but acted in neutral or passively resistant ways to enacting many of the changes requested by the GSA such as flying a Pride flag at school or putting an LGBTQIA+ resources button on the school's website.

Watson et al.'s (2010) study also addressed the individual factors that impacted advisors such as their sexual identities, knowledge of LGBTQIA+ issues, personal experiences, and personality characteristics. These also served as both barriers and facilitators for advisors in my study. Cisgender, straight advisors acknowledged their limitations in not being a part of the LGBTQIA+ community and their strengths as allies who are able to take more risks and use their relative privilege to speak up and support marginalized students (Meyer & Kurtz, 2024). They also reported being able to maintain healthier boundaries and not take the stress of the job home with them as much as LGBTQIA+-identified advisors. What this suggests is that there is power in collaboration and relationships. If you are the sole advisor of your GSA, perhaps consider reaching out to a colleague to share the responsibilities of this role. You can cofacilitate some meetings and take turns planning and supporting meetings to give each other a break. Finding someone who offers some diversity can help balance out what you may lack in terms of personal experience, knowledge, and connections to various social groups.

Many advisors I have spoken with described their choice to let the students lead and to "take a backseat" and just provide a space for students to meet. While I agree that supporting student initiative is valuable, many students need some structured supports to help them channel their energy and make sure the GSA is open and welcoming to all interested students. Finding the balance between guiding and letting students lead is an ongoing challenge. I encourage GSA advisors to provide some support with structures and active facilitation in the beginning of the school year and with more long-term public activities. Try to meet with the GSA leadership to check in and make sure they are getting the information and supports they need to meet their goals. Talking with other club advisors and school staff about how they work with their students and can support LGBTQIA+ students is another way to get ideas and find a balance that reflects the needs of your students and school community. Just remember: Your students can't do this without you, so you need to take care of yourself so you can continue to be present for them.

CONCLUSION

Starting and maintaining a justice- or activist-oriented club is important and hard work. There are many obstacles and rewards along the way. Please remember to connect, laugh out loud, share successes, and celebrate victories as well as share difficult times and face your fears. Never underestimate the value of showing up consistently. Try to lead with love and best intentions. I hope this book helps you go out and, in the words of civil rights leader and Senator John Lewis, "get in good trouble, necessary trouble."

DISCUSSION QUESTIONS

1. What are some aspects of your club/student community that you are proud of and are going well? What could be improved?
2. How are communications between students and the advisor(s) in your GSA? Would you like things to be any different?
3. What is the balance like between social and fun time versus work and project time in your club? Do you want more or less of something? Why?
4. What ideas from this chapter were most interesting to you? What do you want to learn more about?

KEY TERMS

- Equal Access Act
- restorative justice

CHAPTER 6

Express Yourself

> My silences had not protected me. Your silence will not protect you.
>
> —Audre Lorde

Please forgive me and my 80s inner queer child needing to use the title from a Madonna song for this chapter. This chapter is all about the First Amendment and free speech—specifically, the rights and limits for expression in K–12 public schools in the United States. Have you ever been told you can't wear a certain t-shirt or button to school? Or were prevented from writing a newspaper article or class paper on a project of interest to you? Were you asked to take down flyers or not announce information about an event or club? Have books been removed from your school or classroom library? Have students been punished or prevented from participating in a student protest or walkout? These are all examples of how expression might be limited at school. I use the term "expression" broadly to describe any act of speech or communication. This can include spoken and written messages as well as other things such as how you dress, how you protest things you disagree with, the curriculum (assigned texts and topics taught in classes), the content and message of school plays and assemblies, social media posts about people and events at school, the contents of school publications (including yearbooks and newspapers), art displays, and other forms covered by the U.S. Constitution. The First Amendment states, "Congress shall make no law respecting an establishment of religion, or prohibiting the free exercise thereof; or abridging the freedom of speech, or of the press; or the right of the people peaceably to assemble, and to petition the Government for a redress of grievances" ("U.S. Const. amend. I," 1791).

There are three main categories of expression the law recognizes in school: student expression, school-sponsored expression, and *government speech*. Four major Supreme Court decisions provide guidance on how K–12 public schools need to think when addressing First Amendment concerns regarding student speech: *Tinker v. Des Moines School District* (1969), *Bethel v. Fraser* (1986), *Hazelwood v. Kuhlmeier* (1988), and *Morse v. Frederick* (2007). These four cases are each about incidents when students were punished for expressions made at school and provide basic principles for how schools can respond to student expression. These famous cases, along with a few others, will be addressed in this chapter so you can understand these basic guidelines and consider them when planning action in and around school events. I want to start by pointing out that First Amendment issues are handled differently in K–12 public schools than in universities, workplaces, and public spaces. Educational law experts have argued that there are special characteristics of public K–12 schools, including (1) age of students, (2) attendance requirements, (3) multiple school constituencies, (4) heightened safety considerations, (5) need for public accountability, (6) school-associated nature of much student speech, and (7) the need to promote educational goals (Warnick, 2009). Due to these various factors, the rules in K–12 public schools are different from most other places, which is why these three different categories of speech are helpful to understand, as they shape how judges interpret and apply the First Amendment in school settings. This chapter starts with a section on forms of student expression including protests, dress codes, prom and Pride, and online expression and then moves on to address school-sponsored speech such as assemblies and newspapers before addressing staff speech rights and limitations. The chapter then takes up the issues of hate speech and student privacy in the context of new "parents' rights" bills.

STUDENT EXPRESSION

Students have First Amendment rights in schools. This was clearly established in 1969 in a case you will read about in the first section on protests. Students also have the right to wear clothing that reflects their culture and gender, as this is seen as "expressive" conduct, though schools can place limits on messages printed on clothing, which will be addressed in the second section on dress codes. Students must also be allowed to bring the date of their choice to proms and other school events, as this is also seen as a form of expression. The third section on proms and Pride will provide more details on this topic. This section concludes with a discussion of online speech and where schools have the right to limit and address student speech on websites, social media, and other online expression.

Protests

The long history of student activism and First Amendment law starts in the late 1960s when three students opted to wear black armbands with white peace symbols on them to school to protest the Vietnam War even after the school had expressly prohibited them. The students were suspended when they refused to remove the armbands at school. In 1969, the Supreme Court decided in favor of the students and established the long-standing precedent protecting students' right to expression and famously wrote that teachers and students do not "shed their constitutional rights . . . at the schoolhouse gate" (*Tinker v. Des Moines School District*, 1969). The *Tinker* decision protects students' speech rights by outlining two key prongs of when schools could limit student speech. If the expressive act causes either a (1) material and substantial disruption or (2) collides with the rights of others, K–12 public school leaders can legally restrict student speech. What this tells us is that students have the right to peacefully protest social issues if it doesn't disrupt the school environment. Students can walk out, distribute information, circulate petitions, and peacefully disengage from activities that they find offensive or harmful. If such expression impacts your participation in a graded assignment or exam, teachers are within their rights to assign the grade you earned (a zero if you missed a complete test), but you shouldn't experience punishment or other sanctions for participating in such protests. Students can also display buttons, bracelets, stickers, armbands, or other symbols that show their stance on a political issue if they aren't "lewd" or "vulgar" and don't "collide with the rights of others," which leads us to a discussion of dress codes and t-shirts.

Dress Codes and T-Shirts

Federal courts have determined that student clothing and hairstyles can have "communicative content" and that they may symbolize "ethnic heritage, religious beliefs, and political and social views" (Imber & Van Geel, 2010, p. 119). Many schools have dress codes with specific guidelines for male and female students or that prohibit words of any kind on clothing. In one case, a male kindergartner in Texas who is Apache was suspended for wearing his hair past his collar, in a long braid, to school. The courts found that the school violated the student's religious rights (free exercise) and his rights to free expression (*AA v. Needville Independent School District*, 2010). Chapter 7 will discuss more about the harms of school policies, facilities, and procedures that enforce conformity to stereotypical gender norms and how to work to make them more inclusive. In addition to dress codes, t-shirt cases have showed up in courts repeatedly in cases exploring the limits of free speech at school.

A school outside San Diego, CA, had a case where a student wore a t-shirt that stated: "Be ashamed. Our school embraced what god has condemned. Homosexuality is shameful" (*Harper v. Poway Unified School District*, 2006). In this case, the principal gave the student a few choices to conceal the message (tape over it, turn the t-shirt inside out), but the student refused and spent the day in the office. When the student's family filed a lawsuit against the school, the Ninth Circuit Court decided that "vulgar, lewd, obscene, indecent, and plainly offensive speech, may well 'impinge upon the rights of other students,' even if the speaker does not directly accost individual students with his remarks" (Chandler, 978 F.2d at 529 [quoting

Tinker, 393 U.S. at 509]). The court concluded, "Harper's wearing of his T-shirt 'collides with the rights of other students' in the most fundamental way" (p. 1178) and supported the principal's intervention. The student and his family lost this case. An important additional factor in this decision was the history of previous homophobic events at Poway High School. This included several altercations surrounding the "Day of Silence" and a recent San Diego Superior Court decision to award damages to two former students ($175,000 and $125,000) because of the school's failure to protect them from sexual orientation harassment by peers. This prior context and specific examples of "substantial disruption" are taken into consideration when applying these principles to student expression cases. This means that a legal decision based on the facts of a case in California might not have the same outcome to a similar case for schools in other districts or regions of the United States. This case was decided in a federal district court, so it only applies to other states in the Ninth District (Alaska, Hawaii, California, Arizona, Nevada, Idaho, Montana, Washington, and Oregon).

In a similar case, a slightly different t-shirt message in Illinois resulted in a different outcome. A student in a suburb of Chicago wore a shirt that stated, "Be Happy, Not Gay" during the school's Day of Silence event (*Zamecnik v. Indian Prairie School District # 204 Board of Education*, 2011). The school asked the student to tape over the message, and a lower court issued an injunction preventing the student from wearing the shirt to school. In the appeal to the Seventh District Court, the judges found that the "substantial disruption" had not been proven and the school was wrong in limiting student speech in this case. The judges wrote in their decision that "a school that permits advocacy of the rights of homosexual students cannot be allowed to stifle criticism of homosexuality." In this case the message on the shirt was perceived as more benign, and there was no related evidence of ongoing homophobic harassment at the school to impact the judge's decision. This decision only applies to states in the Seventh Circuit which are Illinois, Wisconsin, and Indiana. A complete listing of all the U.S. appeals courts is presented in Table 6.1.

What these two cases show is that if the expression isn't clearly "vulgar, lewd, obscene, indecent, and plainly offensive speech" or doesn't "collide with the rights of other students," then school officials should generally allow it. These two cases also show that there is no easy line for schools to draw and that these decisions are often judgment calls made by administrators. Such judgements are often influenced by a principal's professional priorities as well as the local values and dominant norms of a school community.

In a different kind of t-shirt case, Rachel Bavaro, a high school student in Massachusetts, wore a t-shirt that read "all the cool girls are lesbians." The student was sent to the assistant principal and was told that she needed to cover up her shirt and not wear it to school again. Ms. Bavaro then wrote a letter to her mayor, who then spoke up on Rachel's behalf. At a school committee meeting, the mayor publicly promised that Rachel could wear

Table 6.1. U.S. Courts of Appeal (United States Courts, 2024)

First Circuit	Maine, New Hampshire, Massachusetts, Rhode Island
Second Circuit	Vermont, New York, Connecticut, Puerto Rico
Third Circuit	Pennsylvania, New Jersey, Delaware, U.S. Virgin Islands
Fourth Circuit	West Virginia, Virginia, Maryland, North Carolina, South Carolina
Fifth Circuit	Mississippi, Louisiana, Texas
Sixth Circuit	Ohio, Michigan, Kentucky, Tennessee
Seventh Circuit	Indiana, Illinois, Wisconsin
Eighth Circuit	Minnesota, Iowa, Missouri, Arkansas, North Dakota, South Dakota, Nebraska
Ninth Circuit	Alaska, Hawaii, California, Arizona, Nevada, Idaho, Montana, Washington, Oregon, Guam
Tenth Circuit	Kansas, Oklahoma, New Mexico, Colorado, Wyoming, Utah
Eleventh Circuit	Alabama, Georgia, Florida
District of Columbia Circuit	Washington, DC
Federal Circuit	The U.S. Court of Appeals for the Federal Circuit is unique among the 13 circuit courts of appeal. It has nationwide jurisdiction in a variety of subject areas, including international trade, government contracts, patents, trademarks, certain monetary claims against the U.S. government, federal personnel, veterans' benefits, and public safety officers' benefits claims.

the shirt and that faculty would be given training on free speech topics (CBS staff, 2012). Since this t-shirt wasn't lewd or offensive and didn't "collide with the rights of others," it seems that the school district agreed that it was wrong to limit this student's expression. With the mayor's support, no further legal action was necessary. This is a helpful example of engaging local allies and influential leaders if and when you experience inappropriate resistance or backlash from your school or district administration.

What is interesting about the first two of these cases was the fact that the schools were trying to limit student expression that appeared to "collide with the rights of others" or "interfered with the pedagogical mission of the school"—both of which are legally justifiable. School leaders must realize that they need to have very specific reasons to limit student expression, and disagreeing with the viewpoint or believing it *could have been* disruptive don't meet this test. There needs to be evidence of a "material and substantial disruption" before schools can censor expression. Rachel Bavaro's story is an example of what is possible when youth feel confident and empowered to take a stand and seek additional support on issues that matter to them at school. The next set of cases address controversies over events such as prom, homecoming, and Pride.

Prom and Pride

As Chapter 4 discussed, controversies over proms have endured over the past several decades, and in Chapter 1, I shared the story about Aaron Fricke, who sought permission to bring a male date to his prom (*Fricke v. Lynch*, 1980). Aaron's principal denied permission based, in part, on fears of physical harm to Aaron and his companion and concerns from the community. Fricke brought a complaint against his school alleging that this denial limited his First Amendment rights to freedom of expression and association. The judge in that case did not accept the school district's "heckler's veto" argument that the potential for violence and the safety of others at the prom superseded Fricke's First Amendment rights. A *heckler's veto* is when an opposing group shouts down or otherwise prevents someone from expressing themselves. In this case the heckler's veto was the possibility of violence against Aaron and his date. The court concluded that bringing a date or displaying affection at a school event was communicative and "[t]he first amendment does not tolerate mob rule by unruly school children" (*Fricke v. Lynch*, 1980, p. 387), and it was the school's duty to keep students safe at school events. Four decades following Justice Pettine's conclusion, same-sex couples attending school dances remains controversial in many communities.

In another case of restricting LGBTQIA+-positive messages, a principal in Florida tried to prohibit students from writing "gay pride" on their arms or wearing rainbow paraphernalia to school (*Gillman v. Sch. Bd. for Holmes Cnty., Fla.*, 2008). Heather Gillman tried to work with her school, with the support of the American Civil Liberties Union (ACLU), to identify what phrases or attire would be permitted. Sadly, the school wouldn't allow any such expression to be worn. even "I support my gay friends," due to the "substantial disruption" they argued it might cause. The U.S. District Court for the Northern District of Florida ruled that the principal's decision violated the students' right to free speech and concluded that the school district could not justify banning the speech. The judge stated that the school's actions "constituted impermissible viewpoint discrimination" based on the principal's religious views on homosexuality (Florida, 2008). What this means is that the court saw that the personal values of the administration caused them to act in ways that were discriminatory by trying to limit speech they disagreed with. Such *viewpoint discrimination* is not allowed in schools. Now let's turn to the most recent and complex form of expression: social media and online communication.

Online Expression

The next area of expression is that of online expression through social media such as YouTube, Facebook, Instagram, X (formerly known as Twitter), and other such platforms. In a case in Florida in 2007, a student, Katherine Evans, created a Facebook group about a teacher that included several negative comments including, "Ms. [teacher name] is the worst teacher I've ever met!" She closed the group down after 2 days. Two months later, the school suspended Evans for 3 days. Evans and her family sued to have the suspension removed from her record. The judge who decided this case found that this expression did not take place on school grounds or use school equipment; was not defamatory, threatening, or harassing; and did not substantially disrupt the learning environment and therefore was protected speech. He wrote, "This Court finds that the facts are such that under any form of the *Tinker* test, Evans's actions cannot be construed as even remotely disruptive, nor was her speech in any way lewd, vulgar, defamatory, promoting drug use or violence as seen in other cases." As a result, the school district decided not to proceed to trial and agreed to a $1.00 settlement and to pay $15,000 in attorney's fees to the student (*Evans v. Bayer*, 2010). Although this wasn't a political statement or a form of protest, it helps illustrate how courts consider online expression about school.

In another case that started in 2001, a student named Taylor Bell posted rap songs and lyrics on Facebook under his nickname "T-Bizzle" where he named White football coaches who had been accused of sexually inappropriate comments toward African American female students at his school in Mississippi. Bell was suspended for 7 days and transferred to an alternative school for 5 weeks for "harassment and intimidation of teachers and possible threats against teachers." Initially, a three-judge panel ruled against the school district, saying there was no "true threat" or evidence of a substantial disruption. The school district, Itawamba Schools, appealed this case to the Fifth Circuit. In a full bench (*en banc*) review of the decision, the judges ruled 5–4 in favor of the school district based on a "reasonable forecast of a substantial disruption" (*Bell v. Itawamba County School Bd.*, 2012), citing concerns of increasing school violence. Four judges dissented in support of the student—particularly in his role as a whistleblower about the inappropriate behavior of school personnel, which was backed up by official statements by four female students. While this case was decided well after Bell had left high school and served his punishment, it still provides important insights as to how courts will use current events and the local context to inform how they apply the principles of the First Amendment in schools. For a concise summary of these student rights and how they apply to you, please see Table 6.2. Now we will turn to the second form of expression: school-sponsored speech.

Express Yourself

Table 6.2. Know Your Rights: Student Expression

First Amendment Rights: Student Expression

Students MAY:	Students MAY Not:
1. Opt out of standing for the Pledge of Allegiance or national anthem
2. Distribute materials about political or religious events and activities as long as they respect policies about "time, place, and manner"
3. Wear clothes and symbols that represent their gender and cultural identities.
4. Participate in walk-outs and silent protests but may be subject to discipline due to unexcused absence policies
5. Express themselves freely on social media as long as they post using their own devices outside of school time and as long as it does not "substantially disrupt" the learning environment at school	1. "Substantially disrupt" the learning environment *(see section A later)*
2. Engage in vulgar, lewd, obscene, or plainly offensive speech or make threats of physical violence
3. Use school-sponsored activities to express viewpoints that are not consistent with the pedagogical mission of the school *(see section B later)*
4. Wear clothing that has words or symbols that have a history of inciting violence locally (racist, homophobic, antireligious, etc.)
5. Damage school property (vandalism, graffiti, etc.) and expect to be protected by the First Amendment

A) What Counts as a "Material and Substantial Disruption"?

1. Interrupting class so that instruction or learning activities cannot continue
2. Threats of violence
3. Racially harassing conduct
4. Fights or violent behavior on school grounds
5. School must have evidence that a disruption will occur in order to limit speech; prior events at the school and in the community may be sufficient (protests, targeted violence, etc.)

B) What Counts as "School-Sponsored Speech"?

1. School-run publications (newspapers, yearbooks, literary journals, etc.)
2. School-funded performing arts activities (plays, concerts, etc.)
3. Activities occurring at athletic events
4. Content occurring at other competitions/practices of school clubs and organizations (band, chorus, cheerleading, debate, chess, math club, etc.)
5. Expression occurring during field trips

Source: (Meyer, 2019)

SCHOOL-SPONSORED SPEECH

The first section of this chapter focused on student expression that was clearly attached to an individual through their actions, clothing, or social media accounts. The *Tinker* case has informed how we think about individual expression, but now it's time to learn from the other three Supreme

Court cases mentioned earlier: *Bethel School District No. 403 v. Fraser* (1986), *Hazelwood School District v. Kuhlmeier* (1988), and *Morse v. Frederick* (2007). These all address the second category of speech referred to as *school-sponsored speech*. This has to do with student expression that occurs in the context of a formal school setting such as a newspaper, assembly, sports competition, or other school-sanctioned event.

The *Fraser* case (1986) was about a student government election speech which was full of sexual innuendo and allowed schools to limit student speech that was lewd, vulgar, or counter to the educational mission of the school. Two years later in *Hazelwood* (1988), the Court established that school officials could exert editorial control in school-sponsored expressive activities, such as the student newspaper. In a 5–4 decision, the Court held that "... educators do not offend the First Amendment by exercising editorial control over the style and content of student speech in school-sponsored expressive activities." In *Morse* a student held up a banner with a pro-drug message during a field trip to watch the Olympic flame relay. While the event was off campus, it was during the school day at a sanctioned event, and the message conflicted with the pedagogical mission of the school. In short, school personnel control school-sponsored expression that could reasonably be seen as bearing the stamp of approval of the school. These three cases provide the foundation for legal interpretations of school-sponsored speech.

In a Kentucky case we can learn about how this impacts efforts to address LGBTQIA+ equity at school. In *Morrison v. Board of Education of Boyd County* (2006), the Boyd County School District agreed to develop written policies and mandatory student training as part of their consent decree (a legal agreement) with the ACLU and Boyd County Gay-Straight Alliance to address the widespread homophobia at school. The training—consisting of a 1-hour video, an explanation of the policy, and comments from the instructor as well as an opportunity for students to respond with written comments—was mandatory. At least one set of parents contended that the written policy violated their First Amendment rights and that the training violated their religious beliefs that homosexuality is harmful and a destructive lifestyle. The court found that mandatory student training to reduce homophobic harassment is speech by the school and need not be viewpoint neutral as long as the viewpoint is consistent with the educational mission of the school. It is clear that student safety and prevention of harmful behaviors such as bullying and harassment are consistent with the educational mission of the school. This case seems quite relevant at this writing in 2024, due to the rise in anti-LGBTQIA+ policies restricting curriculum and texts that include LGBTQIA+ topics in some states. Although the U.S. Constitution is written to provide basic protections nationwide, federal courts are hesitant to get involved in educational decisions, which are state government responsibilities. When considering free speech concerns, it is important to also understand the laws in your state impacting the discussion of LGBTQIA+ topics at school.

STAFF EXPRESSION AND GOVERNMENT SPEECH

While we have been talking about students' rights up until now, teachers and other school staff also have rights and restrictions related to their expression at school. "Homosexuality is a perverted spirit . . . I know sin and it breeds like a cancer," reads an excerpt from New Jersey teacher Viki Knox's Facebook page. She was responding to a bulletin board in her school that posted information about the contributions of gay, lesbian, bisexual, and transgender individuals in recognition of LGBT History Month and National Coming Out Day. Her post continued, "Why parade your unnatural immoral behaviors before the rest of us? AND YOU ARE WRONG! I/WE DO NOT HAVE TO ACCEPT ANYTHING, ANYONE. ANY BEHAVIOR OR ANY CHOICES! I DO NOT HAVE TO TOLERATE ANYTHING OTHERS WISH TO DO" ("NJ teacher criticized for Facebook remarks on gays," 2011). This incident is reminiscent of another teacher's post in August 2011. A Florida teacher, Jerry Buell, posted a response to the legalization of same-sex marriage in New York by saying he was "sickened" by the news and that it was a sin and New York was part of a "cesspool" (HuffPost staff, 2011). As a result, he was reassigned during an ethics investigation and returned to work a week later with a letter placed in his file (Sentinel Staff, 2011). This begs the question: What are the limits of staff expression? Teachers do have a right as private citizens to engage in political activity and express personal viewpoints on matters of public concern (*Pickering v. Board of Educ*, 1968). However, when they are acting in their role as educators either during the school day or speaking as professional educators "pursuant to their duties," schools have the right to discipline them for speech that goes against the interests of their employer (*Garcetti v. Ceballos*, 2006). In a research project I did in which I talked with teachers about free speech, I learned about how this played out informally for educators working to support LGBTQIA+ student activism.

SILENCING ALLY EDUCATORS: TWO STORIES

The first incident involves a teacher who described herself as an out-lesbian who was married to another female teacher in the same school. One day she was pulled from her classroom and notified that she was under investigation after a complaint about content in her math classroom. This happened the day before the school's Day of Silence, being run by the students in the Gay-Straight Alliance (GSA), for which she served as the faculty advisor. This investigation was triggered due to complaints from the Liberty Counsel, a far-right, evangelical Christian organization that the founders describe as "an international litigation, education, and policy ministry." The Southern Poverty Law Center's website lists the Liberty Counsel as a hate group. The teacher told me that a student from her class gave the Liberty Counsel information about posters asserting safe space for LGBTQIA+ youth in her classroom, and a complaint was filed that she was teaching inappropriate content in her math class. She was suspended for 2 weeks while the school investigated. The district found no basis in the complaint. She explained how this impacted her—even after she was cleared of any wrong-doing. "My personal experience and what happened to me has also made other teachers a little nervous about what they can and can't say [in the classroom]. So being that I had an outside group actually come after the district, it's made everyone a little more cautious."

The second event involved an English teacher who, in her role as the GSA advisor, took the club to protest anti-LGBTQIA+ bills on a particular lobbying day at the state capitol. A local LGBTQIA+ advocacy group provided transportation, and the teacher secured permissions and approval from the district following standard field-trip policies. The bus also transported nonschool individuals, including a public radio reporter. At the capitol, the students encountered two legislators, one who made openly transphobic comments and another whose comments made him seem more sympathetic to queer folks than his constituents might like. The reporter included these comments in her coverage of the event, and the legislators complained that she did not identify herself as a reporter. Because this incident made the local news, the GSA was also in the news, including the fact that some of the older students had spoken to the reporter. The teacher was reprimanded by the superintendent, and a letter was put in her file. She was untenured at the time. She explained how it impacted her:, "It's a very conservative and religious community. I'm all about equal rights and taking care of my LGBT kids and talking to my Black students about police brutality and their right to protest and all of that. I feel very much like I have to just be careful and watch what I say." In both cases the teachers identified the chilling effect of the investigation on their words and actions and those of their colleagues. The second teacher also explained, "As a teacher, I wanted to keep my job. I couldn't be like, 'Hey guys this is wrong. They're trying to censor people.' If I didn't have to worry about my job, I would have been shining a big spotlight on that." It is likely that incidents like these stoke fear in other educators and limit their willingness to plan and support student-led initiatives that might be connected to larger movements for justice and equity (Meyer & Quantz, 2019). While students might be anxious for their teachers to take risks and speak out more against injustice, possibilities for job sanctions and other backlash make it very complicated for school staff to speak out. Having students take the lead while the educators provide support with information and ideas is one way for teachers to protect their jobs while continuing to be

Table 6.3. Know Your Rights: School Employees

What Counts as "Government Speech?"

1. All curricular content: materials, lessons, and classroom displays, including teacher expression during the school day, at official school events, and on school grounds.
2. School mascots, logos, uniforms, and other official publications that represent the policies, procedures, and views of the school and district (Meyer, 2019).

Teachers and Administrators MAY:	Teachers and Administrators MAY Not:
1. Take immediate action if a student's expression constitutes a "true threat."	1. Discipline a student for creating/sharing expression that they disagree with or dislike.
2. Take punitive action if student expression is causing a "material and substantial disruption."	2. Use class time or school activities to express personally held political or religious views (spoken, posted, on clothing, etc.).
3. Make decisions over curriculum and course content (consistent with district policies and procedures).	3. Refuse to teach required curricula that go against their personal beliefs (evolution, patriotic activities, LGBT inclusion).
4. Restrict the "time, place, and manner" of student expressive activities as long as the application of these policies is reasonable and nondiscriminatory.	4. Make curricular decisions without following district policies and procedures.
5. Enforce antibullying and nondiscrimination policies to ensure student safety at school.	5. Lead prayers or other religious or political activities as part of official duties at school.
6. Decorate their classrooms, understanding that the school has a right to restrict certain displays if they are political or religious in nature.	6. Post on social media about students, school, work-related matters, or content that may impair their functioning as an educator.
7. Engage in political or religious activities as private citizens on their own time.	

a support for student efforts for many years to come. A concise summary of staff speech rights is provided in Table 6.3

OTHER SPEECH ISSUES

Hate Speech: What Counts?

Since the 2016 presidential campaign, there has been a rise in extreme viewpoints represented in mass media, in public spaces, on college campuses, and in K–12 schools (Rogers et al., 2017; Southern Poverty Law Center, 2016).

President Trump's campaign modeled such expression and empowered many individuals who align with far right, antigay, anti-immigrant, and White supremacist ideologies. The increased visibility of such viewpoints emboldened individuals and organizations to act out in individual and collective acts of expression that resulted in many people feeling threatened, scared, at risk, and unsafe. There have been renewed debates in the media and in schools about what constitutes "hate speech" and what sorts of expression can legally and ethically be limited in K–12 classrooms.

Since K–12 schools have a different legal context, the concept of hate speech isn't as relevant. However, college campuses have much more latitude in First Amendment cases, so hate speech may be used as the floor: What is the absolute lowest form of expression that campuses can legally restrict? The legal definition for hate speech in general is quite limited and based on a 1942 Supreme Court decision (*Chaplinksy v. New Hampshire*, 1942) that defined it as "insulting or 'fighting' words—those which by their very utterances inflict injury or tend to incite an immediate breach of the peace." This was later clarified in a 1969 Supreme Court decision that protected a KKK member's racist speech and created the "imminent danger" test (*Brandenburg v. Ohio*, 1969). This response to hate speech was reinforced in the *Snyder v. Phelps* (2011) decision that upheld the right of the Westboro Baptist Church to publicly protest (in this case at an Iraq veteran's funeral) with antigay signs with phrases such as "God hates fags." The Court found that speech in a public setting, about a public issue, couldn't be liable for emotional distress, even if the speech is found to be "outrageous." The Supreme Court continues to uphold a very broad protection of the First Amendment rights of adults in public venues, as long as the speech is not promoting violence.

Fortunately, educational institutions do have a different set of policies and protocols at their disposal to limit and respond to acts of hate speech that might not rise to the legal definition established by the Supreme Court. Most educational institutions have provisions against discrimination, bullying, and harassment that include physical, verbal, and psychological behaviors and a list of "protected classes." K–12 schools have a duty to maintain a safe learning environment. Therefore, if speech acts are targeted at an individual or group and violate your school or campus policies, you should be able to stop it (if safe to do so), report it, and seek some sort of remedy and support.

I would encourage any educator to keep the following principles in mind in deciding when and how to limit student speech. Some guiding questions to consider how to respond if you see offensive or harmful expression at school include:

1. Did the speech act cause a "substantial disruption" to the learning environment?
2. Does it harm or "substantially collide with the rights of others" (threats of violence, or psychological violence)?

3. Does it violate other school policies (bullying, harassment, nondiscrimination)?
4. Does it contradict the educational mission and values of the school?

If you can answer yes to any of these questions, then I would argue that you have the right and a duty to limit that speech act in order to limit its negative impact on others. You should also follow any policy or response protocols that should be in place to address incidents of harassment and discrimination. Some examples that might be relevant at your school include:

1. In t-shirt cases, schools have given students the option of turning the shirt inside-out, putting another shirt on over it, or taping over the offending message.
2. In classroom discussions, you can name what a student has just said: "that statement is harmful to LGBTQIA+ students and families and goes against our inclusive mission" or "what you just said is insulting to students who are new arrivals to this country and is not acceptable in this school" and take immediate action—either by publicly addressing the class or privately engaging with the student. You might also say: "that comment is insulting to the identities of students in our school and is against [school policy/our community guidelines], let's talk more after class."
3. If students are posting signs or other symbols that have histories of violence (Confederate flag, swastikas, etc.), I suggest removing them, having the administration ask them to stop posting, and informing students that those images contradict the educational mission of the school, as they put other students in harm's way as targets for verbal and psychological harassment.
4. In cases of cyberbullying or online speech, school leaders should act if the expression is having an impact on the school environment or a student's access to educational opportunities such as missing school, quitting a team or club, or their grades are falling.

One of the more challenging decisions is deciding whether to suppress student speech since the hope of many educators is to teach students how to engage respectfully in thoughtful debate and critical thinking. However, when speech acts denigrate groups of people and promote hate or violence, educators must take action. Silence in the face of oppressive acts can be viewed as a sign of tacit support. Overall, the duty to keep students safe and protect the integrity of the learning environment should override any concerns about free speech.

Student Privacy vs. Parental Rights

The last speech issue I will address in this chapter is that of student privacy and parents' rights. In 2022–2023 there was a rise in bills passed under the umbrella of parents' rights in states like Georgia, Florida, and Arizona. These bills give more power to parents over the curriculum, library materials, and access to student information (Schultz, 2022). However, over the years courts have found that parents can remove their children or "opt out" of certain public school offerings but that the government has a vested interest in ensuring all students get access to an education that prepares them to function in a diverse democracy.

Since May 2022, six states (Alabama, Arkansas, Indiana, Iowa, North Dakota, and Utah) have passed laws requiring teachers to inform families if students are using a different name or pronouns at school (Pendharkar, 2023). At the most extreme end, lawmakers in Missouri proposed a law in 2024 that would charge teachers with a felony and require them to register as sex offenders if they affirm a transgender student's identity at school (Alfonseca, 2024). In general, sharing private information about a student without their consent could violate state and federal laws, including the Family Educational Rights and Privacy Act (FERPA). Until a child is 18, parents do have the right to review any official records maintained by the school, but schools must not divulge "identifying" information to anyone without a "legitimate educational interest." This is an important distinction, as most of the time when a student comes out as LGBTQIA+ at school, official records are not impacted; therefore, parents should not need to be notified. However, if a student wants to change their name in their official school record, the parents would need to be informed. The ACLU released an open letter in 2020 detailing the privacy rights of LGBTQIA+ youth at schools and the legal precedents supporting them. The letter states:

> Students have the constitutional right to share or withhold information about their sexual orientation or gender identity from their parents, teachers, and other parties, and it is against the law for school officials to disclose, or compel students to disclose, that information. Even when students appear to be open about their sexual orientation or gender identity at school, it remains the student's right to limit the extent to which, and with whom, the information is shared. (Essecks, 2020)

It also goes on to say that outing a student could be interpreted as an act of sex discrimination and a violation of Title IX. The ACLU letter provides valuable legal frameworks and clear information for students and educators with questions about their rights and responsibilities. Students, or any supportive ally, can file a complaint with the U.S. Department of Education's

Office for Civil Rights (OCR) if they feel student rights have been violated. For more information about the complaint process see: https://www2.ed.gov/about/offices/list/ocr/complaintintro.html. You can also get more information about Title IX or other civil rights laws by contacting the OCR at OCR@ed.gov or 800-421-3481, TDD 800-877-8339.

What is new about the legislation in Florida (HB 1557) and other states is it is using the language of parents' rights. In addition to limiting the curriculum, it provides parents the right to sue the school district if they violate this law. The legal strategy of leveraging parental rights has been effective in advancing individual rights over efforts to promote educational opportunity and equity in public schools (Mead & Lewis, 2016) and violates the concept of *parens patrae,* which is explained as follows: "the principle of *parens patriae* provided state and district officials the authority to dictate what a child is required to learn in a public school. That result is even true in the case of controversial topics such as sex education (e.g., *Brown v. Hot, Sexy, Safer Productions, Inc., 1995; Leebaert v. Harrington, 2003*). Parents who objected to such curriculum had no choice but to withdraw from public schools" (Mead & Lewis, 2016, p. 125).

Fortunately, the youth of Florida are voicing their concern with this bill and organizing walk-outs and demonstrations against it. One student, Jack Petocz, an 11th grader at Flagler School District, was suspended for his role in organizing a protest that allegedly went longer than the approved 15-minute rally (Palmer, 2022). Due to public uproar, Jack was allowed to return to school after 4 days; however, it left a permanent "level 3 infraction" on his school record that prevented him from running for class president (Belle, 2022).

CONCLUSION

As you can see, the way free speech plays out at school can be complicated and confusing. Oftentimes school leaders don't have the background knowledge or the time to act thoughtfully in the face of expression they don't like or disagree with. It is my hope that with this new knowledge of relevant laws and awareness of how it can be applied in different contexts, you will be able to make thoughtful and informed decisions about the kind of activism and educational activities you want to engage in at school. Many school districts have policies about student protests or controversial issues. My advice is to be sure your student group and faculty advisor are aware of your local school policies as well as your rights as private citizens. Activities that may be prohibited at school are often completely permissible in the community context—after school hours or off school grounds (protests, marches, rallies, etc.). Be courageous, be creative, be strategic. Consider what actions will best serve your community's needs and interests immediately as well as in the long term. How can you use your newfound knowledge to advocate for the changes you want to see at your school?

DISCUSSION QUESTIONS

1. Which student expression case was most interesting to you? Why?
2. What does a "material and substantial disruption" look like? What gets in the way of your teaching and learning at school?
3. Have you ever felt censored (officially or unofficially) at school? What happened? Would you respond differently after reading this chapter?
4. Are there anti-LGBTQIA+ laws limiting discussions at school or student rights in your state? How can you find out who is organizing against them, and how can you be involved in their efforts?

KEY TERMS

- government speech
- heckler's veto
- school-sponsored speech
- viewpoint discrimination

CHAPTER 7

Busting Binaries

> The appropriate focus for schools should be on *transitioning the school community away from the binary system of gender* and finding ways to interrupt and change other oppressive dynamics.
>
> —Travers

Transgender and *nonbinary* youth and educators are in every community. Some school leaders and educators do not imagine that they have people in their classrooms and schools who identify outside of the *gender binary*. Thus, school leaders commonly choose to ignore or refuse to consider changing their practices to be more affirming of gender diversity. Gender diversity in K–12 schools has been expanding rapidly in the past decade, with growing numbers of young people proudly asserting identities that fall under the category of "transgender." In this book, this term embraces all individuals whose gender identity and/or expression transcends the binary categories of *cisgender* girl and boy or man and woman. It includes people who identify as agender, gender fluid, gender creative, gender independent, gender-free, gender nonconforming (GNC), nonbinary, trans boys, and trans girls as well as other terms that may still emerge. This group is also sometimes referred to as *gender minorities*. In the 2021 GLSEN *National School Climate Survey* (NSCS), of the 22,298 students who responded, 33.8% identified as cisgender, 26.9% as transgender, and 31.5% as nonbinary (Kosciw et al., 2022, p. 7). This is a change from the 2019 survey with 16,713 LGBTQIA+ youth (ages 13–21) where 51% identified as cisgender, 28% identified as transgender, 15% identified as nonbinary, and 5% identified as questioning their gender (Kosciw et al., 2020). In the research methodology section for the 2019 survey, the authors shared the following insights about changes in these categories over time:

> In 2001, there was one instance of a student identifying as "genderqueer," and the number of students identifying their gender in this way continued to grow. Before being added as an option on the gender identity item in 2013, the only non-cisgender options listed for students to select were transgender identities. "Nonbinary" first appeared in the write-in responses in 2011 and was written

in by a small number of students in 2011 and 2013. However, a much larger number of students identified as nonbinary in 2015, and it was added to the survey in 2017. (Kosciw et al., 2019, p. 10)

These numbers indicate the expanding gender diversity in school-aged youth and the related need for schools, classrooms, curricula, and pedagogies to be more carefully designed to support this population.

More expansive gender-affirming practices in schools can support youth in understanding gender beyond the binary and teach against harmful gender stereotyping that harms us all. This chapter starts by exploring the historical and cultural contexts that gave rise to the *cisheteronormativity* in public schools and then presents how *Title IX* is connected to this topic. I then address several areas of ongoing struggle related to gender binaries in schools: use of names and pronouns, access to bathrooms and locker rooms, and participation in sports teams. The chapter concludes with a discussion of nonbinary students and individualized gender support plans as temporary supports until we can fully bust the gender binary structures at school. So let's start with the first question: How did we get here?

ROOTS OF CISHETERONORMATIVITY

Public schools in the United States have a long history of serving a variety of roles: preparing workers for jobs, preparing citizens to participate in democracy, serving public health needs, and "Americanizing" immigrants. As a result, schools have—by design—been a normalizing force in our society. They teach the books, the science, and the histories that represent the interests of the dominant culture. This repetition of facts and perspectives throughout the K–12 schooling system is a form of *normativity*. It produces what the people in power want us to believe is normal, acceptable, or "common sense" (Apple, 2004; Kumashiro, 2002). Teacher preparation schools even used to be called "normal schools" (Neem, 2017). Some foundational elements of normative thinking that are part of U.S. history and culture are that this land and its original inhabitants were colonized by European settlers who established a capitalist economy based on the Protestant work ethic. This is also a country that was made wealthy because of the transatlantic slave trade that exploited the labor and lives of enslaved people mostly from Africa. The land that makes up our country was taken by force, and the pioneers benefitted from the slaughter and forced relocation of millions of Indigenous people to "settle" the West and expand our country's borders. The newly established U.S. government was designed to serve the vision of the "Founding Fathers" who were white, land-owning, Protestant men. As a result of this history, the norms and values taught in schools reflect a White, colonial, cisheteropatriarchal, capitalist, Christian worldview. *Patriarchy* is a term used to describe cultures that are organized around male power and perspective. Examples of this include overrepresentation of cisgender men and their perspectives in leadership positions in government (legislative, executive, and judicial branches), religion (priests, rabbis, imams), culture (artists, writers, directors, producers), and the workforce (CEOs and pay gap). *Cisheteropatriarchy* is a term used to describe the cultural norms and practices that privilege and normalize cisgender identities and heteronormative relationships in a patriarchal society. This worldview has been slow to expand to incorporate the interests and perspectives of those who weren't considered citizens—or even people—at the time of the founding of this country. Schools are a site where many of these controversies and "*culture wars*" play out. Debates over religion's place in public schools (*Lemon v. Kurtzman*, 1971), the integration of students of diverse races and ethnicities in schools (*Brown v. Board*, 1954), and supporting the language learning needs of immigrants (*Lau v. Nichols*, 1974) are all controversies that have shaped the structure of schools today. In each of these cases, the Supreme Court decided that public schools should be for all children in the United States and that these institutions need to work to ensure fair access to learning for all while not valuing one set of religious values and traditions over any other. Schools reflect and help produce the culture that we live in.

One example of dominant cultural norms and practices is the prevalence of the gender binary. The gender binary, which refers to the ways bodies and identities are reduced to only two possible categories, structures the ways we think, talk, and are recognizable in official structures and institutions as male or female only. Schools play an important role in reinforcing this binary in various ways. For example, schools teach and reinforce stereotypes and expectations for "girls" and "boys," buildings mostly only provide for male and female bathrooms and locker rooms, and student data systems often only allow documentation of two legal sexes: M or F. From the moment children start preschool or kindergarten, they are socialized to conform to their teachers' expectations for good behavior and how to "appropriately" dress, play, and act according to their perceived *gender role*. In most cases, this gender role expectation is tied directly to one's legal *sex assigned at birth*. Children learn and internalize gender role expectations through extensive segregation as well as heterosexual teasing and rituals in elementary schools (Renold, 2000, 2002, 2006). These early experiences with gender in schools shape the "sexual scripts of early adolescence" and are an essential element of "borderwork" that strengthens the boundaries (and binaries) between boys and girls (Thorne & Luria, 1986).

In high school, there are many examples of the ways that gender—and masculinity in particular—is socialized. In many schools, the use of the term "fag" was commonly used to monitor the boundaries of acceptable masculinity and is still used against any boy who "fails" to conform to the narrow boundaries of stereotypical masculinity: tough, jock, strong, unemotional, etc. (Pascoe, 2007). This culture of what is referred to as *hegemonic masculinity* seems most prevalent in comprehensive high schools that have large athletics programs and include traditions such as homecoming dances and pep rallies. Alternative high schools (such as arts-based schools, social justice programs, Waldorf schools, etc.) can have very different cultures that allow for more gender expansiveness and creativity of all forms to flourish (Meyer, Tilland-Stafford, and Airton, 2016). GLSEN has reported the ways that many schools reinforce traditional gender norms through dress codes, student databases, and access to sex-segregated facilities. For example, 28% of LGBTQ students reported they were prevented from using a bathroom that aligned with their gender identity, 22% were prevented from using their chosen names and pronouns at school, and 18% had been prevented from wearing certain clothing based on their gender (Kosciw et al., 2020, p. 42). Schools also reinforce gender binaries through traditions and school-sanctioned events. Students reported gender-specific practices such as homecoming court with "kings" and "queens" (45%), graduation attire separated by gender (26%), and yearbook photos with gender-specific attire (25%) (Kosciw et al., 2020, p. 42). These formal policies and long-standing traditions work together to maintain cisheteronormative cultures in schools. Now that we understand where these limiting binaries come from, let's address some of the ways we can change practices at school, starting with a basic overview of a federal law designed to prohibit forms of sex discrimination in schools: Title IX.

KNOW YOUR RIGHTS: TITLE IX

Title IX of the Educational Amendments of 1972 is a federal law that applies to all educational institutions that receive federal funding in the United States. It mandates that no person shall be discriminated against in educational institutions "on the basis of sex" ("Title IX of the Education Amendments of 1972," 1972). Many people know of Title IX primarily as a tool that has worked to improve opportunities for female athletes in college athletics programs; however, that was not its intended goal, and it impacts many more aspects of education than just college sports. One of the reasons this law was introduced was due to a lawsuit filed in 1969 by the Women's Equity Action League. They argued that colleges and universities were engaged in employment discrimination against women based on President Johnson's Executive Order 11246, which prohibited federal contractors from discriminating on the basis of race, color, religion, national origin, and sex (Daley, 2019). President Nixon then convened a task force in 1970 that documented discrimination in education and recommended legislation that was partly included in Title IX. Congressional hearings on sex discrimination in education began in 1970 and led to a proposal which became Title IX of the Education Amendments of 1972. The language in this legislation was explicitly based on the Title VI of the Civil Rights Act of 1964 (Kemper, 1980, p. 33), which states, "No person in the United States shall, on the ground of race, color, or national origin, be excluded from participation in, be denied the benefits of, or be subjected to discrimination under any program or activity receiving federal financial assistance."

Since 1972, Title IX has been interpreted to apply to a diverse array of educational issues, including (1) recruitment, admissions, and counseling; (2) testing and financial aid; (3) athletics funding; (4) sex-based harassment; (5) pregnant and parenting students; (6) discipline; (7) single-sex education; (8) employment; and (9) retaliation (U.S. Department of Education Office for Civil Rights, 2015). The Obama administration strengthened Title IX by clarifying protections for transgender students (Lhamon & Gupta, 2016) and expectations for Title IX coordinators (Lhamon, 2015) with *Dear Colleague Letters (DCLs)*. DCLs are issued by the federal government to provide legal guidance on how laws are to be interpreted, applied, and enforced; are written by employees of federal offices such as the Department of Education and the Department of Civil Rights; and, in the case of Title IX, are distributed to educational institutions receiving federal funds. A 2016 DCL stated, "A school's Title IX obligation to ensure non-discrimination on the basis of sex requires schools to provide transgender students equal access to educational programs and activities even in circumstances in which other students, parents, or community members raise objections or concerns" (p. 2). It went on to clarify that schools ". . . must allow transgender students access to such facilities consistent with their gender identity" (p. 3).

This guidance provided visibility and a set of principles for schools to apply but was met with resistance. Many states have since introduced anti-trans bills prohibiting trans people from using public, sex-segregated facilities that do not match the sex assigned to them at birth (Philips, 2017) or participating in sex-segregated sports programs (Movement Advancement Project, 2023a). The Trump administration rescinded many of these protections by issuing a new DCL during his first administration (2016–2020) (Battle & Wheeler, 2017). Fortunately, in June 2021, President Biden's Department of Education announced that Title IX would again be interpreted and enforced to include protections for transgender youth (Rogers, 2021). While the legal definition of "sex" under Title IX was clarified with the *Bostock v. Clayton County, Georgia* (2020) Supreme Court decision to include gender identity and sexual orientation, the Biden administration's executive order (Executive Order 13988, 2021) explicitly extends this protection to LGBTQIA+ youth in any school funded by the federal government. In April 2024, the Biden administration issued new rules for applying Title IX that formalize the guidance introduced in the executive order from 2021 (Binkley, 2024).

Most public schools get 8–12% of their funds from the federal government and the rest comes from state and local taxes; therefore, a loss of federal funding would be significant to a school district's budget. While these formal rules and guidance are relatively new, Title IX has been interpreted to include gender identity and sexual orientation since as early as 2000. A summary of key Title IX lawsuits related to gender identity and sexual orientation is provided in Table 7.1. Now that we have reviewed the federal legal protections prohibiting discrimination on the basis of sex and gender, let's talk about some of the specific challenges caused by binary structures at school.

Table 7.1. Title IX Lawsuits Related to Gender and Sexual Orientation

Year	Case(s)	Issues
2000	*Ray v. Antioch Unified School District* (California) and *Montgomery v. Independent School District no. 709* (Minnesota)	School failed to protect students from antigay sexual harassment by peers based on gender and perceived sexual orientation; staff knew about "repeated, severe, and pervasive" harassment and were "deliberately indifferent"
2003	*Flores v. Morgan Hill Unified School District* (California)	School failed to protect multiple students (six plaintiffs) from antigay sexual harassment by peers; district staff knew about "repeated, severe, and pervasive" harassment and were "deliberately indifferent." Led to a $1.1 million settlement
2005	*Theno v. Tonganoxie Unified School District* (Kansas)	School failed to protect students from sexual harassment by peers due to gender nonconformity; staff knew about "repeated, severe, and pervasive" harassment and were "deliberately indifferent." Led to a $440,000 settlement.
2017	*Whitaker v. Kenosha Unified School District* (Wisconsin)	Title IX and Equal Protection Clause require schools to respect students' gender identity and provide access to sex-segregated facilities. Led to a $800,000 settlement.
2017, 2020	*G.G. v Gloucester County School Board* (Virginia)	Upheld DCL guidance allowing transgender students' right to access sex-segregated facilities. Led to a $1.3 million settlement.
2022	*Soule et al v. CT Association of Schools et al* (Connecticut)	Upheld DCL guidance for transgender students to compete in a sport aligned with their gender. Case is listed as ongoing at the time of this writing.

NAMES AND PRONOUNS

How others talk to us and treat us is an important part of feeling seen, supported, and valued in a community. The name or nicknames and pronouns we use help form our identities and are a way others can show that they respect and value who we are. When thinking about names and pronouns, there are two main levels of changes to consider: unofficial and official changes. Unofficial changes involve asking people to call you what you want to be called and can be done anytime you decide with as many or as few people as you choose. Formal changes are more time-consuming, are more long-lasting, are harder to change, and require filling out official paperwork and the signature of a parent or guardian if you are still a legal minor (under the age of 18). Let's start with exploring unofficial changes.

Unofficial Changes

An unofficial change to names or pronouns can happen organically over time or after a direct request by you or someone on your behalf. For example, someone named Jennifer may naturally become Jenny over time if friends and teachers start shortening the name and Jenny doesn't object. When I was in first grade, I remember trying various versions of Elizabeth. Every day for several weeks I wrote a different nickname on my paper: Beth, Lizzie, Eli, Betsy, Liz, Betty, Liza . . . you get the idea. The teacher (in Mississippi in 1976) didn't make a fuss out of this or notify my parents, and I eventually settled on Liz after a few months. I also remember being a teacher in schools and universities with international students who preferred anglicized nicknames since Americans often had difficulty pronouncing their legal names. Nobody corrected me or notified me that I couldn't call students by the name they chose. I just wrote the student's chosen name on my attendance sheet and called the student that name for the rest of the term. If the name change also includes a pronoun change, this has suddenly become a bigger issue. It shouldn't be. We don't need a legal name change form to call somebody the name they want and use pronouns that makes them feel seen, safe, and recognized.

Teachers can set the tone and make it seamless and low-stress for students to share their chosen name and pronouns at the start of the school year. There are several strategies I use at the beginning of a new term that provide opportunities for students to introduce themselves and build community at the same time. In my roles as a high school French teacher, substitute teacher, and university professor, I have developed some different strategies summarized in Figure 7.1 that have been helpful for me to learn about my students and ensure I get their names right from the beginning—and leave the opportunity open for them to let me know if it changes at any time we are working together.

Figure 7.1 Classroom Routines to Affirm Gender Diversity

1. **Introduce yourself:** This is a standard first-day thing we all do, but the way you do it will impact students differently. You can tell your students you are going to introduce yourself using the name and pronouns you want people to use in interacting with you and then you will ask them to do the same (in small groups or to the whole room). One script I have used goes as follows: "My name is Dr. Meyer; please address me as Dr. Meyer or Professor. I am happy with either; please use what feels best for you. I use she/her and am also comfortable with they/them pronouns. When you introduce yourselves, please give us the name you want us to use in this class and the pronouns that you want us to use today. Some possibilities include he/him, she/her, they/them, xey/xem, and ze/hir. If this changes at any time, please let me know so I can be sure to recognize you the way that feels most affirming to you."
2. **Last name roll call:** When I am a substitute teacher I use this approach. I call students out by last name if a roll call is necessary. I then ask students to tell me what name they want me to use that day and I write it on my seating chart or attendance sheet. I use they/them pronouns for all students when substitute teaching.
3. **Line up:** The first week of classes I like to incorporate team-building activities. The first one is for students to complete a silent group challenge. Without writing or talking, I give them 1 minute to put themselves in a line in alphabetical order by last name. I then go down the line with my roster and ask them to introduce themselves to the class using the name they want to be called and make a note of the names on my class list. We then talk about active participation, group work expectations, and developing positive communications strategies for the class.
4. **Bathroom policies:** Explain your bathroom policy on the first day and make sure students know the locations of any all-gender or single-user toilets in the building.
5. **All about me:** I have a Google form that I ask students to complete the first week of class. I ask questions like: What name and pronouns do you want me to use in class? What are your learning strengths? Challenges? Personal interests? Responsibilities outside of school? Anything about yourself that would help me support you better? Concerns about this class?
6. **One-on-one meetings:** I make a point out of having one-on-one check-ins with every student the first 3 weeks of school. At the university, students sign up to come to office hours, but in high school, you can do this during independent work time and rotate through everyone so you have a chance to connect and follow up on any items from the "all about me" form.

If other teachers aren't using any of these practices and students aren't sure how to start asking people to use a different name or pronouns, I suggest starting small: Ask one or two close friends to start using it privately with you to see how it feels. As students feel more confident, try expanding the group of peers and maybe ask a trusted teacher or adult to start using it. The beauty about informal name and pronoun change requests is that most people can adjust and adapt quite quickly and easily. If something doesn't feel right or isn't working, then try something else out until you find the one that fits you best. If you ask and you don't get a supportive reaction, you may want to share the website from this book or other resources to help educate the people who are resistant to your request. If a teacher isn't respecting your request, you may be able to file a complaint with the school or district, but this route will likely require the support of a trusted adult to help you navigate the process and connect you to resources if you need additional support with this transition.

In most states, students should be able to ask for teachers to use different pronouns and have that request be respected. However, in 2023 Florida passed HB 1069, part of a so-called "Let Kids Be Kids" bill package that prevents school staff from asking about students' pronouns or using pronouns that do not "correspond to such person's sex" (Atterbury, 2023). If you live in a state like Florida, you may not be allowed to make such a request, or making such a request may put you and your teachers in a more risky or vulnerable position. In cases where it doesn't feel safe or comfortable to request an unofficial name or pronoun change, I suggest getting in the habit of using gender-inclusive language and asking for other teachers and students to do so as well. Even in places where name and pronoun changes are supported, using gender-inclusive language is a good practice to help us expand the way we talk and think about gender. See Figure 7.2 for some sample phrasing and ways to start integrating this into everyday speech. The more you practice, the easier it gets. The next section provides information for students who are ready and want to formally change their name at school.

Official Changes

If a student has the support of a parent or guardian or is no longer a minor, then they can approach the school about officially changing the name and pronouns in school records. School districts have varying policies on name changes, but generally there are two approaches: one first requires a legal name and legal sex marker change through the state, and one involves simply adding a preferred name and pronoun entry into a student's data file. If you are going through a legal name change and correcting the information on all legal documents to reflect your gender, then the school district must update its records to reflect these legal changes to your official documentation. Since students going through such a process have already secured the support of an adult legal guardian and/or legal services, the rest of this section will discuss the second type of change: an update to your chosen names and pronouns that does not delete or overwrite the existing legal documentation the district has on file from when the student entered their system.

There are two common barriers to official name changes in school data systems: individual resistance by district personnel and structural limits caused by how some student information systems (SIS) are constructed. When faced with individual resistance, this can commonly be overcome through education

Figure 7.2. Gender-Inclusive Language

It takes practice shifting the way we speak and think to use more inclusive language. By modeling this language, you are communicating that you recognize gender diversity and want everyone to feel seen and supported in your presence. The more you practice, the more comfortable you will get, and it may help expand the way you think about gender as well!

1. Practice addressing groups with gender-inclusive language such as students, scholars, learning community, y'all, people, future leaders, friends, team, changemakers, or nongendered school mascot (Bobcats, Eagles, Warriors, Bears, etc.).
2. Intentionally disrupt binary language: Instead of "opposite sex" say "different sex"; instead of "boys and girls" say "kids" or "children"; instead of "boy/girlfriend" say "crush" "person you are dating" "significant other" or "special someone."
3. Use gender-inclusive terms consistently when talking about families and guardians: parents, caregivers, siblings, spouse, partner, family members, grown-ups, responsible adult, guardian, etc.
4. Model using third-person pronouns they/them when the gender of a person isn't known or when referring to a generic person: "Someone left their water bottle in class yesterday." "I just met a new student today and they seemed really nice." "Jenny just asked me to start calling them Jimmy, but they didn't tell me what pronouns they are using now." This third-person singular use of "they/them" is grammatically acceptable and has been used by writers such as Chaucer, Shakespeare, and Jane Austen.

Visit the companion website for additional links and resources about gender-inclusive language and information: www.elizabethjmeyer.com/queer-justice

---

and collaboration. While this is time consuming, the advocacy for changing such systems and processes will benefit many students and families for years to come. If students want to take this on as an action project, they can develop a long-term plan to provide information and educational opportunities to the decision-makers about the importance and benefits of providing access to name changes in the SIS. Some school administrators refuse because they know that they are legally responsible for maintaining an official legal record of a student's time in their district. Sharing this chapter, ideas in Figure 7.3, and the resources available on the companion website are a few places to start.

As trans scholar Heath Fogg Davis (2017) argues, schools should carefully re-examine practices of student record-keeping to minimize the audience for students' sex markers and legal names. By removing the display of sex markers from records open to a wide audience, student privacy can be protected and the ways that sex or gender are recorded and displayed can be limited. Schools can also make it easier for students to have their preferred name listed on such documents. With so many other new technologies offering ways to verify identities and ensure accurate tracking of individuals through bureaucratic systems, legal sex markers are generally outdated and unnecessary and should be removed except where absolutely

Busting Binaries

Figure 7.3. Creative Solutions to Name and Pronoun Change Requests

Gender Spectrum is a California-based organization that provides education and resources to schools and families supporting gender-diverse youth. They offer some additional ideas for navigating requests for changes to a student's data in official school district information systems. As mentioned in Chapter 6, all students have a right to privacy, and their transgender status, medical history, and sex assigned at birth are all protected by a law called the *Family Educational Rights and Privacy Act (FERPA)* and should not be shared with anyone who doesn't have a "legitimate educational interest" to have that information. With that in mind, here are some possible approaches for official name change requests:

1. Have the district store a copy of the student's original legal birth certificate locked in the principal's office and update the database to reflect the student's chosen name and gender marker. Include a note that there is confidential documentation associated with the file available in the principal's office. Sample language for such a note could read: "I have reviewed the cumulative enrollment file for _____ and acknowledge that the site file is incomplete but assert that all of the necessary documents for enrollment are appropriate and accounted for. Please direct any questions to [name/role/contact information] should you require access to this student's record."
2. Apply for a passport using the student's updated name and gender marker and then re-enroll them at school with the new documentation. For U.S. citizens, getting accurate passports can be easier than changing official birth certificates.
3. Ask the school district to request their database provider to create two new data fields for "chosen name" and "pronouns" that are public and have the database mark the legal name and sex marker fields as private, so they are not included in any printouts for attendance, testing, or other widely disseminated school reports.

These ideas were taken from: https://genderspectrum.org/articles/student-information-systems (accessed August 2023)

---

required by law. Another set of school structures that are difficult for many students to navigate are sex-segregated bathrooms and locker rooms.

BATHROOMS AND LOCKER ROOMS

Research consistently shows that sex-segregated spaces–particularly bathrooms—are sources of ongoing trauma for transgender youth (Price-Feeney, 2020). Studies found poorer mental health outcomes (including depression and suicidality) (Wernick et al., 2017) and reduced feelings of school safety and well-being (Movement Advancement Project & GLSEN, 2017) when students are denied access to bathroom facilities that align with their gender. Seventy percent of trans students avoid bathrooms at school because they feel unsafe or uncomfortable, 60% were forced to use facilities that did not match their gender, and 75% felt unsafe at school because of their gender expression (Movement Advancement Project & GLSEN 2017). By forcing individuals to publicly enter a space marked "male" or "female," you expose those who don't visibly conform to sex stereotypes to *gender policing*, which can range from stares, mean looks, and rude comments to verbal and physical assault. It often means that transgender folks avoid going to a public bathroom because it can be a dangerous place. This leads to urinary tract infections, kidney diseases, and digestive system problems that can have long-term negative health impacts. In many schools, transgender youth are asked to use the nurse's bathroom or a staff bathroom to avoid the perceived complications of using the boys' or girls' bathroom. This temporary solution can isolate them from their peers and often makes them late to school obligations due to the location of these spaces. For transgender people who have *socially transitioned* and are living publicly based on their affirmed gender, which is different from their sex assigned at birth, laws excluding them from gender-appropriate bathrooms and locker rooms put them in a very vulnerable and dangerous position, which forces them to "out" themselves as transgender and use a bathroom that does not align with their gender identity.

Why are binary bathrooms such a barrier? For now, the international building code requires that there are a certain number of male-designated toilets and female-designated toilets in each building based on some formula related to building size and number of users. As a result, most bathrooms built must be designated to be single-sex, for either males or females (Spula, 2017). We have enshrined the gender binary in our buildings and building codes. As a result, individuals who are transgender, gender fluid, nonbinary, agender, or genderqueer are often left struggling to find a safe place to complete everyday bodily functions.

"Bathroom bills," or bills that restrict access to single-gender public facilities, are on the rise. I encourage readers to work to repeal or revise these laws to ensure everyone can access safe and accessible bathrooms in public spaces. Fortunately, more and more jurisdictions are finding ways to make more affirming and accessible bathrooms for more people. Some jurisdictions have passed laws requiring any single-user bathroom to be signed as available for people of all genders, which reduces the need for additional individual accommodations (Chapter 10 Plumbing Code, n.d.; AB1732, 2016) or have required the inclusion of "an appropriate number of gender-neutral restrooms . . . into the design of new schools and school renovations" (Gender Spectrum, 2022, n.p.). Washington, DC, has required single-person toilets to be labeled "restroom" or have some other gender-neutral sign since 2006. Does anyone remember the TV show *Ally McBeal* (1997–2002)? The law firm in that show had a multistall unisex bathroom, and the characters were constantly breaking into song and dance numbers by the sinks in that bathroom. Why can't we have more of that?

I really don't understand why people feel so threatened by transgender people in the bathroom. There are no documented incidents of transgender people assaulting a cisgender person in the bathroom. However, there are

Busting Binaries

countless reports of transgender people being assaulted and harassed in public spaces. The bathroom is a place where everybody goes to deal with personal hygiene and bodily functions. In schools where students don't have access to appropriate facilities, they experience many barriers to full inclusion and participation. It can also "push out" these students and give them another reason to give up on school. In my own research with teachers who work with transgender and gender-creative students in schools, we found that schools that had fewer sex-segregated spaces were more welcoming and supportive of all kinds of diversity and creativity. We learned about school communities that asked for and created all-gender bathrooms to reduce the harmful impacts of the sex-segregated spaces on their school community (Meyer et al., 2016).

If your student group wants to advocate for more all-gender bathrooms or more access to single-user facilities in your school, Figure 7.4 offers some ideas and strategies. If you are having difficulty as an individual getting access to appropriate bathrooms at school, you can consider requesting a

Figure 7.4. Advocating for All-Gender Bathrooms

Ensuring everyone has safe and reliable access to appropriate facilities is an important goal for queer justice. While some students may have negotiated individual access to private facilities, a more universal approach can ensure any student can access a single-user or all-gender space for any reason. Here are a few approaches you can consider:

1. Bathroom audit: Get a blueprint or detailed map of the school and go and count toilets that are marked male, female, and single-user. You can color-code your map to identify parts of the school that lack single-user toilets or that are extremely far from existing gender-inclusive bathroom spaces. Use this map to educate building admin about "toilet deserts" for students who need privacy or accessible bathrooms.
2. Accessibility audit: Having more private and fully accessible bathrooms is also a disability rights issue. How many bathrooms have wheelchair-accessible stalls? Have handrails? What supports exist for people using mobility aids (walkers, scooters, wheelchairs) to access all parts of the school building? Advocating for more gender-accessible spaces can be paired with coalition work to support the needs and interests of people with disabilities.
3. Building-level ask: Request that at least one single-user bathroom on each floor or wing of the school building be reassigned and clearly designated for general student use.
4. District-level ask: Request that the school district retrofit selected current bathrooms to have floor-to-ceiling stall doors and remove any exterior doors to the space and label them as all-gender.
5. Advocate for *Universal Design*: This principle is one that many people can benefit from and can inform long-term building design and renovation plans. Ask the school board for their long-term facilities plan and budget to identify potential areas for renovation that can be updated using principles of Universal Design. Read more about Universal Design at the companion website.

gender support plan, which is discussed later in this chapter. Another sex-segregated space that reinforces gender binaries and that has been at the center of national gender controversies is school sports.

ATHLETICS

The third main area of binary boundaries is school sports. Sports are part of the educational opportunities offered by schools and can help contribute to positive feelings of belonging at school. As of August 2023, however, 23 different states had enacted legislation that would ban or restrict opportunities for transgender youth to participate in school sports (Movement Advancement Project, 2023a), whereas 17 other states and Washington, DC, currently have guidance that facilitates participation by transgender youth in school sports (GLSEN, 2023). I want to distinguish between elite sports competition and general K–12 sports programs. In elite competition, all athletes are exceptional in some way; they are the best in their country or state. This is often due to different kinds of naturally occurring variations in human physiology and the environmental supports they have access to in order to train and be competitive at such a high level. Consider Simone Biles, Michael Phelps, Lebron James, Katie Ledecky, or Serena Williams. They're all exceptional in different ways, and that's what we celebrate when they win—their exceptionality. Trans athletes don't have any different kind of advantage than these athletes whose naturally occurring variations in their bodies make them ideally suited for excellence in their chosen sport. This idea of an unfair competitive advantage has been disproven by many scientists (Turban, 2021).

In public schools, sports programs are considered part of the "educational opportunities" offered by schools and are subject to civil rights protections to ensure equitable access. Sports are an important part of a school community, and we know that participating in sports and teams offers different kinds of learning and development that benefit and keep youth engaged at school much like music and arts programs. We know from years of research that sports participation provides both physical and psychosocial benefits, including improved bone health, weight, cardiorespiratory and muscular fitness, cognitive function, and a reduced risk of depression as well as higher levels of perceived competence, confidence, and self-esteem; reduced risk of suicide and suicidal thoughts and tendencies; and improved life skills, such as goal setting, time management, and work ethic. Additionally, youth can develop social and interpersonal skills, such as teamwork, leadership, and relationship building (U.S. Department of Health and Human Services, 2019). As such, from both a legal and ethical perspective, if sports programs are available to some students in a school community, they should be available to all students.

So what does this mean for trans girls? I am addressing the issue of trans girls in particular since there have been few public concerns expressed about trans boys. This is likely because there's not a perception that higher levels of estrogen make you stronger or faster. So, athletes who were assigned female at birth (*AFAB*) aren't seen as much of a threat in the athletic arena—except to the perceived masculinity of the other male athletes they are competing against. In any case, with trans girls, most of them are taking hormone blockers or puberty suppression medication prescribed by their endocrinologists once they start puberty. This is to help pause puberty so their bodies don't go through changes that would cause them psychological distress. As such, they won't have higher or elevated levels of testosterone that would put them in a category of having some kind of "unfair" advantage—which, as noted earlier, has not been proven to exist. However, I do want to point out that there are athletes who have naturally occurring size advantages unrelated to sex and gender, and we don't exclude them—even though they can pose some physical danger to the other athletes. If we want to regulate school sports to keep them "fair" and "safe," then why don't we consider height and weight limits to athletes in sports that may involve contact? For example, introduce a safety rule that states you can't play contact sports like football, hockey, basketball, or lacrosse if you're over 6 feet tall or weigh more than 200 pounds. This could make school sports safer and more fair for the average student athlete, but no one is seriously proposing such a restriction.

Involvement in sports offers health benefits to all participants. Most kids just want to have a social activity with their peers, and being part of a team provides this space. Having a broader set of adult mentors and role models is another benefit youth can access by being part of a team. School teams are often more about student engagement and school pride than preparing for elite levels of competition. Blocking young people who already experience significant obstacles due to transphobia from having a valuable—and potentially lifesaving—set of experiences is wrong. This doesn't even address the challenges faced by agender, gender-fluid, and nonbinary youth who want to play sports since there are very few facilities or programs designed to ensure their inclusion.

As the earlier section on Title IX demonstrates, all students have a right to participate in school activities and not be discriminated against based on their gender. The confusing aspect of this is that some states are passing laws that contradict Title IX and explicitly require students to enroll in sports based on their sex assigned at birth. Until these state laws are struck down, it will be very difficult to compete as an out trans athlete in many of these states. But if you are in a state that doesn't specifically prohibit such access to sports teams, then every student should be allowed to play. You might also consider advocating for more all-gender (what historically is referred to as co-ed or "mixed") teams and sports opportunities. In sports such as track, swimming, cross-country, and tennis, there are established opportunities for mixed-gender competitions (relay teams, running the same course, doubles competitions, etc.). Think about ways you can request your school district or state to expand these opportunities—maybe even just at field day or fun run events—to help bust some binaries. This brings us to a specific discussion of nonbinary students.

NONBINARY STUDENTS

The term nonbinary emerged in the early 2010s to refer to anyone whose gender identity does not fit within the binary categories of man or woman. Nonbinary people may feel like they have elements of both masculinity and femininity in them or neither. Many nonbinary people identify as part of the transgender community; some don't. What most nonbinary people have in common is that they are not comfortable with the gender role and norms that accompany the sex assigned to them at birth (and related names and pronouns). Nonbinary folks typically experience their gender as more expansive than the normative legal and linguistic binary systems currently used in societies colonized by European settlers like the United States and Canada.

While many school districts have created policies and guidance that signal support for transgender students, they often don't consider nonbinary students. Trans-affirming policies and guidance documents can provide support to binary trans youth and their families, but also may create narrow guidelines that often do not consider nonbinary or agender students, thus limiting their impact on improving the experiences of all trans students (Meyer & Keenan, 2018). Language that narrowly reinforces binary gender norms unintentionally undermines policies intended to affirm gender diversity. Sociology of sport scholar Travers argues for the concept of "gender justice" in sport by ensuring youth of all genders can participate. Travers recommends investing more funds in community-based sport and recreation programs rather than elite athletics as well as "no-user-fee, sex-integrated sport and recreational opportunities" that "incorporate egalitarian values in the organization and culture" (Travers, 2019, p. 209–210). They also recommend eliminating all "male-only" sports teams at all levels of play while maintaining "girl-only" spaces with "no questions asked trans-inclusive boundaries as an interim measure" (Travers, 2019) (p. 210). Sex-segregated sports spaces can create unnecessary stress and danger for many trans and nonbinary youth. Working to expand these possibilities for yourselves and those after you can be really impactful. The final section of this chapter presents the idea of a gender support plan to ensure trans and nonbinary youth are seen and respected at schools that still have many harmful gendered spaces.

GENDER SUPPORT PLANS

Gender support plans (GSPs) don't bust binaries but can provide temporary relief and support to students who are not getting access to all educational opportunities due to gender-related institutional barriers. What is a GSP? It is a document codeveloped by the school with a trans or nonbinary student and their parent(s) or guardian(s) to ensure the student can safely access educational opportunities and facilities. In an ideal world, we wouldn't need to write out a GSP because the school would already be designed in ways that are inclusive and affirming of gender diversity. Unfortunately, in most schools I have seen, we aren't there yet. Figure 7.5 offers a list of elements to consider when drafting a GSP. Another approach that can be helpful for younger students is to do a safety audit of the school. I learned about this from an educator in Canada. They worked with an elementary student to walk through the school and label different spaces as "comfy" or "uncomfy." Once these spaces have been identified, you can talk through why the uncomfy spaces are difficult to be in and start working to correct those issues (Meyer, Tilland-Stafford, & Airton 2016). Other climate and mapping activities are discussed in Chapter 4.

CONCLUSION

As most readers of this book know, schools and society continue to be bound by restrictive gender binaries that infuse and shape our language, thoughts, norms, buildings, policies, and practices. Trying to get people in power to rethink how these binaries impact the everyday lives and experiences of gender minorities is an important first step to change. Once you have educated your teachers, administrators, and school board about the harms of this binary structure, you can begin to advocate for system-wide change that goes beyond individual accommodations through GSPs and other exceptions made for trans and nonbinary students. I hope the information and

Figure 7.5. Elements in a Gender Support Plan (GSP)

1. Student's chosen name and pronouns
2. Level of parent/guardian involvement and support (scale 1–10)
3. Level of privacy/disclosure (district staff only; building admin; some/all teachers; some students)
4. Safety plan: adult contact, safe space when needed, regular check-ins, etc.
5. Student Information System (SIS) strategy
6. Use of facilities (bathrooms, changing rooms, field trips, etc.)
7. Response plan for if a student is misgendered or inadvertently outed by school staff
8. Extracurricular activities and related supports
9. Other: dress codes/uniforms, sibling considerations, transportation issues, school security protocols
10. Action and communication plan

For additional and updated resources see the companion website: www.elizabethjmeyer.com/queer-justice.

resources shared here provide some ideas and direction to support the next steps that will matter most to students in your school community.

DISCUSSION QUESTIONS

1. What other examples can you come up with that illustrate how cisheteronormativity and patriarchy are present in your community?
2. How does the gender binary come up in everyday language and interactions? (The term "opposite sex" or the design/layout of toy and clothing stores are some examples.)
3. What are the biggest challenges trans and nonbinary students are experiencing at your school? If you don't know, how can you learn more?
4. What terms do you prefer to use: gender diverse, gender minority, trans and nonbinary (TNB), noncisgender, any others? Why? What makes one term more supportive or helpful than another?

KEY TERMS

- assigned female at birth (AFAB)
- cisgender
- cisheteronormativity
- cisheteropatriarchy
- culture wars
- Dear Colleague Letter (DCL)
- Family Educational Rights and Privacy Act (FERPA)
- gender binary
- gender minority
- gender policing
- gender role
- gender support plan (GSP)
- hegemonic masculinity
- nonbinary
- normativity
- patriarchy
- sex assigned at birth
- social transition
- Title IX
- transgender
- Universal Design

CHAPTER 8

Strategies for Action

> Fight for the things you care about, but do it in a way that will lead others to join you.
>
> —Ruth Bader Ginsburg

Here we are at the last chapter in the book; maybe you read everything in order, and maybe you jumped around and decided you wanted to learn more about activism strategies before reading other sections. Any way you read this book is great as long as you are able to make it work for you and your particular school community. Each school, school district, and community is unique, which is why grassroots activism is so important. You know your community better than someone from the outside, so you are the expert(s) who can figure out which of these issues to prioritize, which ideas to put into action, and which resources to use. You, your peers, and supportive staff are the ones whose voices matter and are best situated to inform, educate, and act to demand the changes that you have identified as most urgent (immediate needs) or most important (longer-term priorities).

This final chapter is written to help you think and act strategically to help use your limited energy and resources wisely. Taking action to change institutions is difficult and demanding work that requires endurance. Schools are inherently conservative institutions that are slow to change. I heard someone once compare it to trying to steer an ocean liner: These ships are large, heavy, and slow, while also being powerful, complex ecosystems that rely on vast numbers of people working together to function effectively. To get your school "ocean liner" to change course, you need to think and act strategically and recognize that such activist work is more of a marathon than a sprint. It is easy to burn all your energy early on because the work is urgent and demanding; however, it is a long journey to institute lasting change, so you need to pace yourself as you run this marathon to turn this ship (apologies for mixing metaphors). As such, this chapter's first section focuses on creating the context for change. This includes learning the terrain, building trust, responding to resistance, and choosing your battles. The second section focuses on various ways to amplify student voices so they can be heard more clearly. Strategies discussed in this section include various forms of advocacy and activism that range from private advocacy for an individual student to public activism in your school or community. The last two sections focus on finding the joy and focusing on the possible futures created by engaging in advocacy and activism. We'll talk about ways to sustain your spirit through cultivating queer joy, strengthening your community, and learn about the practice of freedom-dreaming. Now let's start with creating the context for lasting change.

CREATING THE CONTEXT FOR CHANGE

A good friend of mine and brilliant scholar-activist, Bethy Leonardi, wrote about a middle school in California that was making meaningful changes to support LGBTQIA+ youth and talked about the importance of "tilling the soil" before planting seeds that can take root and grow into long-term changes in a school (Leonardi, 2014). "Tilling the soil" is a metaphor to describe the work of preparing an environment so that new ideas and practices have an opportunity to take root, or establish themselves, and grow. If you don't till the soil by building trust and learning the terrain, then it will be much more difficult to create change that will endure after you have graduated or left the school. Since one major goal of activism and advocacy is making long-term changes that will last—not just temporary fixes that can be easily undone—this preparatory work is important. What does it mean to "till the soil"? For those of you who have never planted a garden, it is the prep work that you do before planting any seeds. It can include breaking up dried and hardened portions of dirt, pulling weeds, adding fertilizer, and watering the ground so it is softer and easier to work with. Each of these acts is an extensions of this metaphor to help you think about what is involved in tilling the soil. An important part of preparing any garden is learning the terrain.

Learning the Terrain

Learning the terrain means understanding the landscape of your community and any prior efforts to make changes at your school. This may include finding answers to questions like: What is the history of efforts toward LGBTQIA+ equity in your community? Who has helped support and lead such changes? What resistance did they come up against? Who are influential people in the school and district, and how do they make decisions? Who is on the school board, and what are their positions on topics related to equity, diversity, and LGBTQIA+ rights? What other teachers and student groups are possible allies who can provide networks of support to your projects? Finding answers to these questions might be a helpful fall semester activity for a student organization or class to understand and map

Strategies for Action 121

out the history of LGBTQIA+ equity efforts as well as the sources of power and decision-makers in your school or district.

Who are the decision-makers in a school community? Generally, elected school board members oversee the superintendent, who is responsible for all business in the district. Building principals report to the superintendent (or in larger districts, assistant superintendents) and are responsible for all business in their buildings, including evaluating and supporting the development of all professional staff and implementing district policies. In addition to these formal hierarchies of decision-making, informal power networks exist. Oftentimes there are community organizations and leaders who are highly respected and can influence school leaders through writing letters, speaking at school board meetings, or through informal interactions. There may also be parents' groups and civic leaders who are influential and may be another source of support— or possible resistance. The more you are aware of how power works in your school community and the histories of these power dynamics, the more effective you will be in identifying sources of influence and support so that your requests for action have a higher likelihood of success. Figure 8.1 provides a suggested activity for mapping power structures and identifying who's who in your school community. When thinking about other sources of support, consider regional chapters of national LGBTQIA+-affirming community organizations like GLSEN, PFLAG, and the American Civil Liberties Union (ACLU).

Figure 8.1. Mapping School District Power Structures

For this activity write the name and email address for each person listed and mark any known allies and supporters with a "+" and any known sources of resistance with a "–". You can also draw arrows to indicate who has influence over people in the hierarchy of decision-making.

1) School board members: _____
2) Superintendent _____
3) School district equity director(s) _____
4) Title IX coordinator _____
5) Principal _____
6) Informal leaders in the school (staff) _____
7) Student council officers _____
8) Other student leaders _____
9) Parents' group(s) _____
10) Community organization leaders _____
11) Other anticipated sources of support (group name and/or contact information) _____
12) Anticipated sources of resistance (group name and/or contact information) _____

Building Trust

An essential part of developing a broad range of support for your efforts is establishing positive working relationships with various stakeholders and supporters in the school, district, and larger community. These working relationships should be built on a foundation of trust and shared goals so you can work together guided by common commitments and principles. This trust is essential to hold a community together even if there are disagreements or miscommunications. When feelings are hurt or people feel misunderstood, trust can be eroded and must be rebuilt to keep your relationships strong. Some ways I have found that trust can be established and strengthened include showing up, being consistent, listening, and following through.

Even though it may sound simple, showing up consistently to meetings or events is the best way to start building relationships. Being a regular presence is one way to show others that you are committed to the cause and can be reliable. In addition to being reliable, working well with diverse people is another important skill, and listening is one way to learn and collaborate with others. Although many folks appreciate a strong leader who shares ideas and works hard, an undervalued quality of leadership and community organizing is that of listening: being able to make sure there is space for multiple ideas to be shared and then draw from the perspectives of the various people who are interested in being involved. Being willing to listen and learn and allow various viewpoints to emerge is essential to building support and trust.

Finally, the idea of following through is also important. This means that if you say you are going to do something, you do it. If something comes up, then you communicate with others about the obstacles you are facing and ask for help. It also means that if there is a misunderstanding or hurt feelings, you follow through by being willing to hear how your actions may have hurt others, work on repairing the damage caused, and learn from your mistakes. Activism can be complicated, stressful, and full of challenges while also being empowering, exciting, and fun. We need to be able to stay in the work together and trust that everyone involved is willing to learn, grow, and change, while remaining committed to the shared values and goals that brought you together in the first place. Resistance is something that all activists face, so as long as you have a strong trust built within your club or coalition, you will be more successful in responding to resistance.

Responding to Resistance

When seeking to make changes to a school or any other institution, activists always know that we will encounter resistance. If change was easy, we wouldn't have to put so much time, thought, and energy into making it happen. Resistance can come in many forms, but two main kinds of resistance I have seen in my work are what I refer to as active and passive resistance.

Active Resistance. I define active resistance as any planned action or activity to prevent change from happening. In the case of this book, it would include blocking any efforts to improve the climate at school for LGBTQIA+ people. It can include actions such as preventing or making it very difficult for gender and sexuality alliance (GSA) clubs to meet, using anti-LGBTQIA+ language or comments framed as "jokes," stopping the use of LGBTQIA+-inclusive materials and curriculum, canceling LGBTQIA+-themed events or professional learning activities, and supporting or promoting anti-LGBTQIA+ groups. While this form of active resistance is more visible and actively harmful, it is actually sometimes easier to deal with because the barriers are clear and you know exactly where people stand on an issue.

When working to resolve and address active resistance, it can be helpful to try and identify the reason for the resistance: Is it personal values? Religious beliefs? A narrow interpretation of a policy? Response to public pressure? Once you have diagnosed the root cause for the resistance, you can more effectively respond with information, resources, public support, or legal counsel to help shift the resistance into a more supportive position. For example, one school board in my research passed a resolution stating that LGBTQIA+ topics were not "controversial" and did not need to follow the district's *controversial topics policy*. However, even after this resolution had been passed, a principal in that district told one teacher that LGBTQIA+ topics were still "contentious" and the teacher should still send home a permission slip before teaching a class that included LGBTQIA+ content. In this case, this high school social studies teacher was able to rely on the district's new policy and the support of the superintendent to ensure his principal was enforcing the new policy consistently with the language and vision of the district. He went ahead and taught the lesson without sending home a permission slip.

In some cases, the active resistance is due to deeply held personal values that are often connected to a religious viewpoint. If this is the case, you may be able to draw on some of the information from Chapter 6 on the First Amendment in schools. The *Establishment Clause* of the First Amendment states, "Congress shall make no law respecting an establishment of religion or prohibiting the free exercise thereof," which ensures the separation of church and state. This has been interpreted by the Supreme Court to mean that publicly funded schools may not endorse a particular religious worldview over any other. Another way to think about this that I find helpful when working with educators with religious views that inform their anti-LGBTQIA+ position is that there is a difference between behaviors and beliefs. Everyone is entitled to their own belief system; however, when your belief system leads you to behave in a way that is discriminatory or prevents others from feeling safe and being able to learn, then that needs to be corrected. Public schools in the United States are *secular* (nonreligious) by law, so any overt expression or endorsement of any set of religious values is explicitly prohibited in public schools. In addition to active resistance, the second kind to be prepared for is passive resistance.

Passive Resistance. Passive resistance is any action that allows the status quo to stay in place and slows forward motion toward change. Some examples of passive resistance I noted in my research include being given approval to create more all-gender bathroom spaces but no actions are taken for over 2 years, turnover in building or district leadership slowing action on previously approved changes, lack of leadership by the principal for equity work, preventing GSA clubs from making schoolwide announcements since they aren't part of student council, using student privacy as a reason to prevent collecting data on LGBTQIA+ students' experiences, and not planning a staff workshop on LGBTQIA+ topics even when a trained facilitator was available on staff. For this last example, one teacher told me, "I have said that to a new [principal]. I've said, 'Look, you don't have to look any further. I'm trained. I have had a lot of experience. I have a lot of experience on boots on the ground. I've been trained by the professionals.' . . . So hopefully we get moving on that."

These examples show that while in many cases the principals and superintendents might be supportive of LGBTQIA+ inclusivity in principle, they aren't willing to lead or take action to support changes that require them to publicly endorse LGBTQIA+ equity. Many teachers in my research talked about administrators' fears of public attacks from anti-LGBTQIA+ parents and community members. As a result, the administrators' inaction and lack of leadership prevented changes at the school through such passive resistance. A middle school teacher in a politically progressive suburb best described the problems with passive resistance by stating, "It's almost like because they aren't adversarial, that provides its own set of challenges." When faced with passive resistance, my advice is to explicitly name it and document the repeated requests and lack of action. By keeping track of the various times and formats you have asked for changes (emails, private meetings, GSA meetings, school board public comment, staff meetings, etc.), you can make visible to the leaders and other involved parties how their inaction is preventing positive change from happening and hopefully generate more momentum toward taking supportive actions.

I created a scale to better understand the responses from people in power on this spectrum of active resistance to active support with passive resistance and passive support as intermediate steps between the two (Figure 8.2). The more clearly you can identify the types of resistance and support you are experiencing, the more focused and strategic you can be about working with folks to move decision-makers along from being resistant to showing support. To build positive rapport with leaders to help them move from resistance to support, you sometimes have to be thoughtful about when you ask them to make a big change and how often you are asking them to make such efforts. The next section talks about the strategy of choosing your battles.

Strategies for Action

Figure 8.2. Forms of Resistance and Support

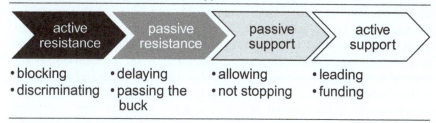

Choosing Your Battles

I used to hate it when my parents or supervisor told me to "pick your battles." It was irritating and frustrating because it felt like every issue was important and I needed to take them all on at once. At the time, I didn't realize that humans and institutions only have the capacity to do so many things simultaneously and too much change at once can cause chaos and result in no real lasting changes. I also didn't realize the importance of having positive relationships with those who can lead and institute such changes, that by being the "squeaky wheel" or the "thorn in someone's side" I wasn't helping others to get invested in solving problems with me.

Over time, I learned that complaining about everything that wasn't working made people tune me out so when I tried to bring important matters to the attention of others they were more easily ignored. I also learned how slow big institutions are to change and no matter how loud and organized my groups were, some lasting changes required slow, thoughtful groundwork to be laid before a major policy or practice shift could happen. Over my years of activism, I have learned the value of choosing my battles and thinking strategically about prioritizing when and how to ask others for changes to improve the likelihood of success. This may be difficult as a student who might only be at a school for 3–5 years and realizing that the groundwork you laid may not result in lasting changes until after you have left the school. However, the power of building activist movements is to also inspire and educate others to keep working for change even after you are gone. This enduring form of activism is one of the best ways to ensure that the movement keeps going and that your school will continue evolving to be better each year. So be strategic, prioritize the issues and actions you want to focus on, and celebrate each small success as it happens.

AMPLIFYING STUDENT VOICE: IDEAS FOR ACTION

There are many forms of advocacy and activism that you can engage in that range in difficulty and risk, from more private to more public, and degrees of planning and coordination. In my research I developed another scale to help think about what types of action seem possible and what factors to consider when planning larger, more public forms of action. This scale helps define forms of advocacy and activism (Meyer & Kurtz, 2024). In this project we talked with educators who supported student activism for LGBTQIA+ equity and used this information to create this scale and refine our definitions of these terms. For me, when use the term advocacy, I am talking about ways to speak up for yourself or others to get someone to make a change. *Advocacy* tends to be a more private, less risky act that often involves sharing information that can improve a situation for an individual or a smaller group of people. When I use the term *activism*, I use it to describe more public, more risky acts that are intended to make changes that will impact a larger group such as the entire school, school district, or community. The next two sections talk about various forms of advocacy and activism that you may consider taking up in your school community.

Advocacy

The educators I spoke with in my research were much more comfortable talking about forms of advocacy because it was less risky for them since they felt it was part of their job to advocate for students. To be more specific about the different kinds of advocacy and activism we have seen in schools, we created a scale from 1 to 8, with 1–4 describing forms of advocacy and 5–8 describing forms of activism (Figure 8.3). For example, a level 1 form of advocacy (private, individual) includes a teacher suggesting that a specific transgender student get a gender support plan (GSP) at school or helping one student get connected to an LGBTQIA+ youth group in the community. Level 2 advocacy (private, group) would be asking for any student who needs more privacy in the bathroom to have access to single-user (often designated as staff bathrooms) toilets in school. Level 3 advocacy (semi-public, group) includes supporting groups of students through voluntary clubs or gatherings such as being part of the GSA either as an advisor or student leader. We defined level 4 advocacy as public advocacy by providing education. This can include either providing a workshop for school staff on supporting LGBTQIA+ students, offering an optional LGBTQIA+-inclusive health education class, designing a lesson that discusses sexual orientation and gender identity, or leading a professional learning community (PLC) on gender and sexual diversity at your school or school district.

One example that came up in my research included multiple examples of advocacy and shows how having multiple supports in place can create more space for students to speak up and feel supported. This is a story from a librarian who was also the GSA advisor at a middle school in a rural community and describes an experience of a transgender student who was new to the school in the middle of the year (see Figure 8.4). This story shows

Strategies for Action

Figure 8.3. Advocacy and Activism Scale

multiple forms of advocacy by several staff members and students. What this example helps illustrate is how just by engaging in consistent work with a variety of people, you can create the context for change to happen in ways that are positive and powerful for people you don't even know yet.

While your club or student group might not have the time, energy, or support to plan more public or large-scale events, just continuing to show

Figure 8.4 Advocacy in Action

We've had the [GSA] club (Level 3 advocacy). This year it's been a really slow start. It's been just a few kids come in. We do it in the morning before school. I had a counselor who's not the one I work with in the club come in and introduce the kid to me and say, "This kid really wants to come to GSA club but it's going to involve a lot of bus transfers and it's going to be a big deal to get there." I was like, "Oh, please come, we're going to be so excited, but also don't get your hopes up because it's a really small group, but we're so excited you're coming." (Level 1 advocacy) The kid came to GSA club. I've talked to this kid a bunch because they're new to the school and they have been coming to the library to get books and talk and hang out, and play chess, but they hadn't asked for name and pronouns or anything like that. I didn't know anything about their identity, but in the GSA meeting, which was I think just three kids total or four kids total. Maybe four kids that day. We always start with saying what we want to be called and what pronouns to refer to us every meeting.

The student got to say their preferred name and their pronouns, which were she and they, and their name is [name]. I was like, "Wow, I didn't know that. Thanks for sharing that." The meeting was just like what I was describing before

(continued)

Figure 8.4. (*continued*)

as social silliness. I don't really remember if we talked too specifically about anything around activism during the meeting, but when we were leaving to go to class, I was writing students' passes to class. I asked the student if she wanted me to use her name that she had shared with me, and she said, "No, my teachers wouldn't know who that is." I said, "That makes total sense. Let me know if you ever want support in how you might talk to them about that." The student standing next to her, who is a very loud and wonderful student, was like, "Here's how I did it. I just asked my teachers if we could stand in the hall and if I could ask them something in the hall. Then we went in the hall and then I told them, 'These are my pronouns, and can you call them to me? And this is the name I want you to use.' The student said, like, "Oh, I never thought of that. That's interesting, thank you," and then left.

    I had put the dead name, birth name on the pass because that's what she asked, but about 15 minutes later, I got an email from her teacher that said, "I just had a student ask me to step in the hall and they told me that they want to use she or they pronouns but I don't really understand what that means. Can you just help me understand? Is it she or they? Which one is it? I don't know what that means." (Level 1 self-advocacy) Which was really cool for me because I was like, "Oh my god, she did it. She just did it right now. It did not seem like that was going to be where the student was at today at all, it seemed like maybe an idea for the future." That was really cool. It was also cool because the teacher, a cis male hetero-type teacher, was taking a PLC class with me on supporting LGBT youth. I feel like he knew that he had support. He knew he had someone to ask, because he was like, "We've been talking about this, but I don't know what that means." (Level 4 advocacy) I said, "Well, I think it means that you can call her 'she' or 'they'. [laughs] I think that if she changes her mind and wants to have it be one or the other, then she'll let you know. I'm so excited. Thank you for being a teacher who she felt comfortable speaking to." I just saw her in [GSA] today, first day in [GSA]. That's amazing. Trying to really celebrate her for getting to do that. Also, him for responding well, but also reaching out for help if he didn't know what to do, or what that meant.

    It was a very cool day, because next thing I know, the kid came back at lunch, and wanted to talk about it, and she was just beaming, and all smiles. I said, "Did you tell anyone else?" She said that she told her other cis male teacher that, and he has little popsicle sticks with kids' names on them that he uses to call kids randomly. He brought over the stick to her. She told me that he brought over the stick that had her dead name on it, and said, "You can do whatever you want with this." Then handed her a clean stick, and said, "Would you like to put your name on this one?" She felt like it was just amazing, such a good feeling, so symbolic to get to just break that stick, and throw it away, and get the new stick. For me, it was an amazing moment, because I was pretty down on [GSA] being so small, and like, "What do we need to do differently?" All those things. Being like, "Ugh, we still have a space." We had a space that the counselor knew to recommend, and then one meeting of talking with other LGBT kids, this kid felt comfortable speaking up to their teachers. I felt just super stoked about it.

up, be visible, and build relationships can lead to powerful outcomes. Some other forms of advocacy you can consider exploring that I documented in this research project are presented in Table 8.1. If you are energized and ready to take on more public and time-intensive activism activities, the next section talks about examples and ways to organize and plan for successful forms of public activism.

Activism

It is important for school staff to educate themselves about speech rights, district policies related to so-called "controversial topics," LGBTQIA+ content, and public-facing projects. I recommend asking for official support or approval from your department chair or administrator before pursuing public-facing projects with students. This will enable chairs and administrators the chance to proactively support such efforts and be prepared to offer affirming responses to complaints if and when they arise. Teachers can increase their chances of administrative support by providing school leaders with clear learning objectives aligned to state standards, potential positive impacts for students and the school, and related legal support and research evidence for the projects. This practice is also useful if the public-facing projects receive backlash because then the teachers would have documentation of administrative support, which should protect them from disciplinary action. If school staff are subject to formal complaints or investigations, you should reach out to union representatives and/or local advocacy organizations such as the ACLU or the Southern Poverty Law Center to ensure your *due process* and professional rights are respected. It is important to ensure professional staff are fairly represented in meetings with district officials and don't get intimidated into agreeing to any sort of personnel action without due process. For ideas on various forms of more public activism to work on together, please see examples offered in Table 8.2.

SUSTAINING YOUR SPIRIT

When I was a young activist, I was hurt and angry a lot. To be honest, I still am. That energy motivates me and keeps me invested in this work. However, I also realized that hurt and anger can only get me so far. I learned that if I only operated from a place of hurt or anger, I am not able to stay in the work because I burned out frequently, and many people didn't want to be around that constant negative energy. I still feel justified in my anger, but I have learned to balance it out with other restorative and sustaining emotions and actions including joy, being in community, and taking time to rest and imagine a better future. I have long appreciated the idea of "sustaining

Table 8.1. Advocacy Activity Ideas

1) Private/ individual		• Supporting a student coming out to their family • Connecting a student to an LGBTQIA+ community organization • Developing a gender support plan (GSP) for a transgender or nonbinary student • Helping a student decide when and how to share their chosen name and pronouns with peers and/or staff • Connecting a student to affirming mental health supports
2) Private/ group		• Inviting staff to post Pride flags or other visible signs of support in their classroom and providing stickers, posters, or other sample displays • Requesting more LGBTQIA+-inclusive materials in the school library • Advocating for student access to single-user bathrooms and getting signage changed • Nominating LGBTQIA+ students to serve on a district equity committee • Educating staff in informal conversations about LGBTQIA+-inclusive practices • Making your classroom an open and welcoming space for students to visit and check in during the day • Requesting that information be added to the school website about the GSA and LGBTQIA+ community resources • Emailing PE teachers and coaches about private changing spaces for students who request it
3) Semi-public/ group		• Helping start or lead/advise a GSA club • Inviting the principal in to listen to the experiences and requests of students in the GSA club • Inviting an outside expert in to consult with your GSA or your school's administration • Inviting local LGBTQIA+ organizations to come speak or share information with the GSA club • Providing a safe and joyful space for students to socialize (board games, coloring, dance party, art activity, etc.) • Role-playing conversations to help students to self-advocate • Offering voluntary LGBTQIA+-inclusive sexuality education workshops • Speaking up when you hear anti-LGBTQIA+ language or behavior

Strategies for Action

Table 8.1. (*continued*)

4) Public education	• Designing and teaching lessons that address gender and sexual diversity
	• Establishing and reinforcing inclusive and affirming classroom communities (language, behavior, classroom décor)
	• Inviting local LGBTQIA+ organizations to present at a staff meeting
	• Presenting workshops at educator conferences about LGBTQIA+-inclusive practices
	• Leading a professional learning community (PLC) on gender and sexual diversity
	• Presenting to a school district committee about LGBTQIA+ student needs
	• Asking the librarian to purchase more books that address LGBTQIA+ topics and/or to create a display of books that address LGBTQIA+ themes
	• Creating posters or bulletin boards to educate the school community about LGBTQIA+ history and culture
	• Creating a list of examples of how teachers misgender students and how it makes them feel to share with school staff
	• Offering a staff training for the teachers in your school on LGBTQIA+-inclusive classroom practices

your spirit," which was introduced to me by Perotti and Westheimer in their book, *When the Drama Club Is Not Enough: Lessons from the Safe Schools Program for Gay and Lesbian Students* (2001). Some strategies they share include connecting with colleagues, laughing out loud, sharing success stories, celebrating small steps, remembering progress is not always obvious, creating symbols and rituals to build community, spending time with young people, sharing difficult times, and seeing the work in a broader context (pp. 171–180). To this valuable list of ideas, I want to add the concepts of queer joy, rest as resistance, and freedom-dreaming. I invite you to think about how these concepts may become a part of your life and relationships to help you stay supported and energized as you engage in various forms of advocacy and activism.

Queer Joy

The concept of *queer joy* builds on lessons learned from the Black and African American justice communities who advanced concepts such as "Black girl magic" (Osterheldt, 2021) and "Black joy" (Love, 2019; Nichols, n.d.). These ideas capture the importance of celebrating self-love and resilience and strengths that are often overlooked and derided by White supremacist culture.

Table 8.2. Activism Activity Ideas

5) School level (students)	• Inviting the principal to a GSA club meeting to listen to the ideas on how to improve schools for LGBTQIA+ students • Creating weekly announcements that share quotes and facts about LGBTQIA+ history or culture • Designing and distributing a school survey to collect data on a topic of interest (antigay bullying, bathroom access, etc.) • Requesting the school display a Pride flag during LGBTQIA+ history month (October) or Pride month (June) • Creating rainbow ribbons, lanyards, scarves, or beaded keychains to distribute to allies to wear and show their support for the LGBTQIA+ community • Working with a local artist to design a mural to paint with students to show support for the LGBTQIA+ community • Requesting more access to all-gender and single-user restrooms for students • Working with coaches and gym teachers to ensure all students have access to safe and private changing spaces for trans and nonbinary students • Working with the sexuality education staff to offer an optional workshop on LGBTQIA+-inclusive health and sexuality education • Writing letters to the editor or opinion columns for the school newspaper • Planning school-wide awareness events mentioned in Chapter 4
6) District level (students)	• Inviting the district superintendent to a GSA club meeting to listen to the ideas on how to improve schools for LGBTQIA+ students • Writing and practicing speeches to present at public comment during school board meetings on priority areas of concern and suggestions for change • Researching state laws and curriculum standards that can provide support for the policy changes you are requesting • Volunteering/nominating GSA leaders to serve on district-level equity and policy committees or working groups • Working with the health and sexuality education staff to ensure the curriculum is inclusive of LGBTQIA+ bodies and identities

Strategies for Action 133

Table 8.2. (*continued*)

7) Community level (students)	• Marching in a local Pride parade or hosting a booth at a Pride event • Planning a community-wide event (march, rally, dance, etc.) for National Coming Out Day (October) or Pride Month (June) • Drafting letters to the editor or opinion columns for the local newspaper • Planning a fundraiser (bake sale, craft sale, etc.) to support a local LGBTQIA+ organization
8) professional activism (staff)	• Speaking at a school board meeting in your role as a staff member/GSA advisor • Marching in a Pride parade with your GSA club or school district • Organizing a field trip to the state capitol with local LGBTIQA+ advocacy groups for youth to engage in lobbying

Black joy is seen as an "essential act of survival and development" (Nichols, n.d.), and Black girl magic is "celebrating this uncontrollable, relentless, beautiful joy that exists despite any obstacles" (Osterheldt, 2021). Queer joy draws from these important concepts of not allowing oneself to internalize the negative messages society has historically shared about people like you and has been described as "happiness against insurmountable odds, being your authentic self" (Khou cited in Luong 2023) and "the meticulous practice of rest in order to access pleasure, care, abundance, and liberation" (Malament cited in Luong, 2023). Queer joy can include creative and artistic expressions of queerness, defying cisheteronormativity and other norms in playful and celebratory ways, and seeking out pleasurable and joyful expressions of queerness (Wilson, 2024). As noted earlier, one element of queer joy is a form of self-care that prioritizes rest and quiet.

Rest as Resistance

Rest as resistance is a term coined by Tricia Hersey (2022), an artist who founded "The Nap Ministry." The idea behind centering rest is to disrupt what she calls "grind culture" and the ways White supremacy and capitalism foster a culture of working ourselves to exhaustion. Hersey argues that by taking time to rest and restore, we are engaging in resistance against the structures that harm us. I love this idea and want to apply it to the frame of activism for LGBTQIA+ equity. Sometimes it is okay to say you have done enough and now it's time to rest. One GSA advisor in my study explained that after a year of intense activism in the face of lots of anti-LGBTQIA+ efforts in her community, she and her students decided to "look inward" and "focus on ourselves." What that meant was to have more time for coloring, board games, and quiet reading during GSA meetings. It might also mean canceling a meeting when people are getting sick or other stresses are piling up. It's okay to take a break and recognize that rest is resistance. Living and thriving as your full self is enough.

Freedom-Dreaming

The last concept I want to share with you is that of *freedom-dreaming* which I learned about while reading *We Want To Do More Than Survive: Abolitionist Teaching and the Pursuit of Educational Freedom* by Bettina Love (2019). She describes this radical action as "critical and imaginative dreams of collective resistance" (p. 101) and goes on to explain that, "Freedom dreaming is imagining worlds that are just, representing people's full humanity, centering people left on the edges, thriving in solidarity with folx from different identities who have struggles together for justice, and knowing that dreams are just around the corner with the might of people power" (p. 103). This means we are all called to draw from our individual and collective creativity, joy, and brilliance to imagine and move toward a more liberatory world. This requires rest, creativity, love, and community. I hope you and your allies, peers, and fellow community members can work together to engage in some freedom-dreaming to imagine and create a brighter world in your school.

CONCLUSION

I am so energized and hopeful when I see and read about young people who care enough to speak up, stand up, and try to make this world a better place. The dreams and possibilities that live in the next generation combined with the foundations laid by our queer ancestors will make new futures and better lives possible for so many people. This does not absolve the adults from doing the work of teaching, supporting, advocating, and radically loving the young people leading many of these changes. While youth have so many strengths and contributions to offer the world, they deserve to have adults in their lives that offer them safe havens, inspiration, information, and connections. Together students and educators can combine their strengths and energies to continually improve and ensure our schools are safe, engaging, and welcoming places for all students to thrive.

I want to remind you of the importance of doing work for justice and equity that is always attentive to intersectional forms of oppression so that we can work together to challenge ableism, classism, colonialism, racism, sexism, xenophobia, and other forms of violence and exclusion while challenging homophobia, transphobia, and cisheteronormativity. We need to continue to draw from the wisdom of black lesbian poet Audre Lorde, who wrote, "There is no such thing as a single-issue struggle because we do not live single-issue lives" (Lorde, 1982/2007). I hope as you finish reading this book you can think about how to continue staying engaged in activism and advocacy to improve the learning and lived experiences of all LGBTQIA+ youth in your community. Take care of yourselves and each other, take breaks, find joy, and then get back out there: agitating, disrupting, challenging, organizing, and asking hard questions—however you feel best meets the situation! We need you to keep working to create the world you want to live in—a world that is more humanizing and just for us all.

DISCUSSION QUESTIONS

1. How long has the GSA been around at your school? When did it start and what projects has it done in the past?
2. What community organizations do you know about that support LGBTQIA+ equity? How can you connect with these groups to build relationships and trust with them?
3. What brings you joy? How can you plan activities that build community and focus on queer joy and creativity?
4. Which examples from Tables 8.1 and 8.2 are ideas you want to try? Which ones feel impossible to try? Why?

KEY TERMS

- activism
- advocacy
- controversial topics policy
- due process
- Establishment Clause
- freedom-dreaming
- queer joy
- rest as resistance
- secular

APPENDIX

Glossary

activism (n.) Taking action to create change in ways that are more public (and thus may involve some professional or personal risk), that address systemic challenges, and that intend to impact large communities of people. This can include public speaking, letter writing, planning protests, press conferences, or other public activities.

advocacy (n.) Taking action to create changes that are more private (and thus less professionally or personally risky) and may impact an individual or a small group of people. This often involves private interactions (written or in person) or educational activities such as bulletin boards, workshops, and invited panels.

AFAB (abbrev.) Assigned female at birth.

AMAB (abbrev.) Assigned male at birth.

bullying (n) A form of interpersonal violence that is common among youth and includes behaviors that are meant to threaten, intimidate, or insult another individual. It can be verbal, nonverbal, or physical and usually involves a power imbalance between the individuals involved (Meyer, 2009). See also *harassment*.

banking education (n.) A concept introduced by Brazilian educational scholar Paulo Freire (1970) to describe and critique traditional models of teaching and learning that prioritize teachers depositing knowledge into the minds of students, who are often treated as passive recipients of new information.

cisgender (adj.) A term that describes people whose gender identity conforms with the social expectations and normative gender categories for their sex assigned at birth. This includes females who identify as girls and women and males who identify as boys and men. People who identify as transgender are NOT cisgender.

cisheteronormativity (n.) A set of social norms and expectations that assumes that all bodies and identities are or should be cisgender and heterosexual. This belief system can lead to discrimination and negative treatment toward people who are gender nonconforming as well as members of the LGBTQIA+ community.

cisheteropatriarchy (n.) The cultural norms and practices that privilege and normalize cisgender identities and heteronormative relationships in a patriarchal society. See also *patriarchy*.

controversial topics policy (n.) A school district–level policy that defines which topics are considered controversial and often adds restrictions and requirements for when teachers might plan to teach this content. This may include requiring signed permission forms from parents, sending home details about an upcoming lesson or topic, and/or providing alternative assignments for students who opt out or do not obtain permission to participate in the lesson.

critical pedagogy (n.) An approach to teaching and learning developed by Brazilian educator Paulo Freire in his book, *Pedagogy of the Oppressed* (1970). Critical pedagogy is a form of teaching that engages with learners in interactive or dialogic ways to help them not only develop essential literacy skills but also learn to "read the world." This form of critical literacy is designed to help students learn to understand how power and oppression operate in order to work toward a more humanizing and liberatory world for all.

culture wars (n.) A term used to describe the collision of different values and belief systems and there is a debate about how such concepts will be addressed in public institutions such as schools. Examples of culture wars in schools include book bans, rights of LGBTQIA+ youth in schools, and the content of health and sexuality education programs.

conscientização (v.) A Portuguese term used by Paulo Freire (1970) to describe a central process in critical pedagogy that is often translated to mean "consciousness-raising." Through this process, students become more aware of how power and oppression work and develop a more critical awareness of the world.

Dear Colleague Letter (DCL) (n.) DCLs are issued by federal government agencies to provide legal guidance on how laws are to be interpreted, applied, and enforced. They are usually written by employees of federal offices such as the Department of Education and the Department of Civil Rights and, in the case of Title IX, are distributed to educational institutions receiving federal funds.

"Don't Ask, Don't Tell" (DADT) (n.) A military policy passed in 1993 under the Clinton administration that allowed gay and lesbians to serve in the military as long as they didn't speak about this aspect of their identity. This policy was seen by some as an improvement from the prior ban against LGBTQIA+ people serving in the military, whereas others argued it caused harm by forcing many gay and lesbian servicemembers to closet themselves in order to remain in the armed forces.

Glossary

due process (n.) A legal concept that describes how a citizen or employee must be treated when charged with a crime or subjected to personnel action (like getting suspended or fired). It means that the school or the government agency needs to follow a specific set of rules and procedures to ensure that the person is being treated fairly and that all required steps are completed before a decision about guilt or innocence is decided by the courts or an administrative review body. The Due Process Clause is part of the Fourteenth Amendment. See also *Fourteenth Amendment.*

enumerated (adj.) A term that describes a specific list of categories used in laws and policies to protect identifiable social groups of people from harassment or discrimination. This can include race, gender, disability, religion, sexual orientation, etc. When bullying policies and nondiscrimination laws are enumerated, they specifically include a list of protected categories under that law or policy.

Equal Access Act (n.) A law passed in 1984 that requires schools to allow noncurricular clubs to meet on school grounds if they are operating a "limited open forum." A limited open forum means that a school has agreed to let a single noncurricular club (like Bible Study, Boy Scouts, or Chess Club) to meet on school grounds. This law has been used to protect the rights of GSAs or other LGBTQIA+-affirming student clubs to meet in public schools ("Equal Access Act," 1984).

Equal Protection Clause (n.) A clause in the Fourteenth Amendment that states "nor deny to any person within its jurisdiction the equal protection of the laws." This clause has been used to ensure people of all races were not subject to discrimination, including the *Brown v. Board* Supreme Court decision that decided that segregated schools were "inherently unequal." It has also applied to discrimination cases based on sexual orientation including *Romer v. Evans* (1996), *United States v. Windsor* (2013), and *Obergefell v. Hodges* (2015) (Constitution Annotated, 2024).

Establishment Clause (n.) A clause in the First Amendment that states "Congress shall make no law respecting an establishment of religion or prohibiting the free exercise thereof," which ensures the separation of church and state. This has been interpreted by the Supreme Court to mean that publicly funded schools may not endorse a particular religious worldview over any other.

Family Educational Rights and Privacy Act (FERPA) (n.) A federal law enacted in 1974 and amended many times since then that provides parents and legal guardians the right to access their children's official "education records" until the student is 18 years of age or enters a postsecondary institution (college or university). For more information see: https://studentprivacy.ed.gov/faq/what-ferpa.

First Amendment (n.) An amendment to the U.S. Constitution that is part of the Bill of Rights that establishes the framework for religious freedom and freedom of expression in the United States.

Fourteenth Amendment (n.) An amendment to the U.S. Constitution passed in 1868 as part of the Reconstruction Amendments after the Civil War to ensure that all citizens were granted equal protection under the laws and were ensured fair treatment through due process under the law.

freedom-dreaming (v.) "Freedom dreaming is imagining worlds that are just, representing people's full humanity, centering people left on the edges, thriving in solidarity with folx from different identities who have struggles together for justice, and knowing that dreams are just around the corner with the might of people power" (Love, 2019, p. 103).

GSA (abbrev.) This is an abbreviation used for many student clubs that work to support LGBTQIA+ equity in schools. The abbreviation originally started from the Gay-Straight Alliance club formed in 1988 by Kevin Jennings and his students at Milton Academy and more recently has shifted to include names such as genders and sexualities alliance, gay-straight activists, and others.

GSD (abbrev.) This abbreviation stands for "gender and sexual diversity." I started using it in my 2010 book *Gender and Sexual Diversity in Schools* to move beyond identity-based discussions of LGBTQIA+ people in schools. The goal was to make clear that everyone has a gender and everyone has a sexuality. When we talk about GSD, we are talking about everyone and ensuring that the ways we talk about gender and sexuality are expansive and inclusive of all genders and sexualities.

gender binary (n.) A term used to capture the ways bodies and identities are discussed as only two possible categories that reflects cisheteronormativity. The gender binary structures the ways we think and talk about gender and limits which genders are recognizable in official structures and institutions. An example of this is when people only refer to "boys and girls" or "men and women" and use terms such as "the opposite sex" to imply that there are only two sexes or genders. See also *gender policing* and *gender role*.

gender policing (n.) A type of informal surveillance or social punishment that involves subtle or overt expressions of disapproval for how people express their gender. This can range from stares, mean looks, and rude comments to verbal and physical assault.

gender minority (adj.) A term used to describe people whose gender identity or expression is outside cisheteronormative expectations for boys and girls and includes gender nonconforming, transgender, nonbinary, and genderqueer people.

gender role (n.) A term used to describe the social expectations placed on a person based on their sex assigned at birth. These social expectations are based on historical norms and stereotyped notions of what girls and boys should look like and how people should behave according to gender binaries and don't reflect the actual broad diversity of interests, strengths, and capacities of individuals of all genders.

gender support plan (GSP) (n.) A document codeveloped by a school or school district with a trans or nonbinary student and their parent(s) or guardian(s) to ensure they can safely access educational opportunities and facilities. See Figure 7.5 for an example.

government speech (n.) A form of expression in First Amendment cases that is understood to be officially endorsed by a government entity and is seen to represent the views and values of that governmental organization. This can include curriculum materials, student handbooks, school yearbooks, and other publications and communications from a school or school district. This can include all curricular content: materials, lessons, classroom displays, including teacher expression during the school day, at official school events, and on school grounds. It also includes school mascots, logos, uniforms, and other official publications that represent the policies, procedures, and views of the school and district (Meyer, 2019).

harassment (n.) A form of interpersonal violence that involves a form of bias such as sexism, homophobia, racism, or transphobia that is either ongoing or severe and has a negative impact on individuals who are targeted as well as on those who witness or are otherwise exposed to the behavior. It can be verbal, nonverbal, or physical, and it can be intentional and sometimes unintentional when forms of bias are repeated or overheard by others (Meyer, 2009). See also *bullying*.

heckler's veto (n.) A form of speech in First Amendment cases that is understood as preventing others from exercising their right to free speech because they are being shouted down or otherwise prevented from being able to freely and safely express their viewpoint. For example, if a group of people stood up and started shouting in the middle of someone's speech such that the speaker could not continue, that could be understood as a "heckler's veto."

hegemonic masculinity (n.) A form of masculinity introduced by gender theorist Raewyn Connell (Connell, 1995; Connell & Messerschmidt, 2005), who argued that the most valued form of masculinity in any culture reflects the values of those in power. In most Western cultures, hegemonic masculinity best describes boys and men who are powerful, dominant, aggressive, assertive, strong, stoic, and heterosexually active. Power can be expressed in many ways including athletically, physically, sexually, socially, politically, or financially. In cisheteropatriarchal Western cultures, White, cisgender, heterosexual, Protestant, able-bodied boys are closest to the hegemonic ideal. See also *hegemony*.

hegemony (n.) A term introduced by Italian philosopher Antonio Gramsci (1971) to describe the dominant values and norms of a culture. Hegemonic norms and values are often implicit and never explicitly written down or otherwise communicated officially. Hegemony can subtly and persistently communicate whose identities and perspectives are most valued and celebrated and those which are not seen as acceptable by those in positions of power and influence.

homophobia (n.) The irrational fear or hatred of people who are attracted to people of the same gender and can result in subtle and overt acts of discrimination and violence.

injunction (n.) A legal action that prevents an entity (school, school district, person) from moving forward with a decision or implementing an action until a court can hear arguments and author a decision on the issue.

intersectional oppression (n.) A term coined by legal scholar Kimberlé Crenshaw (1991) to describe how people from multiply marginalized communities, such as women of color or queer people with disabilities, experience various systems of oppression simultaneously.

LGBTQIA+ (abbrev.) An abbreviation that is used to describe a community of people that includes lesbian, gay, bisexual, transgender, queer, intersex, and asexual. The "+" stands for other folks whose identities and experiences go beyond cisheteronormative expectations and can include multiple other identities including agender, pansexual, and others who don't feel like any of the existing labels accurately describe their identity.

microaggression (n.) A form of interpersonal harm that is biased in nature (racist, sexist, homophobic, transphobic, etc.) and includes smaller, often harder-to-notice forms of exclusion and oppression that can be verbal or nonverbal (Solarzano & Perez Huber, 2020).

National School Climate Survey (NSCS) (n.) A national survey of LGBTQIA+ youth ages 13–19 attending schools in the United States conducted every 2 years by GLSEN since 1999. More information is available at www.glsen.org/nscs.

normative (n.) A term popularized by queer theorists used to describe ideas, behaviors, and concepts that reflect the dominant values and expectations of a culture or community—usually in relation to gender and sexuality. It can be used with prefixes such as cisnormativity, heteronormativity, and even "homonormativity" to describe the dominant norms and expectations for LGBTQIA+ people to fit into a cisheteronormative society (de Jong, 2015). Marriage and monogamy in LGBTQIA+ relationships are some examples of homonormativity.

nonbinary (adj., n.) A term for people whose gender identity is more expansive than the binary labels of "girl" and "boy" can capture. The term emerged in the early 2010s to refer to anyone whose gender identity does not fit within the binary categories of man or woman. Nonbinary people may feel like they have elements of both masculinity and femininity in them or neither. Many nonbinary people identify as part of the transgender community; some don't. See also *gender binary*.

patriarchy (n.) A word that refers to cultures and systems that are organized around male perspectives and protect male power by placing higher value on normative masculine bodies, perspectives, and priorities. Examples can include the overrepresentation of men in positions of power such as elected officials, heads of corporations (including film and publishing companies), and religious institutions.

praxis (v.) A concept drawn from Paulo Freire's (1970) work in critical pedagogy that describes the ongoing process of action and reflection that is required to meaningfully engage in learning activities designed to lead to a more humanizing and liberated society.

queer (n.) A term used to describe an individual (or group of individuals) whose gender and/or sexuality go beyond the norms of a cisheteropatriarchal society and can include people who identify as lesbian, gay, bisexual, transgender, asexual, gender fluid, and pansexual and those whose identities otherwise exceed the concepts of heterosexuality and cisnormativity. While this term was historically used as an insult against LGBTQIA+ people, it has been reclaimed by some and is often also used as a political identity by people who actively challenge dominant norms of cisheteropatriarchy.

to queer, queering (v.) The act of questioning or disrupting normalizing practices, often related to gender and sexuality. It can include asking questions, dressing differently, approaching a familiar problem in a new way, or challenging cisheteronormativity. Queering helps us think outside of dominant categories that shape hierarchies of popularity and power in schools and society. It provides ways to take action to challenge and change ways of speaking, learning, and being that are restrictive and harmful for anyone who doesn't fit the dominant mold.

queer joy (n.) A concept that builds on lessons learned from the Black and African American justice communities who advanced concepts such as "Black girl magic" (Osterheldt, 2021) and "Black joy" (Love, 2019; Nichols, n.d.). Queer joy draws from these important concepts of not allowing oneself to internalize the negative messages society has historically shared about people like you and finding happiness, beauty, and strength in the parts of oneself that haven't been honored or respected in cisheteronormative cultures.

queer pedagogy (n.) A form of teaching and learning that encourages disrupting patterns of normalcy (Bryson & De Castell, 1993) and centers the ideas and knowledge of people and communities that have been historically excluded or marginalized by traditional texts, lessons, and curricula. It expands our ways of thinking, talking, and interacting beyond White, Western, colonial, patriarchal cisheterornormative binaries of right/wrong, good/bad, Black/White, male/female. This also includes explicitly and consistently talking about gender and sexual diversity (GSD) (Meyer, 2010). Queer pedagogies also invite us to focus on joy, pleasure, and desire, or *eros,* in learning (Britzman, 1995).

radical love (n.) A concept from the work of bell hooks (1994a) and Paulo Freire (1970) that describes the conscious and consistent act of loving oneself and others as an act of resistance against forms of domination and oppression. It is a concept rooted in service to others and is seen as a form of critical pedagogy (Colonna & Nix-Stevenson, 2013).

rest as resistance (v.) A concept introduced by Tricia Hersey, aka "the Nap Bishop," designed to disrupt what she calls "grind culture" and the ways White supremacy and capitalism foster a culture of working ourselves to exhaustion. By taking time to rest and restore, we are engaging in resistance against the oppressive structures that benefit White supremacist, capitalist cisheteropatriarchy and often harm individuals marginalized by these systems (Hersey, 2022).

risk narratives (n.) A way of talking about LGBTQIA+ people and other minoritized groups only in terms of the harms or negative aspects they experience due to their minoritized status. This is related to the studies of populations who are "at risk" of dropping out of school or "at risk" for experiencing violence. Some scholars argue that the emphasis on risk and harm detracts from the strength, creativity, brilliance, and resilience that students in these groups also demonstrate, while others point out that researching these risks and harms is an important step in documenting the negative results of systemic racism, sexism, homophobia, and transphobia to motivate changes in practice.

restorative justice (n.) This concept includes four elements: restitution (reparation of harm), resolution (by the parties involved), reconciliation (reason for emotions), and voluntary engagement. Restorative justice activities can be completed between two individuals regarding a specific incident, or the whole club if others have been impacted by the behaviors. Restorative justice can be a complex process that requires knowledgeable leaders to lead well (Morrison & Vaandering, 2012).

Glossary

school climate (n.) A term used to describe the overall safety and experience of a school community and includes five main elements: safety, relationships, teaching and learning, institutional environment, and the school improvement process (Thapa et al., 2013). School climate has been extensively studied by GLSEN and various other researchers with a specific focus on the experience of LGBTQIA+ youth. See Chapters 2 and 4 for more on this topic.

school-sponsored speech (n.) A term in First Amendment cases that describes forms of expression that are not government speech but are still under the control of the school and can include school-run publications (newspapers, yearbooks, literary journals, etc.), school-funded performing arts activities (plays, concerts, etc.), activities occurring at athletic events, and content occurring at other competitions/practices of school clubs and organizations (band, chorus, cheerleading, debate, chess, math club, etc.) (Meyer, 2019).

secular (adj.) A term that describes any group or object that is nonreligious in nature.

sex (n.) A medico-legal category that is initially assigned at birth by medical professionals. Currently the most widely used sex categories are "male" and "female." Some regions have introduced a third legal category, "x," to represent people who do not identify with their sex assigned at birth. This legal category can be altered for transgender people who complete certain legal and medical procedures (Meyer, 2010). See also: *sex assigned at birth*.

sex assigned at birth (n.) A legal category of "male" or "female" that is initially assigned at birth by medical professionals. See also: *AFAB, AMAB*.

social transition (v.) A term used to describe the act of changing one's gender expression and the way one presents oneself in public without undergoing any medical or legal changes. This can include changing one's chosen name and pronouns, the way one dresses and presents oneself in public, and the gendered facilities one uses in public or semi-public spaces.

stakeholder (n.) A person or group of people who have a "stake" or are invested in a particular community. In a public school, some key stakeholders include school board members, district leaders (superintendent, other district office personnel), principals, teachers and other educational staff (librarians, counselors, paraeducators, social workers), students, parents, and other community members. In charter and private schools, there are different stakeholders to consider, including charter network leaders, school board members, heads of school, alumni associations, and religious leaders. Each one of these stakeholders has different priorities, knowledge of the issues, and values shaping their positions on matters related to LGBTQIA+ equity in schools

Title IX (n.) Title IX of the Educational Amendments of 1972 is a federal law that applies to all educational institutions that receive federal funding in the United States. It mandates that no person shall be discriminated against in educational institutions "on the basis of sex" ("Title IX of the Education Amendments of 1972," 1972).

transformative SEL (social-emotional learning) Jagers et al.'s (2019) framework for transformative SEL builds on the Collaborative for Academic, Social, and Emotional Learning's (CASEL's) existing five competencies of self-awareness, self-management, social awareness, relationship skills, and responsible decision-making. The goal is to align SEL frameworks with transformative and justice-oriented notions of citizenship (Westheimer & Kahne, 2004) by integrating four new elements: identity, agency, belonging, and engagement (p. 167). Jagers and colleagues emphasize that since they view SEL as a civic enterprise, political agency or "efficacy" is an important element in SEL—specifically within the second competency of self-management.

transgender (adj.) This term embraces all individuals whose gender identity and/or expression transcends the binary categories of cisgender girl and boy or man and woman. It includes people who identify as agender, gender fluid, gender creative, gender independent, gender-free, gender nonconforming (GNC), nonbinary, trans boys, and trans girls as well as other terms that may still emerge. Current preferred use is as an adjective such as, "transgender person" or "she is a transgender woman" and not a noun. This group is also sometimes referred to as "gender minorities."

transsexual (n.) This term is used to describe transgender people who have gone through medical treatments that can include hormone blockers, hormone supplements, and surgical procedures to have their bodies more accurately reflect their gender. It has fallen out of use in some communities who want to de-emphasize the medical and physical aspects of gender, whereas some transsexual people are recommitting to the use of this term and embracing it as an accurate descriptor of their identity and experience.

transphobia (v.) The irrational fear or hatred of people who are transgender; it can lead to acts of discrimination and violence against transgender and gender-nonconforming people.

Universal Design (n.) An approach to the design of built environments and learning experiences that seeks to remove barriers to access and make communities and classrooms more engaging for people of all abilities. Universal Design in construction can include curb cuts, ramps, elevators, and high-contrast signage. Universal Design for Learning can include lessons and activities that offer students choices and multiple means of engagement and multiple ways to demonstrate what they have learned.

viewpoint discrimination (n.) A form of censorship in First Amendment cases that is not allowed under current interpretations of free speech protections. Schools cannot silence expression simply because they do not agree with the message. They must abide by a set of guidelines and principles that apply to regulating all forms of expression on school grounds. For example see: *Gillman v. Sch. Bd. for Holmes Cnty., Fla.* (2008).

References

AA v. Needville Independent School District, 701 F. Supp. 2d 863 (S.D. Tex. 2009)
AB 1732 Single-user restrooms. (2016). https://leginfo.legislature.ca.gov/faces/bill NavClient.xhtml?bill_id=201520160AB1732
ACLU (American Civil Liberties Union) of Louisiana. (2018). *Transgender student's successful effort to challenge discrimination is people power in action.* American Civil Liberties Union. Retrieved July 21 from https://www.laaclu.org/en/news/transgender-students-successful-effort-challenge-discrimination-people-power-action
ACLU. (2011). *Sturgis v. Copiah County School District.* American Civil Liberties Union. Retrieved July 18 from http://www.aclu.org/lgbt-rights/sturgis-v-copiah-county-school-district
ACLU. (2024). *Mapping attacks on LGBTQ rights in U.S. state legislatures.* American Civil Liberties Union. Retrieved May 15, 2024 from https://www.aclu.org/legislative-attacks-on-lgbtq-rights-2024
ACLU of Florida (2008). *Gillman v. School Board for Holmes County.* ACLU. Retrieved July 27 from https://www.aclufl.org/en/gillman-v-school-board-holmes-county#:~:text=Gillman%20sued%20the%20school%20board,and%20therefore%20must%20be%20permitted.
ACLU staff. (2017). *ACLU of Massachusetts challenges Malden charter school's discriminatory hair policy.* ACLU. https://www.aclu.org/press-releases/aclu-massachusetts-challenges-malden-charter-schools-discriminatory-hair-policy
ACLU staff. (2021). *Gloucester county school board to pay $1.3 million to resolve Gavin Grimm's case.* ACLU. https://www.aclu.org/press-releases/gloucester-county-school-board-pay-13-million-resolve-gavin-grimms-case
Adair, V., Dixon, R. S., Moore, D. W., & Sutherland, C. M. (2000). Ask your mother not to make yummy sandwiches: Bullying in New Zealand secondary schools. *New Zealand Journal of Educational Studies, 35*(2), 207–221.
Alfonseca, K. (2024). Missouri teachers who support a trans minor's social transition could face felony, be put on sex offender list under proposed bill. *ABCNews.* Retrieved March 15, 2024, from https://abcnews.go.com/US/missouri-bill-teachers-support-minors-transitioning-felony-sex-offender-list/story?id=107803364#:~:text=Social%20transitioning%20refers%20to%20changes,%2C%20name%2C%20clothing%20or%20hairstyle.&text=A%20new%20Missouri%20bill%20would,transitioning%20of%20a%20transgender%20minor.
Álvarez, B. (2023). The pride flag flies again. *NEA News.* Retrieved May 29, 2024, from https://www.nea.org/nea-today/all-news-articles/pride-flag-flies-again

Apple, M. (2004). *Ideology and the curriculum* (3rd ed.). RoutledgeFalmer.
Aragon, S. R., Poteat, V. P., Espelage, D. L., & Koenig, B. W. (2014). The influence of peer victimization on educational outcomes for LGBTQ and Non-LGBTQ high school students. *Journal of LGBT Youth, 11*(1), 1–19. https://doi.org/10.1080/19361653.2014.840761
Associated Press. (2022). Missouri high school asks teachers to remove gay pride flags. *NBC News*. Retrieved May 29, 2024, from https://www.nbcnews.com/nbc-out/out-news/missouri-high-school-asks-teachers-remove-gay-pride-flags-rcna44585
Atterbury, A. (2023). Florida lawmakers restrict pronouns and tackle book objections in sweeping education bill. *Politico*. Retrieved August 16, 2023, from https://www.politico.com/news/2023/05/03/florida-lawmakers-restrict-pronouns-and-tackle-book-objections-00095084
Bagemihl, B. (1999) *Biological exuberance: Animal homosexuality and natural diversity*. St. Martin's Press.
Battle, S., & Wheeler, T. E. (2017, February 22). *Dear Colleague Letter: Withdrawing statements of policy and guidance*. Retrieved from https://www2.ed.gov/about/offices/list/ocr/letters/colleague-201702-title-ix.pdf
Bear, G. (2020). *Improving school climate: Practical strategies to reduce behavior problems and promote social and emotional learning*. Routledge.
Bell v. Itawamba County School Bd., 859 F.Supp.2d 834 (United States District Court, N.D. Mississippi, Eastern Division 2012). https://www.leagle.com/decision/infdco20120316b78
Belle, E. (2018). Massachusetts introduces LGBTQ-Inclusive curriculum. *Teen Vogue*. Retrieved July 26, 2023, from https://www.teenvogue.com/story/massachusetts-introduces-lgbtq-inclusive-curriculum
Belle, E. (2022). Don't Say Gay protests: How Florida students like Jack Petocz are fighting against hatred. *Teen Vogue*. Retrieved July 27, 2023, from https://www.teenvogue.com/story/jack-petocz-dont-say-gay-florida
Bethel School Dist. No. 403 v. Fraser, 478 U.S. 675 (1986)).
Binkley, C. (2024). Biden's new Title IX rules protect LGBTQ+ students, but transgender sports rule still on hold. *AP News*. https://apnews.com/article/title-ix-sexual-assault-transgender-sports-d0fc0ab7515de02b8e4403d0481dc1e7
Bond, L., Carlin, J. B., Thomas, L., Rubin, K., & Patton, G. (2001). Does bullying cause emotional problems? A prospective study of young teenagers. *BMJ: British Medical Journal, 323*(7311), 480–484.
Bostock v. Clayton County, Georgia (Supreme Court of the United States 2020).
Boyd County High School Gay Straight Alliance v. Board of Education of Boyd County, Ky (258 F. Supp. 2d 667 (E. D. KY) 2003).
Brandenburg v. Ohio (395 U.S. 444 1969). https://supreme.justia.com/cases/federal/us/395/444/
Britzman, D. (1995). Is there a Queer pedagogy? Or, stop reading straight. *Educational Theory, 45*(2), 151–165.
Bronski, M. (2019). *A Queer history of the United States for young people*. Beacon Press.
Brown v. Board of Education of Topeka (347 U.S. 483 1954).
Brundin, J. (2022). In a divided vote, Colorado's State Board of Education approves new inclusive social studies standards after a tumultuous year-long debate. *Colorado Public Radio News*. Retrieved December 27, 2023, from https://www.cpr

References

.org/2022/11/10/colorado-state-board-of-education-approves-new-inclusive-social-studies-standards/

Bryson, M., & De Castell, S. (1993). Queer pedagogy: Praxis makes Im/Perfect. *Canadian Journal of Education, 18*(3), 285–305.

Caudillo v. Lubbock (311 F. Supp. 2d 550, (N. D. TX, Lubbock Division, 2004).

CBS staff. (2012). Lynn Mayor, ACLU defend student who wore 'Lesbian' shirt to school. *CBS News Boston*. Retrieved July 27, 2023, from https://www.cbsnews.com/boston/news/lynn-mayor-aclu-support-student-who-wore-lesbian-shirt-to-school/

Chaplinksy v. New Hampshire (315 U.S. 568 1942). https://supreme.justia.com/cases/federal/us/315/568/

Chapter 10 Plumbing Code. 10-10-2 Adoption of Plumbing Code with Modifications (n.d.). City of Boulder. https://library.municode.com/co/boulder/codes/municipal_code?nodeId=TIT10ST_CH10PLCO_10-10-2ADINPLCOMO

Choi, A. (2024). Record number of anti-LGBTQ bills were introduced in 2023. *CNN Politics*. Retrieved May 15, 2024, from https://www.cnn.com/politics/anti-lgbtq-plus-state-bill-rights-dg/index.html

Civil Rights Act of 1964. (1964). In: Pub.L. 88-352, 78 Stat. 241.

Coggan, C., Bennett, S., Hooper, R., & Dickinson, P. (2003). Association between bullying and mental health status in New Zealand adolescents. *International Journal of Mental Health Promotion, 5*(1), 16–22.

Cohen, S. (2005). Liberationists, clients, activists: Queer youth organizing, 1966–2003. *Journal of Gay & Lesbian Issues in Education, 2*(3), 67–86. https://doi.org/10.1300/J367v02n03_06

Colonna, S. E., & Nix-Stevenson, D. (2013). Radical love: Love all, serve all. *International Journal of Critical Pedagogy, 5*(1), 5–10.

Connell, R. W. (1995). *Masculinities*. Allen and Unwin.

Connell, R. W., & Messerschmidt, J. W. (2005). Hegemonic masculinity: Rethinking the concept. *Gender & Society, 19*(6), 829.

Constitution Annotated. (2024). Congress.gov: United States Congress Retrieved from https://constitution.congress.gov/browse/essay/amdt14-S1-8-11/ALDE_00000837/

Crenshaw, K. (1991). Mapping the margins: Intersectionality, identity politics, and violence against women of color. *Stanford Law Review, 43*(6), 1241–1299. https://doi.org/10.2307/1229039

D'Augelli, A. R., & Hershberger, S. L. (1993). Lesbian, gay, and bisexual youth in community settings: Personal challenges and mental health problems. *American Journal of Community Psychology, 21*(4), 421–448.

Daley, J. (2019). Remembering "Godmother of Title IX": Bernice Sandler. *Smithsonian.com*. Retrieved June 21, 2019, from https://www.smithsonianmag.com/smart-news/godmother-title-ix-bernice-sandler-180971246/

Davis, H. F. (2017). *Beyond trans: Does gender matter?* New York University Press. http://ebookcentral.proquest.com/lib/ucb/detail.action?docID=4714305

de Jong, D. (2015). "He wears pink leggings almost every day, and a pink sweatshirt. . . ." How school social workers understand and respond to gender variance. *Child and Adolescent Social Work Journal, 32*(3), 247–255. https://doi.org/10.1007/s10560-014-0355-3

De Pedro, K. T., Gilreath, T. D., Jackson, C., & Esqueda, M. C. (2017). Substance use among transgender students in California public middle and high schools. *Journal of School Health*, 87(5), 303–309. https://doi.org/10.1111/josh.12499

Diaz, J. (2022). Florida's governor signs controversial law opponents dubbed 'Don't Say Gay'. *NPR*. Retrieved May 28, 2024, from https://www.npr.org/2022/03/28/1089221657/dont-say-gay-florida-desantis

Dimarco, B. (2023, March 16). *Legislative tracker: 2023 parent-rights bills in the states*. FutureEd. Retrieved May 29, 2024 from https://www.future-ed.org/legislative-tracker-2023-parent-rights-bills-in-the-states/

Drysdale, S. (2023). Massachusetts approves first sex and health education changes in schools in 24 years. *CBS News Boston*. Retrieved February 16, 2024, from https://www.cbsnews.com/boston/news/massachusetts-sex-health-education-changes-schools-lgbtq-dese/

East High Gay/Straight Alliance v. Board of Education of Salt Lake City School District (81 F. Supp. 2d 1166, 1197 (D. Utah 1999).

Elliott, K. O. (2016). Queering student perspectives: Gender, sexuality and activism in school. *Sex Education*, 16(1), 49–62. https://doi.org/10.1080/14681811.2015.1051178

Equal Access Act. (1984). H.R. 5345, 98th Cong.

Espelage, D. L., Low, S., Polanin, J. R., & Brown, E. C. (2013). The impact of a middle school program to reduce aggression, victimization, and sexual violence. *Journal of Adolescent Health*, 53(2), 180–186. https://doi.org/10.1016/j.jadohealth.2013.02.021

Espelage, D. L., Low, S., Van Ryzin, M. J., & Polanin, J. R. (2015). Clinical trial of Second Step Middle School Program: Impact on bullying, cyberbullying, homophobic teasing, and sexual harassment perpetration. *School Psychology Review*, 44(4), 464-479.

Essecks, J. D. (2020). *Open letter to schools about LGBTQ student privacy*. American Civil Liberties Union. https://www.aclu.org/documents/open-letter-schools-about-lgbtq-student-privacy

Evans v Bayer, No. 08-61952-CIV-GARBER (District Court for the Southern District of Florida 2010). https://jolt.law.harvard.edu/digest/evans-v-bayer

Executive order 13988 3 C.F.R. (2021) *Preventing and combating discrimination on the basis of gender identity or sexual orientation*. Retrieved from https://www.whitehouse.gov/briefing-room/presidential-actions/2021/01/20/executive-order-preventing-and-combating-discrimination-on-basis-of-gender-identity-or-sexual-orientation/

Feingold, J., & Weishart, J. (2023). How discriminatory censorship laws imperil public education. Boulder, CO National Education Policy Center.

Fernandez, M. (2007, June 24). School officials black out photo of a gay student's kiss. *The New York Times*. Retrieved May 13, 2011, from http://www.nytimes.com/2007/06/24/education/24yearbook.html?ref=nyregion

Freire, P. (1970). *Pedagogy of the oppressed*. Continuum.

Fricke v. Lynch, 491 F. Supp. 381 (D.R.I. 1980)

Furman, E., Singh, A. K., Wilson, C., D'Alessandro, F., & Miller, Z. (2019). "A space where people get it": A methodological reflection of arts-informed community-based participatory research with nonbinary youth. *International Journal of*

References

Qualitative Methods, 18, 1609406919858530. https://doi.org/10.1177/1609406919858530

Gamarel, K. E., Garrett-Walker, J. J., Rivera, L., & Golub, S. A. (2014). Identity safety and relational health in youth spaces: A needs assessment with LGBTQ youth of color. *Journal of LGBT Youth, 11*(3), 289–315. https://doi.org/10.1080/19361653.2013.879464

Garcetti v. Ceballos, 410, 421 547 (U.S. 2006).

Gardner, M. (2020a). More to *Finding Nemo*: Sex-shifting fish as reproductive strategy. In S. Woolley & L. Airton (Eds.), *Teaching about gender diversity: Teacher-tested lesson plans for K-12 classrooms* (pp. 59–67). Canadian Scholars.

Gardner, M. (2020b). Using school audits as an equity lens: Understanding the experiences of gender diverse students. In S. Woolley & L. Airton (Eds.), *Teaching about gender diversity: Teacher-tested lesson plans for K-12 classrooms* (pp. 235–250). Canadian Scholars.

Garofalo, R., Deleon, J., Osmer, E., Doll, M., & Harper, G. W. (2006). Overlooked, misunderstood and at-risk: Exploring the lives and HIV risk of ethnic minority male-to-female transgender youth. *Journal of Adolescent Health, 38*(3), 230–236. https://doi.org/10.1016/j.jadohealth.2005.03.023

Gender Spectrum. (2022). Excerpts on school bathroom policies. Gender Spectrum. Retrieved January 24, 2022 from https://genderspectrum.org/articles/excerpts-bathroom-policies

Gibson, P. (1989). *Gay male and lesbian youth suicide* ((DHHS Publication No. [ADM]89-1623, pp. 110–142)). (In U.S. Department of Health & Human Services, Alcohol, Drug Abuse, and Mental Health Administration, Report of the Secretary's Task Force on Youth Suicide: Vol 3. Prevention and interventions in youth suicide, Issue.

Gillman v. Sch. Bd. for Holmes Cnty., Fla., 567 F. Supp. 2d 1359 (N.D. Fla. 2008).

GLSEN staff. (n.d.). LGBTQ history timeline lesson. Retrieved from https://www.glsen.org/activity/lgbtq-history-timeline-lesson on June 3, 2024. GLSEN.

GLSEN. (2016). *Educational exclusion: Drop out, push out, & school-to-prison pipeline*. GLSEN. http://www.glsen.org/article/drop-out-push-out-school-prison-pipeline

GLSEN. (2023). *Gender affirming and inclusive athletics participation*. GLSEN. Retrieved August 18, 2023 from https://www.glsen.org/activity/gender-affirming-inclusive-athletics-participation

Gonsalves, A., Wiseman, D., Vanderzwet, L., Spencer, K. R., & Caretier-Archambault, V. (2020). Beyond the binary: Are there really only two sexes? In S. Woolley & L. Airton (Eds.), *Teaching about gender diversity: Teacher-tested lesson plans for K-12 classrooms* (pp. 259–270). Canadian Scholars.

Gramsci, A. (1971). *Further selections from the prison notebooks* (D. Boothman, Trans.). University of Minnesota Press.

Greytak, E., Kosciw, J., & Diaz, E. (2009). *Harsh realities: The experiences of transgender youth in our nations' schools*. GLSEN.

Greytak, E., Kosciw, J., Villenas, C., & Giga, N. (2016). *From teasing to torment: School climate revisited, a survey of U.S. secondary school students and teachers*. GLSEN. https://www.glsen.org/article/teasing-torment-school-climate-revisited-survey-us-secondary-school-students-and-teachers

Hall v Durham Catholic District School Board. (2003). 94 CCR (2d) 1 (Ontario SCJ)).

Halley, J. (2014). *Sexual orientation and the politics of biology: A critique of the argument from immutability*. Routledge.

Harper v. Poway Unified School District (445 F.3d 1166 (9th Cir.) 2006).

Harris & Associates. (1993). *Hostile hallways: The AAUW survey on sexual harassment in America's schools*. American Association of University Women.

Hazelwood School District v. Kuhlmeier, 484 U.S. 260, 108 S. Ct. 562 (1988)

Hersey, T. (2022). *Rest is resistance: A manifesto*. Little Brown Spark.

hicks, b. l. (2020). The festival of puberty. In S. Woolley & L. Airton (Eds.), *Teaching about gender diversity: Teacher-tested lesson plans for K-12 classrooms* (pp. 151–160). Canadian Scholars.

Hill, C., & Kearl, H. (2011). *Crossing the line: Sexual harassment at school*. American Association of University Women. http://www.aauw.org/learn/research/crossingtheline.cfm

Hillier, A., Kroehle, K., Edwards, H., & Graves, G. (2020). Risk, resilience, resistance and situated agency of trans high school students. *Journal of LGBT Youth, 17*(4), 384–407. https://doi.org/10.1080/19361653.2019.1668326

hooks, b. (1984). *Feminist theory: From margin to center*. Routledge.

hooks, b. (1994a). Love as the practice of freedom. In *Outlaw culture* (pp. 243–250). Routledge.

hooks, b. (1994b). *Teaching to transgress*. Routledge-Falmer.

How the parkland students pulled off a massive national protest in only 5 weeks. (2016). Facing History & Ourselves. Retrieved May 23 from https://www.facinghistory.org/resource-library/how-parkland-students-pulled-massive-national-protest-only-5-weeks

Howard, J. P. (2002). Following-up on Jubran: Boards, bullying, and accountability. *Education Canada, 42*(3), 40–41.

HuffPost staff. (2011). Jerry Buell, Florida high school teacher, suspended for anti-gay Facebook posts. *Huffpost*. Retrieved March 15, 2024, from https://www.huffpost.com/entry/jerry-buell-florida-high_n_931941

Hunt, G. L., & Hunt, M. W. (1977). Female-female pairing in Western gulls (Larus occidentalis) in Southern California. *Science, 196*(4297), 1466–1467.

Hurston, Z. N. (1996) *Dust Tracks on a Road*. HarperPerennial.

Imber, M., & Van Geel, T. (2010). *Education law* (4th ed.). Routledge.

Jagers, R. J., Rivas-Drake, D., & Williams, B. (2019). Transformative social and emotional learning (SEL): Toward SEL in service of educational equity and excellence. *Educational Psychologist, 54*(3), 162–184. https://doi.org/10.1080/00461520.2019.1623032

Jennings, K. (2016). Foreword: It's about time. In Sadowski, M. *Safe is not enough: Better schools for LGBTQ students* (pp. vii–x). Harvard Education Press.

Jordan, K. M. (2000). Substance abuse among gay, lesbian, bisexual, transgender, and questioning adolescents. *School Psychology Review, 29*(2), 201–206.

Joyner, C. (2009). Girl in tuxedo denied a place in school yearbook. *USA Today*. Retrieved May 18, 2011, from http://www.usatoday.com/news/nation/2009-10-18-yearbook-photo-lesbian_N.htm

Keenan, H. (2017). Unscripting curriculum: Toward a critical trans pedagogy. *Harvard Educational Review, 87*(4), 538–556.

References

Kemper, D. P. (1980). Intercollegiate athletics and Title IX: Legal aspects of higher education. *Journal of the NAWDAC, 43*, 33–38.

Kosciw, J. G., Clark, C. M., & Menard, L. (2022). *The 2021 National School Climate Survey: The experiences of LGBTQ+ youth in our nation's schools*. GLSEN.

Kosciw, J. G., Clark, C. M., Truong, N. L., & Zongrone, A. D. (2020). *The 2019 National School Climate Survey: The experiences of lesbian, gay, bisexual, transgender, and queer youth in our nation's schools*. GLSEN.

Kosciw, J. G., Palmer, N. A., & Kull, R. M. (2014). Reflecting resiliency: Openness about sexual orientation and/or gender identity and its relationship to well-being and educational outcomes for LGBT students. *American Journal of Community Psychology, 55*(1–2), 167–178. https://doi.org/10.1007/s10464-014-9642-6

Kosciw, J., Diaz, E., & Gretytak, E. (2008). *2007 National School Climate Survey: The experiences of lesbian, gay, bisexual, and transgender youth in our nation's schools*. GLSEN. www.glsen.org/research

Kosciw, J., Greytak, E., Giga, N., Villenas, C., & Danischewski, D. (2016). *The 2015 National School Climate Survey: The experiences of lesbian, gay, bisexual, transgender, and queer youth in our nation's schools*. GLSEN. www.glsen.org

Kumashiro, K. (2002). *Troubling education: Queer activism and antioppressive pedagogy*. Routledge Falmer.

Kumashiro, K. (2004). *Against common sense: Teaching and learning toward social justice*. Routledge Falmer.

Labaree, D. F. (1997). Public goods, private goods: The American struggle over educational goals. *American Educational Research Journal, 34*(1), 39–81. https://doi.org/10.3102/00028312034001039

Labuski, C., & Keo-Meier, C. (2015). The (mis)measure of trans. *TSQ: Transgender Studies Quarterly, 2*(1), 13–33. https://doi.org/https://dx.doi.org/10.1215/23289252-2848868

Ladson-Billings, G. (2014). Culturally relevant pedagogy 2.0: Aka the remix. *Harvard Educational Review, 84*(1), 74–84. https://doi.org/10.17763/haer.84.1.p2rj131485484751

Lane, S. (2018). *No sanctuary: Teacher and the school reform that brought gay rights to the masses*. University Press of New England.

Lau v. Nichols, 414 U.S. 563 (1974).

Lemon v. Kurtzman, 411 U.S. 192, 93 S. Ct. 1463 (1973).).

Leonard, A. S. (2004). *Unusual gay student loss*. Gaycitynews.com. Retrieved October 15 from http://www.gaycitynews.com/site/index.cfm?newsid=17005271&BRD=2729&PAG=461&dept_id=568864&rfi=8

Leonardi, B. (2014). *Tilling the soil for LGBTQ inclusive policies: A case study of one school's attempt to bring policy into practice*. University of Colorado at Boulder. http://libraries.colorado.edu/record=b7876820~S3

Leonardi, B., Farley, A. N., Harsin Drager, E., & Gonzalez, J. (2021). Unpacking the T: Understanding the diverse experiences trans students navigating schools. *Berkeley Review of Education, 10*(2), 274–303. https://doi.org/http://dx.doi.org/10.5070/B810245267

Lhamon, C. (2015). *Dear Colleague Letter on Title IX coordinators*. U.S. Department of Education, Office for Civil Rights Retrieved from http://www2.ed.gov/about/offices/list/ocr/letters/colleague-201504-title-ix-coordinators.pdf

Lhamon, C., & Gupta, V. (2016). *Dear Colleague Letter on transgender students.* Department of Education, Office for Civil Rights Retrieved from http://www2.ed.gov/about/offices/list/ocr/letters/colleague-201605-title-ix-transgender.pdf

Lorde, A. (1982/2007). Learning from the 1960s. In *Audre Lorde, sister outsider: Essays & speeches by Audre Lorde* (pp. 134–144). Crossing Press.

Love, B. (2019). *We want to do more than survive: Abolitionist teaching and the pursuit of educational freedom.* Beacon Press.

Luong, M. (2023). The art of queer joy. *Yes!* https://www.yesmagazine.org/social-justice/2023/06/29/queer-joy

Macgillivray, I. K. (2007). *Gay-straight alliances: A handbook for students, educators, and parents.* Harrington Park Press.

Mackenzie, S., & Talbott, A. (2018). Gender justice/gender through the eyes of children: A photovoice project with elementary school gender expansive and LGBTQ-parented children and their allies. *Sex Education 18*(6), 1–17. https://doi.org/10.1080/14681811.2018.1456915

Massachusetts Department of Elementary and Secondary Education (1999). *Massachusetts high school students and sexual orientation: Results of the 1999 Youth Risk Behavior Survey.* Retrieved from http://www.doe.mass.edu/hssss/yrbs99/glb_rslts.html January 3, 2005

Mayberry, M. (2006). The story of a Salt Lake City gay-straight alliance: Identity work and LGBT youth. *Journal of Gay & Lesbian Issues in Education, 4*(1), 13–31. https://doi.org/10.1300/J367v04n01_03

Mayo, C. (2014). *LGBTQ youth and education: Policies and practices.* Teachers College Press.

McCabe, A. (2022). Frustrated by society's erasure, the Lesbian Avengers fought back. *Morning Edition.* https://www.npr.org/2022/06/24/1106444650/frustrated-by-societys-erasure-the-lesbian-avengers-fought-back

McCready, L. T. (2004). Some challenges facing queer youth programs in urban high schools: Racial segregation and de-normalizing whiteness. *Journal of Gay & Lesbian Issues in Education, 1*(3), 37–51. https://doi.org/10.1300/J367v01n03_05

McGuire, J. K., Anderson, C. R., Toomey, R. B., & Russell, S. T. (2010). School climate for transgender youth: A mixed method investigation of student experiences and school responses. *Journal of Youth & Adolescence, 39*(10), 1175–1188. https://doi.org/10.1007/s10964-010-9540-7

McMillen v. Itawamba County School District, 702 F. Supp. 2d 699 (N.D. Miss. 2010).

Mead, J. F., & Lewis, M. M. (2016). The implications of the use of parental choice as a legal "Circuit Breaker". *American Educational Research Journal, (53)*1, 100–131.

Meyer, E. J. (2007a, April 9–13). Bullying and harassment in secondary schools: A critical analysis of the gaps, overlaps, and implications from a decade of research. Annual meeting of the American Educational Research Association, Chicago, IL.

Meyer, E. J. (2007b). Lessons from Jubran: Reducing school board liability in cases of peer harassment. *Proceedings of the 17th Annual Conference of the Canadian Association for the Practical Study of Law in Education*, Vol. 1, 561–576. http://sites.google.com/site/lizjmeyer/publications

Meyer, E. J. (2009a). Creating schools that value sexual diversity. In S. Steinberg (Ed.), *Diversity and multiculturalism: A reader* (pp. 173–192). Peter Lang.

References

Meyer, E. J. (2009b). *Gender, bullying, and harassment: Strategies to end sexism and homophobia in schools*. Teachers College Press.

Meyer, E. J. (2010). *Gender and sexual diversity in schools*. Springer.

Meyer, E. J. (2014a, December 27). "Gender reveal parties" In Utero? *Gender and Education* [blog]. Retrieved from https://www.psychologytoday.com/us/blog/gender-and-schooling/201403/gender-reveal-parties-in-utero

Meyer, E. J. (2014b). New solutions for bullying and harassment: A post-structural, feminist approach. In R. Schott & D. M. Sondergard (Eds.), *School bullying: New theories in context*. Cambridge University Press.

Meyer, E. J. (2019). Student and staff speech rights in K-12 schools [Fact Sheet]. In National Center for Free Speech and Civic Engagement. Irvine, CA. Retrieved from http://www.elizabethjmeyer.com/research.html

Meyer, E. J. (2020). Gender and Bullying. In C. Mayo (Ed.), *Oxford encyclopedia of gender and sexuality in education*. Oxford University Press.

Meyer, E. J., & Keenan, H. (2018). Can policies help schools affirm gender diversity? A policy archaeology of transgender-inclusive policies in California schools. *Gender and Education*, 30(6), 736–753. https://doi.org/10.1080/09540253.2018.1483490

Meyer, E. J., & Kurtz, E. (2024). *Advocating for activism: Teachers' experiences supporting student activism for LGBTQ Equity*. [Roundtable Session]. The Annual Meeting of the American Educational Research Association, Philadelphia, PA.

Meyer, E. J., & Quantz, M. (2019). *Free speech in the Trump era: A mixed-methods investigation of K-12 and university faculty*. The Annual Meeting of the American Educational Research Association, Toronto, CANADA.

Meyer, E. J., Leonardi, B., & Keenan, H. (2022). Transgender students and policy in K-12 public schools: Acknowledging historical harms and taking steps toward a promising future. Boulder, CO:. National Education Policy Center. http://nepc.colorado.edu/ publication/transgender

Meyer, E. J., Quantz, M., & Regan, P. (2022). Race as the starting place: Equity directors addressing gender and sexual diversity in K-12 schools. *Sex Education*, 23(5), 491–505. https://doi.org/10.1080/14681811.2022.2068145

Meyer, E. J., Taylor, C., & Peter, T. (2014). Perspectives on gender and sexual diversity (GSD)-inclusive education: Comparisons between gay/lesbian/bisexual and straight educators. *Sex Education: Sexuality, Society and Learning*, 15(3), 221–234. https://doi.org/10.1080/14681811.2014.979341

Meyer, E. J., Tilland-Stafford, A., & Airton, L. (2016). Transgender and gender-creative students in PK-12 schools: What we can learn from their teachers. *Teachers College Record*, 118(8), 1–50. http://www.tcrecord.org.colorado.idm.oclc.org/library ID Number: 21368, Date Accessed: 12/15/2016 4:13:57 PM

Miller, K. (2019). The end of a captivating journey and beginning of a new chapter. *Medium*, 2019, December 21. https://kcmilleredu.medium.com/the-end-of-a-captivating-journey-and-beginning-of-a-new-chapter-26e6ea274d5d

Mitchell, J. (2023). Mississippi trans teen finally gets to walk across stage in her graduation dress and heels. *Sun Herald*. Retrieved July, 21, 2023, from https://www.nola.com/news/mississippi-trans-teen-finally-wears-graduation-dress/article_fc924a0a-03b0-11ee-87fc-2302dacea0f5.amp.html

Morrison v. Board of Educ. of Boyd County, 419 F. Supp. 2d 937 (E.D. Ky. 2006).

Morrison, B. E., & Vaandering, D. (2012). Restorative justice: Pedagogy, praxis, and discipline. *Journal of School Violence*, 11(2), 138–155. https://doi.org/10.1080/15388220.2011.653322

Morse v. Frederick, 93 551 (U.S. 2007). https://supreme.justia.com/cases/federal/us/551/393/

Movement Advancement Project, & GLSEN. (2017). *Separation and stigma: Transgender youth & school facilities*. GLSEN. http://lgbtmap.org/transgender-youth-school

Movement Advancement Project. (2023a). *Bans on transgender youth participation in sports*. Movement Advancement Project. Retrieved August 18, 2023 from https://www.lgbtmap.org/equality-maps/youth/sports_participation_bans

Movement Advancement Project. (2023b). *LGBTQ curricular laws*. Retrieved December 14 from https://www.lgbtmap.org/equality-maps/curricular_laws

Movement Advancement Project. (2024). *Equality maps: Nondiscrimination laws*. Retrieved February 12 from https://www.lgbtmap.org/equality-maps/non_discrimination_laws/public-accommodations

Mullender, A., & Ward, D. (1991). *Empowerment in action: Self-directed groupwork*. Palgrave MacMillan.

Murchison, G. R., Agenor, M., Reisner, S. L., & Watson, R. J. (2019). School restroom and locker room restrictions and sexual assault risk among transgender youth. *Pediatrics*, 143(6), 1–10. https://doi.org/10.1542/peds.2018-2902

Nabozny v. Podlesny, 92 F. 3d 446, (7th Cir. 1996).

Nadal, K. L., Issa, M.-A., Leon, J., Meterko, V., Wideman, M., & Wong, Y. (2011). Sexual orientation microaggressions: "Death by a thousand cuts" for lesbian, gay, and bisexual youth. *Journal of LGBT Youth*, 8(3), 234–259. https://doi.org/10.1080/19361653.2011.584204

National Coalition to Support Sexuality Education. (2003). *Gay straight alliance (GSA) allowed at Texas school*. National Coalition to Support Sexuality Education. Retrieved January 3 from http://www.ncsse.org/mandates/TX.html

Neem, J. N. (2017). *Democracy's schools: The rise of public education in America*. Johns Hopkins University Press.

Nehm, R. H., & Young, R. (2008). "Sex hormones" in secondary school biology textbooks. *Science & Education*, 17(10), 1175–1190.

Nichols, E. (n.d.). *Black joy: Resistance, resilience and reclamation*. National Museum of African American History and Culture. Retrieved June 6, 2024 from https://nmaahc.si.edu/explore/stories/black-joy-resistance-resilience-and-reclamation#:~:text=Black%20Joy%20demonstrates%20that%20internal,uplifting%2C%20and%20life%2Daffirming.

Nittle, N. (2022). Lawsuits, complaints and protests are upending sexist school dress codes. *The 19th News*. Retrieved December 7, 2023, from https://19thnews.org/2022/01/school-dress-code-challenges/

NJ teacher criticized for Facebook remarks on gays. *ABC7 Chicago*. (2011). Retrieved March 15, 2024, from https://abc7chicago.com/archive/8390754/

Olweus, D. (1993). *Bullying at school: What we know and what we can do*. Blackwell Publishing.

Oregon N. O. W. (2016). *Model student dress code*. Retrieved December 7, 2023 from https://noworegon.org/issues/model-student-dress-code/

References

Orwell, G. (1945). *Animal farm*. Signet.
Osterheldt, J. (2021). What we mean by Black Girl Magic. *The Boston Globe*. https://www.bostonglobe.com/2021/12/01/metro/what-we-mean-by-black-girl-magic/
Palmer, E. (2022). Florida students who organized 'Don't Say Gay' protest is suspended. *Newsweek*. Retrieved July 27, 2023, from https://www.newsweek.com/florida-student-dont-say-gay-protest-suspended-jack-petocz-1684830
Pascoe, C. J. (2007). *Dude, you're a fag: Masculinity and sexuality in high school*. University of California Press.
Pascoe, C. J. (2023). *Nice is not enough: Inequality and the limits of kindness at American high*. University of California Press.
Payne-Patterson, J. (2023). *The CROWN Act: A jewel for combating racial discrimination in the workplace and classroom*. https://www.epi.org/publication/crown-act/
Pendharkar, E. (2023). Pronouns for trans, nonbinary students: The states with laws that restrict them in schools. *Education Week*. Retrieved March 15, 2024, from https://www.edweek.org/leadership/pronouns-for-trans-nonbinary-students-the-states-with-laws-that-restrict-them-in-schools/2023/06
Pendleton Jimenez, K. (2016). *Tomboys and other gender heroes: Confessions from the classroom*. Peter Lang.
Perrotti, J., & Westheimer, K. (2001). *When the drama club is not enough: Lessons from the safe schools program for gay and lesbian students*. Beacon Press.
Peter, T., Campbell, C. P., & Taylor, C. (2021). *Still every class in every school: Final report on the Second National Climate Survey on Homophobia, Biphobia, and Transphobia in Canadian schools*. Egale Canada Human Rights Trust.
Philips, R. R. (2017). The battle over bathrooms: Schools, courts, and transgender rights. *Theory in Action*, *10*(4), 100–117. https://doi.org/10.3798/tia.1937-0237.1729
Pickering v. Board of Educ, 563 391 (U.S. 1968).
Poteat, V. P., Calzo, J. P., Yoshikawa, H., Miller, S., Ceccolini, C. J., Rosenbach, S., & Mauceri, N. (2018). Discussing transgender topics within gay-straight alliances: Factors that could promote more frequent conversations. *International Journal Transgender*, *19*(2), 119–131. https://doi.org/10.1080/15532739.2017.1407983
Poteat, V. P., Godfrey, E. B., Brion-Meisels, G., & Calzo, J. P. (2020). Development of youth advocacy and sociopolitical efficacy as dimensions of critical consciousness within gender-sexuality alliances. *Developmental Psychology*, *56*(6), 1207–1219. https://doi.org/10.1037/dev0000927
Price-Feeney, M. (2020). Impact of bathroom discrimination on mental health among transgender and nonbinary youth. *Journal of Adolescent Health*, *68*(6), 1142–1147.
Rands, K. (2013). Supporting transgender and gender-nonconforming youth through teaching mathematics for social justice. *Journal of LGBT Youth*, *10*(1–2), 106–126. https://doi.org/10.1080/19361653.2012.717813
Renold, E. (2000). 'Coming out': Gender (hetero)sexuality and the primary school. *Gender and Education*, *12*(3), 309–326.
Renold, E. (2002). Presumed innocence—(Hetero)sexual, heterosexist and homophobic harassment among primary school girls and boys. *Childhood—A Global Journal of Child Research*, *9*(4), 415–434.
Renold, E. (2006). "They won't let us play . . . Unless you're going out with one of them": Girls, boys and butler's "Heterosexual Matrix" in the primary years. *British Journal of Sociology of Education*, *27*(4), 489–509.

Ressler, P. (2005). Challenging normative sexual and gender identity beliefs through "Romeo and Juliet". *English Journal, 95*(1), 52.

Reynolds, D. (2017). Laverne Cox at Grammy Awards: 'Google Gavin Grimm.' *Advocate*. https://www.advocate.com/transgender/2017/2/12/laverne-cox-grammy-awards-google-gavin-grimm

Rizzo, E. (2023). Central Bucks moves forward with policy censoring classroom decor and discussions—Despite federal investigation. *WHYY.org*. https://whyy.org/articles/central-bucks-school-district-pride-flag-ban-lgbtq-advocacy-policy-321/

Rogers, J., Franke, M. Yun, J. E., Ishimoto, M., Diera, C., Geller, R., Berryman, A., & Brenes, T. (2017). Teaching and learning in the age of Trump: Increasing stress and hostility in America's high schools. Los Angeles, CA: UCLA's Institute for Democracy, Education, and Access.

Rogers, K. (2021, June 16, 2021). Title IX protections extend to transgender students, education dept. says *The New York Times*. https://www.nytimes.com/2021/06/16/us/politics/title-ix-transgender-students.html

Rosales, I., Afshar, P., & Garcia, J. (2023). A transgender girl misses her high school graduation after Mississippi judge denies emergency plea to permit her to go in a dress and heels. *CNN U.S*. Retrieved July 21, 2023, from https://www.cnn.com/2023/05/20/us/mississippi-judge-denies-transgender-high-school-graduation-dress/index.html

Ruiz, R. (2022). How Florida's 'Don't Say Gay' bill turned students into activists. *Mashable*. Retrieved December 7, 2023, from https://mashable.com/article/dont-say-gay-florida-young-lgbtq-activists

Russell, S. T., Muraco, A., Subramaniam, A., & Laub, C. (2009). Youth empowerment and high school Gay-Straight Alliances. *Journal of Youth and Adolescence, 38*(7), 891–903. https://doi.org/10.1007/s10964-008-9382-8

Ryan, C. L., & Hermann-Wilmarth, J. M. (2013). Already on the shelf: Queer readings of award-winning children's literature. *Journal of Literacy Research, 45*(2), 142–172. https://doi.org/10.1177/1086296x13479778

Ryan, C. L., & Hermann-Wilmarth, J. M. (2018). *Reading the rainbow: LGBTQ-inclusive literacy instruction in the elementary classroom*. Teachers College Press.

Ryan, C., Russell, S. T., Huebner, D., Diaz, R., & Sanchez, J. (2010). Family acceptance in adolescence and the health of LGBT young adults. *Journal of Child Adolescent Psychiatric Nursing, 23*(4), 205–213. https://doi.org/10.1111/j.1744-6171.2010.00246.x

Schultz, B. (2022). Explainer: The history behind 'parents' rights' in schools. *AP News*. https://apnews.com/article/religion-education-gender-identity-0e2ca2cf0ef7d7bc6ef5b125f1ee0969

Sentinel Staff. (2011). Lake reinstates teacher after Facebook comments about gays. *Orlando Sentinel*. Retrieved March 15, 2024, from https://www.orlandosentinel.com/2011/08/24/lake-reinstates-teacher-after-facebook-comments-about-gays/

Shaffer, B. (2017). Malden charter school drops ban on hair extensions. Retrieved May 28, 2024, from https://www.wbur.org/news/2017/08/12/mystic-valley-hair-extension-ban-ends

Singh, A. A. (2013). Transgender youth of color and resilience: Negotiating oppression and finding support. *Sex Roles, 68*(11–12), 690–702. https://doi.org/10.1007/s11199-012-0149-z

References

Skinner, A. (2022). 'Safe Space' stickers banned by school district following DeSantis Bill. *Newsweek*. Retrieved December 27, 2023, from https://www.newsweek.com/safe-space-stickers-banned-school-district-following-desantis-bill-1739162

Smith, P. K. (2011). The prom as a spectacle of heteronormativity. In D. Carlson & D. Roseboro (Eds.), *The sexuality curriculum and youth culture* (pp. 156–170). Peter Lang.

Snyder v. Phelps (562 U.S. 443 2011).

Solarzano, D., & Perez Huber, L. (2020). *Racial microaggressions: Using critical race theory to respond to everyday Racism*. Teachers College Press.

Solórzano, D., & Huber, L. P. (2020). *Racial microaggressions: Using critical race theory to respond to everyday racism* (e-book ed.). Teachers College Press.

Southern Poverty Law Center. (2016). *After election day: The Trump effect // The impact of the 2016 presidential election on our nation's schools*. SPLC. https://www.splcenter.org/sites/default/files/the_trump_effect.pdf

Spula, I. (2017). An unexpected ally of gender-neutral restrooms: Building codes. *Architect Magazine*.

Staley, S., & Leonardi, B. (2020). A pretty queer thing: Thinking queerly about teachers' gender and sexual diversity-focused professional learning. *Journal of Teacher Education*. 72(5), 511–522. https://doi-org.colorado.idm.oclc.org/10.1177/0022487120971588

Straights and Gays for Equity v. Osseo Area Schools (Civ. No. 05-21000 (JNE/FLN), Mn 2006).

Sturgis v. Copiah County School District (United States District Court, Southern District of Mississippi, Jackson Division 2010). http://www.aclu.org/files/assets/sturgis.PDF

Suarez, M., & Wright, K. (2020). A critical approach to teaching data management and analysis categories. In S. Woolley & L. Airton (Eds.), *Teaching about gender diversity: Teacher-tested lesson plans for K–12 classrooms* (pp. 139–148). Canadian Scholars.

Sue, D. W. (2010). *Microaggressions in everyday life: Race, gender, and sexual orientation*. John Wiley & Sons.

Swearer, S. M., & Espelage, D. (2009). *Bullying prevention and intervention: Realistic strategies for schools*. Guilford Press.

Szlacha, L. (2003). Safer sexual diversity climates: Lessons learned from an evaluation of Massachusetts safe schools program for gay and lesbian students. *American Journal of Education*, 110(1), 58–88.

Taliaferro, L. A., McMorris, B. J., Rider, G. N., & Eisenberg, M. E. (2019). Risk and protective factors for self-harm in a population-based sample of transgender youth. *Archives of Suicide Research*, 23(2), 203–221. https://doi.org/10.1080/13811118.2018.1430639

Taylor, C., & Peter, T. (2011). *Every class in every school: The First National Climate Survey on Homophobia, Biphobia, and Transphobia in Canadian schools. Final report*. Manitoba Teachers Society. http://egale.ca/index.asp?lang=&menu=1&item=1489

Taylor, C., Peter, T., Campbell, C., Meyer, E., Ristock, J., & Short, D. (2015). *The every teacher project on LGBTQ-inclusive education in Canada's K–12 schools: Final Report*. Manitoba Teachers' Society. http://news-centre.uwinnipeg.ca/wp-content/uploads/2016/01/EveryTeacher_FinalReport_v12.pdf

Thapa, A., Cohen, J., Guffey, S., & Higgins-D'Alessandro, A. (2013). A review of school climate research. *Review of Educational Research, 83*(3), 357–385. https://doi.org/10.3102/0034654313483907

The Governor's Commission on Gay and Lesbian Youth: Breaking the Silence in Schools and in Families. (1993). *Making Schools Safe for Gay and Lesbian Youth* Report #: 17296-60-500-2/93-C.R. The Commonwealth of Massachussetts. Boston, MA.

Thorne, B., & Luria, Z. (1986). Sexuality and gender in children's daily worlds. *Social problems, 33*(3), 176–190.

Tinker v. Des Moines Independent School District (393 US 503, 509 1969).

Title IX of the Education Amendments of 1972. (1972). In: 20 U.S.C. § 1681–1688.

Travers. (2019). *The trans generation: How trans kids (and their parents) are creating a gender revolution.* New York University Press.

Truong, N. L., Zongrone, A. D., & Kosciw, J. G. (2020). *Erasure and resilience: The experiences of LGBTQ students of color, Black LGBTQ youth in U.S. schools.* GLSEN.

Truong, N. L., Clark, C. M., Rosenbach, S., & Kosciw, J. G. (2021). *The GSA study: Results of national surveys about students' and advisors' experiences in gender and sexuality alliance clubs.* GLSEN.

Turban, J. L. (2021). Trans girls belong on girls' sports teams. *Scientific American.* Retrieved July 14, 2021, from https://www.scientificamerican.com/article/trans-girls-belong-on-girls-sports-teams/

U.S. Const. amend. I. (1791).

U.S. Const. Amend. XIV. (1868).

U.S. Department of Education Office for Civil Rights. (2015). *Title IX Resource Guide.* Washington, D.C.: U.S. Department of Education, Office for Civil Rights. Retrieved from https://www2.ed.gov/about/offices/list/ocr/docs/dcl-title-ix-coordinators-guide-201504.pdf

U.S. Department of Health and Human Services. (2019). *The national youth sports strategy.* Washington D.C. Retrieved from https://health.gov/sites/default/files/2019-10/National_Youth_Sports_Strategy.pdf

United States Courts. (2024). *Court website links.* Federal Judiciary. Retrieved June 2, 2024 from https://www.uscourts.gov/about-federal-courts/federal-courts-public/court-website-links

Vermont Agency of Education. (2018). Full spectrum: Educators' guide to implementing LGBTQ+ inclusive sex ed. In. Barre, VT: Vermont Agency of Education.

Walton, G., & Niblett, B. (2013). Investigating the problem of bullying through photo elicitation. *Journal of Youth Studies, 16*(5), 646–662. https://doi.org/10.1080/13676261.2012.733810

Warnick, B. R. (2009). Student speech rights and the special characteristics of the school environment. *Educational Researcher, 38*(3), 200–215.

Watson, L. B., Varjas, K., Meyers, J., & Graybill, E. C. (2010). Gay–straight alliance advisors: Negotiating multiple ecological systems when advocating for LGBTQ youth. *Journal of LGBT Youth, 7*(2), 100–128. https://doi.org/10.1080/19361651003799700

Watson, R. J., & Russell, S. T. (2016). Disengaged or bookworm: academics, mental health, and success for sexual minority youth. *Journal of Research on Adolescence, 26*(1), 159–165. https://doi.org/10.1111/jora.12178

References

Wells, K. (2007). Diverse threads in social fabrics: Autobiography and arts-informed educational initiatives for social justice. In I. Killoran & K. P. Jimenez (Eds.), *"Unleashing the unpopular": Talking about sexual orientation and gender diversity in education* (pp. 117–128). Association for Childhood Education International.

Wernick, L. J., Kulick, A., & Chin, M. (2017). Gender identity disparities in bathroom safety and wellbeing among high school students. *Journal of Youth and Adolescence, 46*(5), 917–930. https://doi.org/10.1007/s10964-017-0652-1

Westheimer, J., & Kahne, J. (2004). What kind of citizen? The politics of educating for democracy. *American Educational Research Journal, 41*(2), 237–269. https://doi.org/10.3102/00028312041002237

Whitaker v. Kenosha Unified School District (U.S. Court of Appeals, Seventh Circuit 2017). https://transgenderlawcenter.org/legal/youth/whitakerhttps://transgenderlawcenter.org/archives/13892

White County High School Peers in Diverse Education v. White County School District (Civil Action No. 2:06-CV-29-WCO (N. D. Georgia, Gainesville Division). 2006).

Wilson, A. E. (2024). I research how people creatively express 'queer joy' online—here are three tips for trying it yourself. *The Conversation*. Retrieved June 6, 2024, from https://theconversation.com/i-research-how-people-creatively-express-queer-joy-online-here-are-three-tips-for-trying-it-yourself-224306

Windschitl, M., Thompson, J., & Braaten, M. (2008). Beyond the scientific method: Model-based inquiry as a new paradigm of preference for school science investigations. *Science Education, 92*(5), 941–967.

Zamecnik v. Indian Prairie School District 204, 10-2485, 10-3635 (7th Cir. 2011). https://caselaw.findlaw.com/court/us-7th-circuit/1557587.html

Zongrone, A. D., Truong, N. L., & Kosciw, J. G. (2020a). *Erasure and resilience: The experiences of LGBTQ students of color, Native American, American Indian, and Alaska Native LGBTQ youth in U.S. schools*. GLSEN.

Zongrone, A. D., Truong, N. L., & Kosciw, J. (2020b). *Erasure and resilience: The Experiences of LGBTQ students of color*. GLSEN.

Index

Academics, LGBTQ students, 19–20
Active resistance, 123–124
Activism, 125–126, 129, 137
Adair, V., 60
Adults
   supportive, 24, 26
   and youth collaborations, 6–8
Advocacy, 125–129, 137
   activity ideas, 130–131
AFAB (assigned female at birth), 51, 115, 137
Affirming policies, LGBTQIA+, 27–28
Against Common Sense (Kumashiro), 40
AIDS Coalition to Unleash Power (ACT UP), 11
Alfonseca, K., 98
All-gender bathrooms, 113
Álvarez, B., 44
AMAB (assigned male at birth), 51, 137
American Civil Liberties Union (ACLU), 5, 52, 79, 89, 98
Animal Farm (Orwell), 37
Antibullying, 61
Antiharassment, 61
Apple, M., 102
Aragon, S. R., 20
Art show, 29–30
Assigned female at birth (AFAB), 51, 115, 137
Assigned male at birth (AMAB), 51, 137
Athletics, 114–116
Attendance, LGBTQ students, 19–20
Atterbury, A., 109
Authoritative school climates, 50

Bagemihl, B., 41
Banking education, 33, 137
Bathrooms, 111–114
Battle, S., 105
Bear, G., 50
Belle, E., 70, 99
Bell v. Itawamba County School Bd. (2012), 90
Bennett, S., 60
Bethel School District No. 403 v. Fraser (1986), 92
Bethel v. Fraser (1986), 84
Biden, J., 105
Binkley, C., 105
Black, Indigenous, and People of Color (BIPOC) youth, 43
#BlackLivesMatter movement, 11
Bolden, M., 52–53
Bond, L., 60
Bostock v. Clayton County, Georgia (2020), 57, 105
Britzman, D., 33, 144
Brown v. Board of Education of Topeka (1954), 56
Brundin, J., 35
Bryson, M., 33
Bullying, 17–18, 49, 59–62, 137

California Healthy Kids Survey (CHKS), 25
Carlin, J. B., 60
Caudillo v. Lubbock (2004), 79
Centers for Disease Control Youth Risk Behavior Surveillance System (CDC-YRBSS), 24–25
Central Coast Coalition for Inclusive Schools (CCC4IS), 9, 10, 11

Change the Status Quo (CSQ), 10
Character education, 43–44
Cisgender, 18, 137
Cisheteronormativity, 1, 2, 15, 102, 137
  roots of, 102–104
Cisheteropatriarchy, 103, 138
Civics Renewal Network, 64
Civil Rights Act of 1964, 56
  Title VI of, 105
Civil rights–era protections, 56–57
Clopton, R., 52
Coggan, C., 60
Cohen, S., 69
Collaborative for Academic, Social, and Emotional Learning (CASEL), 43
Colonna, S. E., 144
Community advisory board (CAB), 9
Connell, R. W., 141
Conscientização (consciousness-raising), 9, 138
Controversial topics policy, 123, 138
Cook, D., 5
Cook, M., 5
Courts of Appeal (U.S.), 88
COVID-19 pandemic, 19
Create a Respectful and Open Workplace for Natural Hair (CROWN) Act, 5
Creating Change, 74
Crenshaw, K., 142
Critical pedagogy, 9, 33, 138
Culturally relevant education (CRE), 43
Culture wars, 103, 138
Curriculum
  inclusive, 26–27
  queering, 35–43

Daley, J., 104
Data collection methods
  art show, 29–30
  digital photo essay, 28–29
  local climate survey, 30
  mapping project, 29
  microaggression journals, 30
D'Augelli, A. R., 15

Davis, H. F., 110
Day of Silence, 65
Dear Colleague Letters (DCLs), 105, 138
De Castell, S., 33
de Jong, D., 143
De Pedro, K. T., 19
Diaz, J., 5
Dickinson, P., 60
Digital photo essay, 28–29
Dimarco, B., 46
Dixon, R. S., 60
Don't Ask, Don't Tell (DADT), 7, 138
Don't Say Gay law, 5, 6
Dress codes, students, 86–89
Drysdale, S., 70
Due process, 129, 139

East High GSA v. Salt Lake City Board of Education (1999), 3
Elliott, K. O., 24
Enumerated, 27, 61, 139
Enumerated protections, 58
Equal Access Act, 3, 68, 71, 76–79, 139
Equal Protection Clause, 2, 49, 52, 56, 139
Espelage, D. L., 20, 43
Essecks, J. D., 98
Establishment Clause, of First Amendment, 123, 139
Events, national/international, 62–66
Executive Order 11246, 104
Expression, 84
  government speech, 84, 93
  school-sponsored, 84, 91–93
  silencing ally educators, 93–95
  student (*see* Student expression)

FAIR (Fair, Accurate, Inclusive, and Respectful) Education Act (SB48), 9, 35
FAIR Education Act Implementation Coalition, 64
Family Educational Rights and Privacy Act (FERPA), 98, 111, 139
Feingold, J., 38

Index

Fernandez, M., 52
Fifteenth Amendment, 55
First Amendment, 2, 84, 85, 140
   Establishment Clause of, 123
Flags, 44–47
Fourteenth Amendment, 2, 49, 52, 55, 56, 140
Freedom-dreaming, 134, 140
Freire, P., 9
Fricke, A., 2
Fricke v. Lynch (1980), 2

Gamarel, K. E., 29
Gardner, M., 38, 40
Garofalo, R., 21
Gay and Lesbian Independent School Teachers Network (GLISTEN), 70–71
Gender, 2
Gender and sexual diversity (GSD), 33, 140
   lessons, in sexuality and health education, 40–43
Gender and Sexuality Alliances (GSAs), 9–10, 11, 21, 28, 42
Gender binary, 101, 140
Gender diversity
   classroom routines to affirm, 108
   in public K–12 schools, 101
Gender-inclusive language, 110
Gender minorities, 101, 140
Gender policing, 112, 140
Gender roles, 36, 103, 141
Gender Spectrum, 111
Gender support plan (GSP), 116–117, 141
GLSEN, 71, 75, 104
   National School Climate Survey (*see* National School Climate Survey (NSCS))
Gomez, Javier, 5–6
Gonsalves, A., 39
Government speech, 84, 93, 141
Governor's Commission on Gay and Lesbian Youth, 69–70
Graduation celebration, 53–54
Gramsci, A., 142

Grimm, G., 4
GSA (Gay-Straight Alliance), 3, 68, 140
   advising, 81–82
   building bridges and networks, 79–82
   history of, 69–72
   purposes of, 71–72
   starting/developing (*see* GSA development)
GSA development
   membership/leadership development, 72–74
   strategic planning, 74–76

Hall, M., 3
Hall v. Durham Catholic District School Board (2005), 3
Harassment, 17–18, 49, 59–62, 141
Hate speech, 95–97
Hazelwood School District v. Kuhlmeier (1988), 92
Hazelwood v. Kuhlmeier (1988), 84
Healthy Kids Colorado Survey (HKCS), 25–26
Heckler's veto, 89, 141
Hegemonic masculinity, 104, 141–142
Hegemony, 142
Hershberger, S. L., 15
Homecoming ritual, 51–52
Homophobia, 2, 15, 142
   bullying/harassment and, 17–18
Hooper, R., 60

Inclusive curriculum, 26–27
Injunction, 2, 3, 142
International Day Against Homophobia, Biphobia, and Transphobia (IDAHOBIT), May 17, 66
Intersectional oppression, 30, 142
It Gets Better Project, 17

Jackson, A., 52
Jimenez, K. P., 42

Koenig, B. W., 20
Kosciw, J., 21

Language arts, 37–38
Laws/policies, 54–55
   bullying and harassment, 59–62
   nondiscrimination protections, 55–59
Learning, 33–34
Learning the terrain, 120–121
LGBTQ+ History Cards, 63
LGBTQIA+ History Month, 63–64
LGBTQIA+ (lesbian, gay, bisexual, transgender, queer, intersex, and asexual) people, 1–2, 142
   academics and attendance, 19–20
   affirming policies, 27–28
   coalitions for justice, 8–12
   early activists (1980s and 1990s), 2–4
   history of rights and activism, 7
   impacts of negative school climate, 15–23
   learning the terrain, 120–121
   millennial change-makers, 4–6
   queering curriculum, 35–43
   responding to resistance, 122–125
   students of color, 20–21
   students with disabilities, 22
   transgender/nonbinary students, 21–22
Liberty Counsel, 93–94
Life sciences, 39
Local School Climate Survey (LSCS), 30
Locker rooms, 111–114
Luria, Z., 103
Lynch, R., 2

Mapping project, 29
Maps, creation of, 29
"March for Our Lives," 11
Math instruction, queering, 38–39
Mental health, LGBTQIA+, 19
Messerschmidt, J. W., 141
Microaggressions, 11, 30, 60, 142
Milk, H., 37
Miller, KC, 4–5
Mix It Up at Lunch Day, 63
Moore, D. W., 60

Morrison v. Board of Education of Boyd County (2006), 92
Morse v. Frederick (2007), 84, 92

Nabozny, J., 3
Nabozny v. Podlesny (1996), 56
Names/pronouns, 107
   official changes, 109–111
   unofficial changes, 107–109
National Abortion Rights League (NARAL), 81
National Association for the Advancement of Colored People (NAACP), 5
National Coming Out Day, October 11, 64
National/international events, 62–66
National LGBTQ Task Force, 74
National Organization for Women (NOW), 81
National School Climate Survey (NSCS), 16, 22, 39, 101, 142
   bullying, 18
   curriculum, 27
Negative school climate, impact on LGBTQIA+, 15–16
   academics and attendance, 19–20
   mental health, 19
   safety and well-being, 16–19
   variation in schools and student experiences, 20–23
Nineteenth Amendment, 55–56
Nix-Stevenson, D., 144
No Name Calling Week (NNCW), 65
Nonbinary students, 21–22, 101, 116, 143
Nondiscrimination protections, 55–59
   matrix, 58–59
   state, 57–59
Nonverbal microaggressions, 30
normative, 1, 142–143
Normativity, 102

Office for Civil Rights (OCR), 99
O'Keefe, R., 5
Olweus, D., 58
Online expression, 90
Oppression
   intersectional forms of, 30

Index

Parens patriae, 99
Parental rights, student privacy *vs.*, 98–99
Parental Rights in Education Act, 5
Parents' rights, 45, 46
Passive resistance, 124
Patriarchy, 102–103, 143
Patton, G., 60
Pedagogy
 critical, 33
 queer, 32–35
Peterson, K., 3
Pham, K., 53
Pink Shirt Day (Canada), fourth Wednesday in February, 65
Policies. *See* Laws/policies
Positive school climate, impact on LGBTQIA+, 23–28
 supportive adults, 24, 26
Poteat, V. P., 20
Praxis, 9, 143
Preliminary injunction, 2
Pride, 89
Pride flags, 44, 45–46
Pride Month, 66
Prom, 51–52, 89
Pronouns. *See* Names/pronouns
Public K–12 schools, 84
 characteristics of, 85
 gender diversity in, 101

Queer, 1, 143
Queering, 143. *See also* LGBTQIA+ (lesbian, gay, bisexual, transgender, queer, intersex, and asexual) people
 curriculum, 35–43
 meaning of, 1
 questions, 34
Queer joy, 15, 131, 133, 143–144
Queer pedagogy, 32–35, 144

Racial microaggressions, 60
Racist dress codes, 5
Radical love, 33, 144
Rands, K., 39
Reading the Rainbow (Ryan & Hermann-Wilmarth), 37
Reconstruction Amendments, 55–56

Resistance, 122
 active, 123–124
 forms, and support, 125
 passive, 124
 rest as, 133–134
Ressler, P., 37
Rest as resistance, 133–134, 144
Restorative justice (RJ), 80–81, 144
Risk narratives, 15, 144
Rituals
 graduation celebration, 53–54
 homecoming, 51–52
 prom, 51–52
 yearbooks, 52–53
Rubin, K., 60

Safe Schools Program for Gay and Lesbian Students, 70
Safety, of LGBTQIA+ students in school, 16–19
Same-sex coupling, 41
SB 48, 35
School climate, 49–51, 145
 authoritative, 50
School climate, impact on LGBTQIA+
 negative, 15–23
 positive, 23–28
Schools
 safety, 44, 45
 types of, 22
School-sponsored expression, 84, 91–93, 145
School Success and Opportunity Act (AB1266)0, 9
Science instruction, queering, 39–40
Secular, 123–124, 145
Self-directed groupwork–social action research (SDG-SAR) methodology, 9
Seth's Law (AB9), 9
Sex assigned at birth, 103, 145
Sex discrimination, 57, 98, 104
Sexism, 5
Sex-segregated sports spaces, 116
"Sex-Shifting Fish as Reproductive Strategy," 40
Sexual diversity, 2
Sexuality and health education, 40–43
Silencing ally educators, 93–95

Social-emotional learning (SEL), 43–44
  transformative, 43, 146
Social Identity Wheel, 37
Social studies curriculum, 35–37
Social transition, 112, 145
Spirit Day, 64
Sports, 114–116
Staff expression, 93
Stakeholder, 14, 145–146
Stickers, 44–47
Student clubs, 28
Student expression, 84
  dress codes, 86–89
  Know Your Rights, 91
  online expression, 90
  prom and pride, 89
  protests, 85–86
Student information system (SIS), 109
Student privacy *vs.* parental rights, 98–99
Students with disabilities, 22
Sturgis, C., 52
Supportive adults, 24, 26
Sutherland, C. M., 60

Task Force, 74
Teacher speech and political viewpoint argument, 46–47
Teaching about Gender Diversity (Suarez and Wright), 38
Thirteenth Amendment, 55
Thomas, L., 60
Thorne, B., 103
"Tilling the soil," 120
Tinker v. Des Moines School District (1969), 84, 86, 90, 91
Title IX of the Educational Amendments of 1972, 4, 52, 53, 56, 98, 102, 104–106, 115, 146
  lawsuits related to gender and sexual orientation, 106
Title VII of Civil Rights Act, 57
Title VI of Civil Rights Act of 1964, 56, 105
Tomboys and Other Gender Heroes (Pendleton Jimenez), 42

Trans and nonbinary (TNB) students, 21–22, 101
Transformative SEL, 43, 146
Transgender Day of Remembrance (TDOR), November 20, 64–65
Trans Lifeline, 17
Transphobia, 2, 15, 146
  bullying/harassment and, 17–18
TransPULSE Survey, 38
Transsexual, 146
Trevor Project, 17
Truong, N. L., 21, 71, 72, 73, 76
Trust building, 122
Turban, J. L., 114
Turning gay, 45–46

Universal Design, 113, 146–147
Unofficial changes, 107–109
U.S. Courts of Appeal, 88

Viewpoint discrimination, 89, 147

Weishart, J., 38
Well-being, of LGBTQIA+ students in school, 16–19
Wells, K., 30
"What Works Clearing house," 44
Wheeler, T. E., 105
When the Drama Club Is Not Enough (Perotti and Westheimer), 71
Whitaker, A., 4
Whitaker v. Kenosha Unified School District (2017), 4
Wilson, A. E., 133
Windschitl, M., 39
Women's Equity Action League, 104

Yearbooks, 52–53
Youth
  and adult collaborations, 6–8
  BIPOC, 43
  hotlines, 17
Youthline, 17

Zongrone, A. D., 21

About the Author

Elizabeth J. Meyer is a professor in Educational Foundations, Policy, and Practice at the University of Colorado Boulder. Previously, she served as an Assistant Professor in the School of Education at California Polytechnic State University, San Luis Obispo and Concordia University in Montreal, Canada. She completed her Ph.D. in Education at McGill University in Montreal, Canada. She spent 5 years as a high school teacher, including one year as a Fulbright Teacher Exchange Program grantee in Normandy, France. She is a Fellow with the National Educational Policy Center and received the Distinguished Contributions to Gender Equity in Education Research Award by the American Educational Research Association in 2021. Dr. Meyer's research focuses on issues related to gender and sexual diversity in K-12 education.